LOOKING SOUTH

Australia's Antarctic Agenda

Editors

Lorne K Kriwoken

Julia Jabour

Alan D Hemmings

Foreword by
Professor Stuart Harris

THE FEDERATION PRESS
2007

Published in Sydney by

The Federation Press
PO Box 45, Annandale, NSW, 2038.
71 John St, Leichhardt, NSW, 2040.
Ph (02) 9552 2200. Fax (02) 9552 1681.
E-mail: info@federationpress.com.au
Website: http://www.federationpress.com.au

National Library of Australia cataloguing-in-publication
Looking south: Australia's Antarctic agenda

Bibliography.
Includes index.
ISBN 978 186287 657 6 (pbk)

1. Australian Antarctic Territory (Antarctica). 2. Antarctica – Government
policy – Australia. I. Kriwoken, Lorne K. II. Jabour, Julia. III. Hemmings,
Alan D. IV. Title.

349.94

Text printed on
100% recycled paper

Typeset by Federation Press Pty Ltd, Leichhardt, NSW.
Printed by Ligare Pty Ltd, Riverwood, NSW.

Foreword

Stuart Harris

Emeritus Professor
Department of International Relations
Australian National University

As it approaches half a century of existence, it can be argued that the Antarctic Treaty System (ATS) is a successful – and rather rare – experiment in global civil consciousness. This is despite its basically fragile institutional base. Although Australia's involvement in Antarctica has a much longer history, it is within the ATS that Australia's Antarctic agenda has largely been pursued and is most likely to continue.

Over its almost 50-year lifetime, the ATS has survived various tensions: territorial disputes; Cold War antagonisms; moves to bring Antarctica under UN administration; and proposals to manage Antarctica as a 'wilderness park' to ensure complete environment protection, a proposition with which Australia was associated.

Since the end of World War II, science has been central to human activities in Antarctica, and subsequently became the criterion for Consultative Party status in the Antarctic Treaty. Environmental concerns have also been basic to the ATS from the start, particularly the local issues of native birds, mammals and fauna and flora, for all of which various protective measures have been developed. Eventually, however, the public goods aspects of the environment – the ozone layer, carbon dioxide sinks, the impacts on the climate of ice melts and reflectivity (albedo) and the contributions of ice core measurements and other scientific investigations to an understanding of global weather systems and to the science of global climate change – came to the fore. Antarctica's unique contribution as an indicator of planetary change became and remains important.

Notwithstanding its fragility, the ATS has survived largely because it has adjusted to changing global concerns. This has been important given the voluntary cooperation on which it is based and in particular the agreement to put contested sovereignty issues aside in the interests of cooperative management – and, among other things, to recognise and adjust to the growing interests of non-claimant States. The continuing interests of the ATS members and collaborators in cooperation have survived the various tensions of the past. They will have to face and respond to present and likely future tensions if cooperation is to be maintained.

Since 1984, when the volume to which this present volume is a worthy successor was published, there have been substantial changes that are providing new challenges to the ATS, as the contributions to this volume illustrate. Some of the old tensions – sovereignty for example – have remained even if emerging in new contexts, notably through the Law of the Sea Convention, and new ones have become important.

As the ATS developed, for many of those involved in Antarctic matters, there was a sense in which the ATS would cover within its regulatory processes all things that related to or impinged on Antarctica. This understanding has been reflected in the development of a growing range of conventions, agreements, principles and standards covering an expanding subject matter. Such a coverage, however, has become more difficult as the ability to distinguish Antarctic issues from those of a wider geographic nature, linked to other more broadly based institutional arrangements, has diminished. In part this is a consequence, as the authors in this volume indicate, of the impact of globalisation and the commercial pressures it has facilitated.

Resource issues have been important in the past and provided an important challenge for the ATS. They are currently important for marine resources such as krill, squid and a number of fish species, where an ecosystem management approach has been adopted, and for bio-prospecting. The question of minerals and energy, especially oil, exploitation on land or offshore was much discussed in the mid 1980s. The tensions and potential conflicts of interests reflected at the time in seeking to develop a resources management regime could return more substantially in the longer term, or perhaps sooner if the economic costs, direct and indirect, of resource exploitation are ignored. Tourism is also becoming increasingly important with potential impacts on the environment.

This poses two problems. Although not uncontested, a long held argument by, or belief among, the Treaty States was that they administer the Antarctic in trust on behalf of the wider international community. This was challenged once before, unsuccessfully, in the UN by some developing countries led by Malaysia seeking to treat Antarctica's assumed resource wealth as the common heritage of humankind. Challenges could emerge again from those outside – or possibly from within – the ATS as economic benefit issues appear more important. Moreover, the collaborative basis of the existing system will come under stress, as the authors in the volume indicate, given the competitive processes arising from increased actual or perceived economic benefits to be gained.

For Australia, as for the other claimant States, its scientific research effort has always been central to its role in Antarctica, in part at least, to shore up its claim to sovereignty. But, inconsistent as Australia's policy approach to Antarctica has been at times, developments in recent decades have also influenced Australia's evaluation of its interests. The policy interests in 1984 were summarised at the time as sovereignty, neutrality, environment, science, involvement and benefit. In general terms the policy interests today are not greatly different but in particular cases their meanings may be different or their relative importance changed. Some, such as neutrality have less salience; for others, such as benefit, Australia's policy interests have become more specific.

Australia has generally been active in ATS affairs. As a claimant to 42 per cent of the Antarctic continent and given its relatively close geographic location and substantial influence on Australia's weather systems, Australia will remain interested in what happens in Antarctica and how it is managed. Hence, Australia's sustained political interest in 'involvement'. In recent decades, Australia has been firmer in its financial and other support for scientific and other efforts in the Australian Antarctic Territory but this has also meant a shift in the interests that Australia sees as important in Antarctica. Australia's enhanced support for its Antarctic activities, however, has been associated with a concern shared with other ATS participants, and also with global commercial interests, to gain economic benefit including enhanced resource access from Antarctica.

What this volume illustrates very clearly is that the ATS is facing a variety of new challenges that will require not just adept Australian diplomacy but also a continuing acceptance, by all the Parties and others associated with it, that the System has been, and will remain, a valuable suite of instruments for managing Antarctica. Yet the relationships are not simple. There have always been tensions for Australia (and no doubt for some other countries) between national interests and international collaboration on Antarctica and how those tensions are resolved will largely shape Antarctica's future.

Concern about the limited public understanding of Australia's interests and its role in Antarctica has been a continuing refrain of those closely associated with the continent. While this is understandable it leaves the policies vulnerable to the idiosyncrasies of a narrow decision making framework. The importance of this volume is that it provides a means for raising public interest in the subject and providing a comprehensive and up to date information base for those interested while addressing the increasingly complex range of Antarctic and Southern Ocean issues important to the analyst and policy decision-maker.

Stuart Harris
Canberra
May 2007

Table of Contents

CONTENTS

Acknowledgements

The editors and authors acknowledge the financial support of the Antarctic Climate and Ecosystems Cooperative Research Centre (ACE CRC); ACE CRC Policy Program; the School of Geography and Environmental Studies, University of Tasmania; the Institute of Antarctic and Southern Ocean Studies, University of Tasmania; the Sydney Centre for International and Global Law; the Faculty of Law, University of Sydney and the Sustainable Tourism CRC.

We express our particular thanks to Professor Stuart Harris for writing the foreword; Louise Darko (School of Government, University of Tasmania); Ivana Zovko and Mariusz Bartoszewicz (Sydney Centre for International and Global Law) for their assistance at the workshops; the team at The Federation Press for their editorial assistance; and June Pongratz for graphics.

List of Figures and Tables

Figures

Tables

About the Contributors

Professor Ben Boer, Professor in Environmental Law, Australian Centre for Environmental Law, Faculty of Law, University of Sydney, and International Co-Director and Visiting Professor, IUCN Academy of Environmental Law, Faculty of Law, University of Ottawa.

Dr Rob Hall, Lecturer, School of Government and Antarctic Climate and Ecosystems Cooperative Research Centre, University of Tasmania.

Associate Professor Marcus Haward, School of Government and Program Leader, Policy Program, Antarctic Climate and Ecosystems Cooperative Research Centre, University of Tasmania.

Dr Alan D Hemmings, Research Associate, Institute of Antarctic and Southern Ocean Studies, University of Tasmania and Senior Fellow, Gateway Antarctica Centre for Antarctic Studies and Research, University of Canterbury, New Zealand.

Dr Nick Holmes, Research Associate, School of Geography and Environmental Studies, University of Tasmania.

Mr Andrew Jackson, Senior Policy Adviser, Australian Antarctic Division, Department of the Environment and Water Resources and Honorary Fellow, Antarctic Climate and Ecosystems Cooperative Research Centre, University of Tasmania.

Dr Julia Jabour, Senior Lecturer, Institute of Antarctic and Southern Ocean Studies and Deputy Policy Program Leader, Antarctic Climate and Ecosystems Cooperative Research Centre, University of Tasmania.

Mr Murray Johnson, Research Associate, Sydney Centre for International and Global Law, University of Sydney.

Professor Aynsley Kellow, School of Government and Antarctic Climate and Ecosystems Cooperative Research Centre, University of Tasmania.

Dr Lorne K Kriwoken, Senior Lecturer, School of Geography and Environmental Studies and Antarctic Climate and Ecosystems Cooperative Research Centre, University of Tasmania.

Dr Gail Lugten, Senior Lecturer, School of Law and Antarctic Climate and Ecosystems Cooperative Research Centre, University of Tasmania.

Dr Erik Jaap Molenaar, Netherlands Institute of Law of the Sea, University of Utrecht and Research Associate, Antarctic Climate and Ecosystems Cooperative Research Centre, University of Tasmania.

Dr Stephen Powell, Senior Policy Adviser, Australian Antarctic Division, Department of the Environment and Water Resources.

Professor Donald R Rothwell, Professor of International Law, ANU College of Law, The Australian National University.

Dr Rosemary Sandford, Research Fellow, Policy Program, Antarctic Climate and Ecosystems Cooperative Research Centre, University of Tasmania.

Dr Shirley Scott, Associate Professor of International Relations, School of Social Sciences and International Studies, University of New South Wales.

Dr Tim Stephens, Senior Lecturer, Sydney Centre for International and Global Law, University of Sydney.

Acronyms

AAD	Australian Antarctic Division
AAE	Australasian Antarctic Expeditions
AAP	Australian Antarctic Program
AAT	Australian Antarctic Territory
ACAP	Agreement on the Conservation of Albatrosses and Petrels
ACE CRC	Antarctic Climate and Ecosystems Cooperative Research Centre
ACF	Australian Conservation Foundation
ACS	Australian Customs Service
ACT	Australian Capital Territory
AFMA	Australian Fisheries Management Authority
AFZ	Australian Fishing Zone
AIIA	Australian Institute of International Affairs
ANARE	Australian National Antarctic Research Expeditions
ARAC	Antarctic Research Advisory Committee
ASAC	Antarctic Science Advisory Committee
ASOC	Antarctic and Southern Ocean Coalition
ATCM	Antarctic Treaty Consultative Meeting
ATCP	Antarctic Treaty Consultative Party
ATME	Antarctic Treaty Meeting of Experts
ATS	Antarctic Treaty System
AWS	Australian Whale Sanctuary
BANZARE	British, Australian and New Zealand Antarctic Research Expedition
BoM	Bureau of Meteorology
CBD	Convention on Biological Diversity
CCAMLR	Convention on the Conservation of Antarctic Marine Living Resources
CCAS	Convention for the Conservation of Antarctic Seals
CCSBT	Commission for the Conservation of Southern Bluefin Tuna
CEE	Comprehensive Environmental Evaluation
CEP	Committee on Environmental Protection
CITES	Convention on International Trade in Endangered Species of Wild Fauna and Flora
CLCS	Commission on the Limits of the Continental Shelf
CM	Conservation Measure
CMS	Convention on Migratory Species
COFI	Committee on Fisheries
COLTO	Coalition of Legal Toothfish Operators

COMNAP	Council of Managers of National Antarctic Programs
CoP	Conference of Parties
CRAMRA	Convention on the Regulation of Antarctic Mineral Resource Activities
CSIRO	Commonwealth Scientific and Industrial Research Organisation
DEH	Department of Environment and Heritage
DFAT	Department of Foreign Affairs and Trade
DTAE	Department of Tourism, Arts and the Environment (Tasmania)
EEZ	Exclusive Economic Zone
EIA	Environmental Impact Assessment
ENSO	El Niño-Southern Oscillation
EPBC Act	Environment Protection and Biodiversity Conservation Act 1999 (Cth)
GHG	Greenhouse gases
HIMI	Heard Island and McDonald Islands
HSI	Humane Society International
IAATO	International Association of Antarctica Tour Operators
IASOS	Institute of Antarctic and Southern Ocean Studies
ICG	Intersessional Contact Group
ICRW	International Convention for the Regulation of Whaling
ICSU	International Council for Science
IEE	Initial Environmental Evaluation
IFAW	International Fund for Animal Welfare
IGY	International Geophysical Year (1957-8)
IMO	International Maritime Organization
IPCC	Intergovernmental Panel on Climate Change
IPoA	International Plan of Action
IPY	International Polar Year (1882-3, 1932-3, 2007-9)
ISA	International Seabed Authority
ISOFISH	International Clearing House for Southern Ocean Fishing
ITLOS	International Tribunal for the Law of the Sea
IUCN	International Union for the Conservation of Nature and Natural Resources or World Conservation Union
IUU	Illegal, Unreported and Unregulated
IWC	International Whaling Commission
JARPA	Japanese Whale Research Program under Special Permit in the Antarctic
KSK	Kyodo Senpaku Kaisha
LOS Convention	Law of the Sea Convention
MARPOL	International Convention for the Prevention of Pollution from Ships
MIRAG	Macquarie Island Research Assessment Group
MoP	Meeting of Parties
MoU	Memorandum of Understanding

NGO	Non-government Organisation
nm	nautical mile
NPoA	National Plan of Action
OECD	Organisation for Economic Co-operation and Development
OPEC	Organization of the Petroleum Exporting Countries
PA	Preliminary Assessment
PWS	Tasmanian Parks and Wildlife Service
RAN	Royal Australian Navy
RFMO	Regional Fisheries Management Organisation
RMP	Revised Management Procedure
RMS	Revised Management Scheme
SCALOP	Standing Committee on Antarctic Logistics and Operations
SCAR	Scientific Committee on Antarctic Research
SEA	Strategic Environmental Assessment
SEAFO	South East Atlantic Fisheries Organization
TAC	total allowable catch
TMA	Tourism Management Area
UN	United Nations
UNESCO	United Nations Educational, Scientific and Cultural Organization
UN FAO	United Nations Food and Agriculture Organization
UNFCCC	United Nations Framework Convention on Climate Change
UNGA	United Nations General Assembly
WCPFC	Western and Central Pacific Fisheries Commission
WG-IMAF	Working Group on Incidental Mortality Associated with Fishing
WMO	World Meteorological Organization
WWF	World Wide Fund for Nature

Figure 1: Antarctica and the Southern Ocean

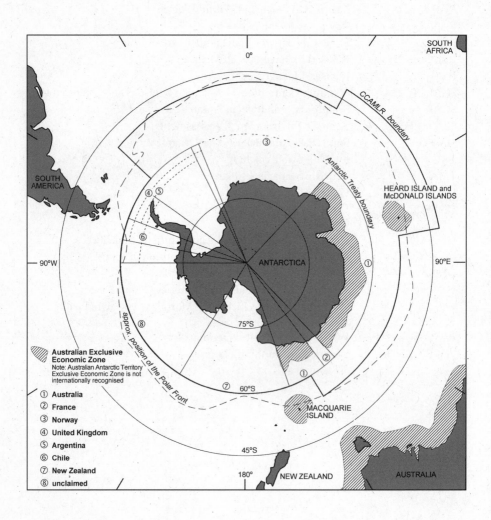

Figure 2: Distances from Australia

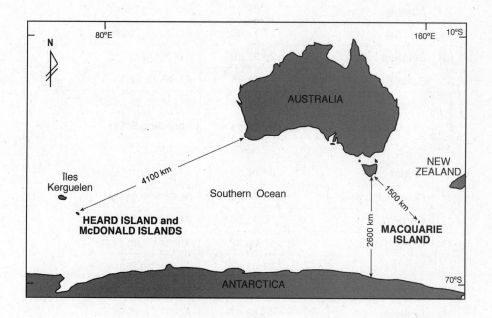

Table 1: Antarctic Treaty Contracting Parties
(Compiled by Dr Julia Jabour, last updated April 2007)

	State	Effective Date	Status
1	*Argentina*	*23.06.61*	*ATCP/OS/C*
2	*Australia*	*23.06.61*	*ATCP/OS/C*
3	Austria	25.08.87	Acceding State
4	Belarus	27.12.06	Acceding State
5	Belgium	26.07.60	ATCP/OS
6	Brazil	16.05.75	ATCP 12.09.83
7	Bulgaria	11.09.78	ATCP 25.05.98
8	Canada	04.05.88	Acceding State
9	*Chile*	*23.06.61*	*ATCP/OS/C*
10	China	08.06.83	ATCP 07.10.85
11	Colombia	31.01.89	Acceding State
12	Cuba	16.08.84	Acceding State
13	Czech Republic	14.06.62	Succeeding State[1]
14	DPR Korea	21.01.87	Acceding State
15	Denmark	20.05.65	Acceding State
16	Ecuador	15.09.87	ATCP 19.11.90
17	Estonia	17.05.01	Acceding State
18	Finland	15.05.84	ATCP 09.10.89
19	*France*	*16.09.60*	*ATCP/OS/C*
20	Germany[2]	05.02.79	ATCP 03.03.81
21	Greece	08.01.87	Acceding State
22	Guatemala	31.07.91	Acceding State
23	Hungary	27.01.84	Acceding State
24	India	19.08.83	ATCP 12.09.83
25	Italy	18.03.81	ATCP 05.10.87
26	Japan	04.08.60	ATCP/OS
27	Netherlands	30.03.67	ATCP 19.11.90
28	*New Zealand*	*01.11.60*	*ATCP/OS/C*

	State	Effective Date	Status
29	*Norway*	*24.08.60*	*ATCP/OS/C*
30	**Papua New Guinea**	**16.03.81**	Acceding State
31	**Peru**	**10.04.81**	ATCP 09.10.89
32	**Poland**	**08.06.61**	ATCP 29.07.77
33	**Republic of Korea**	**28.11.86**	ATCP 09.10.89
34	**Romania**	**15.09.71**	Acceding State
35	**Russian Federation**	**02.11.60**	Succeeding State[3] ATCP/OS
36	**Slovak Republic**	**14.06.62**	Succeeding State[4]
37	**South Africa**	**21.06.60**	ATCP/OS
38	**Spain**	**31.03.82**	ATCP 21.09.88
39	**Sweden**	**24.04.84**	ATCP 21.09.88
40	**Switzerland**	**15.11.90**	Acceding State
41	**Turkey**	**24.01.96**	Acceding State
42	*United Kingdom*	*31.05.60*	*ATCP/OS/C*
43	**United States of America**	**18.08.60**	ATCP/OS
44	**Uruguay**	**11.01.80**	ATCP 07.10.85
45	**Ukraine**	**28.10.92**	ATCP[5] OS
46	**Venezuela**	**24.03.99**	Acceding State

KEY:
ATCP = Antarctic Treaty Consultative Party
OS = *Original Signatory (automatically ATCP)*
C = *Claimant State (automatically ATCP)*

1   The Czech and Slovak Republics inherited Czechoslovakia's obligations as a Contracting Party with effect from 1 January 1993, the date of their succession to the Treaty.

2   The German Democratic Republic was united with the Federal Republic of Germany on 02.10.90. GDR acceded to the Treaty on 19.11.74 and was recognised as an ATCP on 05.10.87.

3   Following the dissolution of the USSR, Russia assumed the rights and obligations of being a party to the Treaty. The USSR had been an original signatory to the Treaty.

4   See note 1 above.

5   Ukraine has asserted that it succeeded to the Treaty following the dissolution of the USSR and should be entitled to ATCP status. Formal Consultative Party status was granted on 27.05.04.

1

Introduction

Julia Jabour, Alan D Hemmings and Lorne K Kriwoken

Looking South in Context

Australia has a long, rich and significant history in Antarctic affairs. Post Federation Australia, through well-known characters such as Sir Douglas Mawson, became a key player in the so-called heroic era of exploration and the opening up of Antarctica. Since 1933 Australia has asserted a claim to 42 per cent of the continent – two separate slices known collectively as the Australian Antarctic Territory (AAT) (see Figure 1 at beginning of book). Australia was an original signatory to the 1959 Antarctic Treaty and has subsequently played an active role in international governance of Antarctica under the Antarctic Treaty System (ATS). Antarctica is not at the forefront of Australia's political agenda, true, but it has held a constant second-order place in the mainstream of national and foreign affairs – and the fact that it has not always been to the fore may be a measure of the success of the Treaty.

Almost half a century after the adoption of the Antarctic Treaty, and in the first decade of the 21st century, the Antarctic is better known but is still not completely understood to science. It has been designated a natural reserve devoted to peace and science and whilst some matters, such as mining, have been put on hold, others present both continuing and new challenges. These include the implications for Antarctica of global climate change, and indeed the continent's role in the generation of the world's weather; the environmental, political and ethical implications of increasing human activity in the region; and the goals of maintaining or developing the most appropriate governance mechanisms given the complex legal circumstances.

Inevitably, examinations of national interest and policy in Antarctica are infrequent. But, 20 years ago as the Antarctic Treaty Parties discussed resource exploitation, there was a flurry of interest in Antarctic affairs across a wider intellectual and public policy community than had been the case previously. In March 1984 a particularly valuable workshop was held

1

in Canberra on Australia's policy options with regard to the Antarctic. That workshop led to the volume *Australia's Antarctic Policy Options* edited by Professor Stuart Harris, a former Secretary of the Department of Foreign Affairs and the then Director of the Australian National University's Centre for Resource and Environmental Studies. The workshop, and the volume that it spawned, brought together a diverse and intellectually powerful array of Australians focused on Antarctic law, policy and the social sciences. In many respects *Australia's Antarctic Policy Options* provided the new departure point for informed consideration of Australia in Antarctica.

At the time of the Harris volume, there were 31 Antarctic Treaty Parties (there are 46 today, see pp xx-xxi); the Southern Ocean fishing regime (Convention on the Conservation of Antarctic Marine Living Resources – CCAMLR) had just entered into force; the international community was mid-way through the long and arduous minerals convention (Convention on the Regulation of Antarctic Mineral Resource Activities – CRAMRA) negotiations. There had been a dramatic increase in the number of Antarctic Treaty Parties (10 new Parties in the four years 1980-84), in large measure a reaction to the annual discussions on the "Question of Antarctica" in the United Nations General Assembly. This was a time of unprecedented global interest in the Antarctic and of challenge to the legitimacy (or at least the hegemony) of the ATS.

Australia was an important player in CCAMLR as host of the new Secretariat in Hobart. Australia was engaged in rebuilding all of its continental stations (itself a reflection of its recognition that Antarctica was elevated to a first-order issue) and within a few years of the appearance of the Harris volume, Australia was, with France, leading the opposition to Antarctic mining and CRAMRA, and proposing instead what became the Protocol on Environmental Protection to the Antarctic Treaty (Madrid Protocol). Australia and a small group of its Antarctic allies took pride in the greening of Antarctica, and it remains in many ways the greatest single policy success in Australia's Antarctic engagement.

The Looking South Project

Australia's Antarctic Policy Options provided a benchmark by which to measure the tenor of Australia's contemporary Antarctic agenda and as such has been of great assistance to us individually and collectively. Consequently 20 years on we thought it timely to explore how the issues identified in that volume might have developed and whether any significant new issues had emerged. Our focus, as with Harris, was on Antarctica from an essentially Australian perspective.

The core project group was drawn from the Institute of Antarctic and Southern Ocean Studies (IASOS) and the Policy Program of the Antarctic Climate and Ecosystems Cooperative Research Centre (ACE CRC, University of Tasmania), the Centre for International and Global Law (University of Sydney Law School), the Australian National University College of Law, and the University of New South Wales (School of Social Sciences and International Studies). Following substantial exchanges and sub-group discussions, the group as a whole came together in two workshops, the first in Sydney in November 2004 and the second in Hobart in July 2005, where we were fortunate to also be able to draw upon expertise from the Australian Antarctic Division (AAD). At the workshops various topics were presented and critiqued, inspiring more free ranging discussion across issues as they emerged. Thereafter authors prepared the chapters you now see in this volume.

The project did not aim to create a unitary interpretation of issues or Australia's engagement with the Antarctic. Nor did we aspire to a systematic coverage of all current Antarctic issues, although we believe that the most significant are in fact addressed. Where linkages between chapters are evident, some cross-referencing has been done, but the chapters are largely stand-alone.

Because the authors represent a range of disciplines, with a corresponding wide range of discipline-specific styles and protocols, we have, with the authors' agreement and cooperation, edited the chapters into a constant house style. We hope this stylistic consistency is an aid to readers. Whilst the editors take responsibility for the overall shape of the volume, individual chapter authors are responsible for the substantive positions adopted in their chapters.

Chapter Coverage

Sovereignty is an enduring issue in Antarctica, given recent new salience through increasing commercial interest and developments in international law. Don Rothwell and Shirley Scott lead this volume with an examination of Australia's sovereignty (Chapter 2). Here they note that sovereignty is legally tenuous but, regardless, Australia continues to solidify its claim. Although Australia has not pushed its sovereignty to the point where it has provoked an attempt at a resolution, which may turn out to be unfavourable, its actions nevertheless raise delicate and contentious issues under the United Nations Convention on the Law of the Sea (LOS Convention) in relation to Article IV of the Antarctic Treaty. They observe that the day may be looming when Australia will face a choice between national and international interests.

Marcus Haward, Rob Hall and Aynsley Kellow (Chapter 3) investigate and describe Australia's Antarctic policy-making environment specifically in relation to the four official government goals. They note that success relies on good relations between members of the policy community (local and international) and that a host of challenges are on the radar, including: consensus decision-making, LOS Convention, climate change, tourism and other human effects, including illegal, unreported and unregulated (IUU) fishing.

Two·AAD officers, Stephen Powell and Andrew Jackson, present a highly valuable insiders' view on Australia's influence in the Antarctic Treaty System (Chapter 4). They conduct a retrospective of the 13th Antarctic Treaty Consultative Meeting (ATCM) in 1985 and the 28th meeting in 2005, examining the emphases on resource potential and the environment respectively. For the insiders, the issues are identical to those of Haward, Hall and Kellow, but also include the International Polar Year (IPY) 2007-09 and the new intercontinental airlink between Hobart and Casey Station, East Antarctica.

In Chapter 5, Tim Stephens and Ben Boer, like Rothwell and Scott, warn of the tenuous position Australia maintains regarding sovereignty. They note that it enacts legislation that it has neither the capacity nor the intention to enforce. Furthermore, in their investigation of enforcement and compliance dilemmas, they argue that any attempt by Australia to enforce its domestic law against non-nationals would be highly controversial. This puts Australia on the horns of a dilemma: on the one hand there will be external pressures requiring it to maintain the plausibility of its claim and on the other, there will be internal pressure to satisfy domestic constituencies. This may mean that Australia will be under increasing pressure to revisit the delicate policy position it seeks to maintain.

The Antarctic and the Southern Ocean play a pivotal role in generating the world's climate, and changes in climate will have global impact, possibly positive, possibly negative. At home, government attention to changing climate is set to become a key election issue in 2007. Rosemary Sandford examines what Australia's Antarctic science programs and their supporting institutions might look like in a correspondingly changing science-policy environment (Chapter 6). She nominates the underlying questions as: what are some of the key domestic and international challenges facing Australia's Antarctic science program as it reviews the way it does business in a changing global climate, and how might or should it respond to these? She suggests that the Antarctic Treaty Parties, including Australia, can no longer remain aloof from the interdependence of climate variability and change, globalisation, population growth, depletion of the global energy reserves and environmental and resource security.

Tourism is the largest commercial activity in the Antarctic. Because only about 10 per cent of tourists are Australian, or served by Australian companies, and tourism activity in the AAT is relatively low, Australia has been able to take a more technical policy approach without risking its sovereign interests. The authors of Chapter 7, Murray Johnson and Lorne Kriwoken, speculate that while the government has a policy on Antarctic tourism, it is arguable whether the existing regulatory approach will prove effective in meeting long-term policy aspirations. Rather, the government would benefit from the inclusion of additional strategic and precautionary provisions to deal with future tourism interests.

According to Gail Lugten (Chapter 8), the second largest commercial activity in the Antarctic – marine living resources harvesting – is reasonably well managed and Australia's own conservation policies are on track, but more needs to be done. She cites examples within the LOS Convention, specifically its anachronistic freedom to fish and the technical requirements of hot pursuit, which would greatly benefit from reform. Furthermore, because Australia has had a number of unsatisfactory outcomes in its courts, she recommends that the Australian government seek reform of domestic legislation to strengthen its ability to successfully deal with IUU fishers once they have been apprehended.

An associated problem to that of IUU is the devastating bycatch of seabirds across the Southern Ocean. Rob Hall (Chapter 9) describes the situation which has led to adoption of the Agreement on the Conservation of Albatrosses and Petrels (ACAP), in which Australia played a pivotal role. Australian scientists provided important information on the scope of problem and a range of mitigation measures, and the Australian government facilitated the development of the Convention, and now hosts the Secretariat in Hobart. Hall sees the fledgling ACAP as a step in the right direction, but more effort needs to be directed at widening the scope of seabird protection.

Another global issue in which Australia plays a key role is that of the conservation of whales. Long-standing protection has permitted conditions in which some stocks of some whale species in some areas (especially minke whales in parts of the Southern Ocean) have recovered to levels conducive to managed, sustainable harvests. Notwithstanding, Australia has adopted a strict policy of seeking a permanent global ban on commercial whaling. The authors of Chapter 10, Julia Jabour, Mike Iliff and Erik Jaap Molenaar, describe the modern scenario in which Australia pursues a seemingly futile but electorally popular total prohibition. They explore the domestic and international bases for the policy and conclude that Australia would better serve whale conservation by putting greater emphasis on threats to whales from activities other than commercial whaling, including bycatch, environmental changes, pollution and stranding.

In Chapter 11, Lorne Kriwoken and Nick Holmes investigate the emerging issues that face Macquarie Island, Heard Island and McDonald Islands – spectacular and remote Australian sub-Antarctic territories. They are critical habitats for a diversity of flora and fauna, in addition to being strategic locations for science and environmental monitoring. The authors discuss science and management, tourism, quarantine, disease and alien introductions, and commercial fishing. They conclude that these island groups provide their own particular challenges to Australia's Antarctic agenda and in order to fulfil World Heritage Area obligations, the government should take a number of important steps as a matter of urgency.

With changes in global climate likely to affect the sub-Antarctic and Antarctic in dramatic ways (the alteration to conditions promoting the colonisation of alien species, for example), Aynsley Kellow (Chapter 12) discusses his notion that the benefits from Antarctic research are problematic and unlikely to result in a clear justification that investment is acceptable. The significance for Australia will come from the fact that its climate system depends in large part on what happens to the south. He concedes, however, that understanding atmospheric and oceanic processes, and any improvement in Southern Ocean weather systems science, promises to be a significant benefit flowing from Antarctic scientific research.

In Chapter 13, Alan Hemmings explores the ending of Antarctic isolation and the effects of the worldwide trend called "globalisation". He identifies technology, six existing and emerging commercial interest clusters within the area, and the extension of human activity up to the boundaries of the Antarctic as significant factors in the transformation of Antarctica. This transformation has profound implications for the manner – indeed the very viability of – cooperative international governance of Antarctica.

Finally, in Chapter 14, the editors take a look forward at Antarctica as an enduring Australian interest, and explore the deep structure of national engagement. We ask what are Australia's interests, whether they are best advanced through the stance of a territorial claimant, and how they might be realised. Inevitably, much remains unclear, but we anticipate that this will at least provide a stimulant to further enquiry.

2

Flexing Australian Sovereignty in Antarctica: Pushing Antarctic Treaty Limits in the National Interest?

Donald R Rothwell and Shirley V Scott

Introduction

Australia has a number of external possessions, such as Lord Howe Island and Macquarie Island which are parts of states, others are formally External Territories. The most significant of the latter is the Australian Antarctic Territory (AAT), which is founded upon Australia's claims to the Antarctic continent.[1] Australia also makes claim to Heard Island and McDonald Islands in the Southern Ocean – which are also part of an External Territory – the Territory of Heard Island and McDonald Islands.

The assertion of these claims by Australia in the Southern Ocean and to parts of the Antarctic continent is legally tenuous. This is because whilst the claims are primarily based upon discovery followed by acts proclaiming sovereignty, there is considerable doubt whether the claims have been satisfactorily "perfected" under international law or recognised by a sufficient number of other States (Brownlie 2003: 142-4). Whilst the exploration of these lands was undertaken following Federation in 1901, many of the initial claims were not made by Australians or on behalf of Australia. It was not until the formal adoption by the Commonwealth Parliament of the *Australian Antarctic Territory Acceptance Act* 1933 (Cth) that the claims were "perfected" under Australian law. However, the Australian claims to the continent have not been widely recognised. Apart from New Zealand and the United Kingdom – whose mutual recognition of the Australian claim is somewhat inevitable given they all sprang from the same foundation – only France and Norway recognise the legitimacy of the Australian claim. Recent events before the Australian courts and public

---

1   The other claimants are Argentina, Chile, France, New Zealand, Norway and the United Kingdom.

statements by government Ministers have underlined the inherent weakness of the Australian sovereign claim to parts of Antarctica. Yet, the claim is persisted with and indeed part of the rationale for the Australian Antarctic Division (AAD) and its scientific program in Antarctica is the promotion of Australian sovereignty.

An ongoing debate has taken place as to the relative weighting of the scientific value of Antarctica as against its economic value. Long term projections over the potential value of Antarctica's mineral wealth have resulted in speculation that some claimant States may be keeping their Antarctic claims "in reserve" for the future (Bergin 1991). In this respect, Australia has increasingly sought to take a more aggressive stand on certain Antarctic matters which go to the heart of Australian sovereignty over the AAT. This chapter will explore the history of the Australian claim and the international legal-political context in which it has been asserted and developed, before addressing the current issues for Australian policymakers charged with ensuring the ongoing strength of that claim.

Australia's Claim to Antarctic Sovereignty

Whilst most parts of the Australian Antarctic claim were asserted following Federation, British or Empire expeditions, many of which contained some Australian personnel, provide the foundation for nearly all of the claim. The first Australian Antarctic Expedition took place in 1911 under the command of Douglas Mawson, and a series of expeditions followed until the creation in 1929 of the British, Australian and New Zealand Antarctic Expedition (BANZARE), also under the command of Mawson. These expeditions had both a scientific and political significance. They represented some of the first Australian-funded external scientific expeditions. Politically they were also of great consequence as each of the early expeditions resulted in the discovery of new Antarctic lands accompanied by the inevitable "planting of the flag".[2] Mawson was well aware of the significance attached to his expeditions, noting in 1911 that:

> If ever in the history of Australia an expedition is to set out under favourable circumstances, it must be immediate. No time is to be lost. So surely as it lapses a moment foreign nations will step in and secure this most valuable portion of the Antarctic continent for themselves, and for ever from the control of Australia. (Mawson 1911)[3]

Formal proclamations of what became the AAT were made in 1930-31, though these claims were accompanied by the hoisting of the British Flag and assertion of British sovereignty (Triggs 1986: 107). The formal transfer

2   The importance of the act of discovery as a basis for a sovereign claim is canvassed by the Permanent Court of International Justice in the *Island of Palmas Case* 2 RIAA 829.

3   See also the discussion in Triggs (1986).

of sovereignty from Britain to Australia took place in 1933 first with a British Order in Council asserting British rights over the AAT and placing it under the administration of the Commonwealth of Australia, followed by the enactment of the *Australian Antarctic Territory Acceptance Act* 1933 (Cth). Australia thereby gained sovereignty over approximately 42 per cent of the Antarctic continent through a mixture of British claims, "Empire" claims, and Australian claims made by Mawson and others. Proclamation of the AAT was contested only by Norway, however this was withdrawn in 1939 following a compromise that Norwegian whalers would not be faced with onerous licensing requirements in waters adjacent to other territorial claims (Triggs 1986: 110). Since 1933 Australia has been engaged in a gradual process of solidifying for international law purposes its claim over the AAT, whilst also working with the international community in the active management of Antarctic affairs.

The Antarctic Treaty System and Antarctic Sovereignty

By 1959 there had emerged a three-way division of positions on the question of Antarctic sovereignty. United Kingdom officials had originally harboured ambitions to acquire the whole Antarctic continent (Chaturvedi 1990: 44) but between the two World Wars it had negotiated a division of the continent with France, Norway, New Zealand and Australia. Australia was a member of a small group of States that had, from the early 20th century onwards, made claims to Antarctica based on the international law of territorial acquisition. As we have seen, it is only the other States within this group that recognise Australia's claim to the AAT.

None of these States recognised the Antarctic territorial rights of the two South American claimants, Chile and Argentina, and Britain's attempts in the immediate post-war period to resolve the issues of its overlapping claim were unsuccessful. Chile and Argentina each asserted territorial rights to the portion of the Antarctic continent nearest to its mainland territory, both recognising the right of the other to a portion of South American Antarctica. These rights were believed to derive from a papal bull of 1493 by which Alexander VI gave, granted and assigned forever to Spain and its successors, all territory from the Arctic pole to the Antarctic pole west of a meridian 370 leagues west of the Cape Verde Islands. Argentina and Chile, as successor States to Spain in South America, each believed they had inherited territorial rights to a portion of Antarctica. At the time when the first group of States was actively engaged in claiming their territorial rights, the South American States believed that their rights were long-standing; for this second group of States all that remained to be done was to negotiate a mutual boundary between their respective portions of the South American Antarctic (Scott 1997).

Members of a third group of States, which included the United States, the USSR, Japan, South Africa and Belgium, had not made formal territorial claims but either asserted their right to do so at a later date or had at least displayed an active interest in the question. While the positions of the first two groups of States had not been reconcilable, the existence of this third perspective further complicated the situation.

This was the background to Antarctic sovereignty and the status of the existing territorial claims which confronted the 1959 Washington Conference called to consider the continent's future. The United States led the way in the negotiations, which resulted in the adoption of Article IV to the Antarctic Treaty and an agreement to disagree regarding Antarctic sovereignty. Article IV provides:

1. Nothing contained in the present Treaty shall be interpreted as:
   (a) A renunciation by any Contracting Party of previously asserted rights of or claims to territorial sovereignty in Antarctica;
   (b) A renunciation or diminution by any Contracting Party of any basis of claim to territorial sovereignty in Antarctica which it may have whether as a result of its activities or those of its nationals in Antarctica, or otherwise;
   (c) Prejudicing the position of any Contracting Party as regards its recognition or non-recognition of any other State's right of or claim or basis of claim to territorial sovereignty in Antarctica.

2. No acts or activities taking place while the present Treaty is in force shall constitute a basis for asserting, supporting or denying a claim to territorial sovereignty in Antarctica or create any rights of sovereignty in Antarctica. No new claim, or enlargement of an existing claim, to territorial sovereignty in Antarctica shall be asserted while the present Treaty is in force.

This article was deliberately ambiguous, providing a basis for inter-State cooperation despite the three-way division in attitudes on the fundamental question of sovereignty. Given the tensions over sovereignty claims in the immediate postwar period, and the Cold War rivalry of the United States and Soviet Union at that time, the reaching of a consensus over the language of Article IV was remarkable. The then Australian Minister for External Affairs, Richard Casey, is credited with having played a major role in securing Soviet support for Article IV (Woolcott 2003: 20).

It has been reinforced by subsequent agreements within the system. Most recently, Article 4 of the 1991 Protocol on Environmental Protection to the Antarctic Treaty (Madrid Protocol) stipulated that it shall neither modify nor amend the Antarctic Treaty and that, by paragraph 2, nothing in the Protocol "shall derogate from the rights and obligations of the Parties to this Protocol under the other international instruments in force within the Antarctic Treaty System". As more States have become Parties to the Treaty and the number of Consultative Parties has increased, so the proportion of States falling into the third category has increased. Of the current 28 Consultative Parties to the Antarctic Treaty, 21 have made no claims to Antarctic Territory to date and do not recognise the existing claims (Australian Attorney-General 2005).

Article IV, which constituted a carefully crafted non-resolution of the sovereignty dispute, necessitated an equally carefully crafted provision on dispute resolution. Article XI emphasised consensual dispute resolution only and, while the Madrid Protocol provides for compulsory dispute settlement, it expressly excludes from that process disputes relating to Article IV of the Antarctic Treaty. Since the negotiating States did not want formal dispute resolution of their basic point of disagreement, they included other substantive provisions in the Antarctic Treaty – such as prohibiting measures of a military nature and guaranteeing freedom of scientific research and activity – which were designed to facilitate their avoiding disputes in the first place (Wilder 1995).

Both before and since the coming into force of the Antarctic Treaty in 1961, Australia has directed considerable diplomatic effort to protecting its sovereignty claim against any weakening from multilateral developments.[4] When it was not possible to formulate a treaty to address the emergent issue of Antarctic mining so as to be at least neutral in its implications for Australia's sovereignty, Australia led the charge to abandon the 1988 Convention on the Regulation of Antarctic Mineral Resource Activities (CRAMRA) and replace it with the Madrid Protocol. While the diplomatic stand gave a boost to Australia's environmental credentials, there is little doubt that a fundamental motivation for Australia's diplomatic actions was the view that CRAMRA had not satisfactorily respected the position of the claimant States (Crawford and Rothwell 1992).

Australian Sovereignty and the Antarctic Treaty System

Australia has developed its Antarctic policy and law within the context of the Antarctic Treaty System (ATS). In practice this has meant seeking to continually strengthen its legal position, without forcing the issue to a point at which another State might pursue some form of dispute resolution. This task was made difficult not only by Article IV but by Article VIII of the Antarctic Treaty, which places significant constraints on the exercise of territorial sovereignty vis-a-vis other Treaty Parties; preferring instead jurisdiction based upon nationality. Australian law has been gradually extended to a variety of activities in Antarctica from criminal and civil law to wide-ranging environmental standards (Crawford and Rothwell 1992: 53-88; Rothwell and Davis 1997; Kaye *et al* 1999). The 1992 report of the House of Representatives Standing Committee on Legal and Constitutional Affairs entitled "Australian law in Antarctica" (House of Representatives 1992), exposed some gaps in the legal regime and concluded that:

---

4   In the immediate postwar years, for example, Australian officials sought the inclusion of Japan's renunciation of territorial rights in the post-War Peace Treaty with Japan (Scott 1999).

[I]t is both in Australia's sovereign interests and consistent with Australia's obligations under the Antarctic Treaty to extend and apply Australian law to foreign nationals in the Australian Antarctic Territory who are not otherwise exempted by Article 8(1) of the Antarctic Treaty.[5]

Australia's intent has clearly been to create a legal regime that reflects Australian sovereignty over Antarctica and also a national policy of promoting the freedom of scientific research and environmental protection. The Australian Government has nevertheless stopped short of enforcing its laws in Antarctica against the nationals of other States Parties to the Antarctic Treaty, except in cases where such persons have voluntarily subjected themselves to Australian laws (Australian Attorney-General 2005: 3). Whilst this position has largely been viable with respect to Australian law on the continent, its application has been tested with respect to the waters of the Southern Ocean offshore the AAT. This has been due to developments in the international law of the sea which have arisen throughout the life of the Antarctic Treaty, and increased activity in the Southern Ocean.

The Third United Nations Convention on the Law of the Sea (LOS Convention),[6] which entered into force in 1994,[7] continued the trend of limiting the freedom of the seas in favour of greater coastal State jurisdiction. In relation to Antarctica this gave rise most fundamentally to the question of whether there are in fact any coastal States in Antarctica (Joyner 1992: 75). Article IV(2) of the Antarctic Treaty, by which "No new claim, or enlargement of an existing claim, to territorial sovereignty in Antarctica shall be asserted while the present Treaty is in force", has created a challenge for States seeking to assert their rights as coastal States under the law of the sea whilst also acting consistently with the Treaty. Australia has asserted a range of claims offshore the AAT which the Government considers to be consistent with both its obligations under the Antarctic Treaty and the LOS Convention. Australia first asserted a continental shelf claim offshore the AAT in 1953 (Kaye and Rothwell 2002; Kaye 2001). In 1973 Australia proclaimed a three nautical mile (nm) territorial sea around all its territory, including the AAT, and in November 1990 extended this from three to twelve nm. Australia proclaimed an Exclusive Economic Zone (EEZ) off the AAT on 1 August 1994 (Opeskin and Rothwell 1991).

In accordance with the need to ensure the strength of its claim while not pushing the sovereignty issue so far as to provoke an attempt at resolution, Australia has adopted the somewhat ambiguous legal position of having asserted these maritime claims without actively implementing its laws within these zones. Indeed due to the uncertainty as to the position of

---

5   Article 8(1) relates to designated observers and scientific exchange personnel.
6   1833 UNTS 396.
7   Australia ratified the Convention on 5 October 1994, five weeks before it came into force on 16 November 1994.

12

the baselines around the AAT, there remains doubt as to precisely how far offshore Australia's maritime claims actually extend (Rothwell 2001). Whilst a good deal of Australian law applies within these various maritime areas offshore the AAT, there has been no instance of such law being applied to the activities of non-Australian nationals or foreign vessels.[8] Australia has thereby sought to maintain the integrity of its claim to sovereignty over the AAT and the accompanying maritime sovereignty and jurisdiction which any coastal State enjoys over its offshore areas, whilst also respecting the limitations on the active assertion of sovereignty and jurisdiction imposed by the Antarctic Treaty.

Current Issues for Australian Sovereignty

The most recent challenges for Australian policymakers have pertained to Australia's delimitation of the outer limit of the extended continental shelf as well as to the possible enforcement of whaling regulations within the EEZ.

Australia's Southern Ocean Extended Continental Shelf Claim

The LOS Convention recognises that every coastal State is entitled to a minimum continental shelf of 200 nm, however some coastal States may be able to claim an extended continental shelf of up to approximately 350 nm depending on their particular offshore geological shelf conditions.[9] The LOS Convention imposes an obligation upon coastal States to submit their claims to an extended continental shelf within a defined time limit and in November 2004 Australia submitted its claim to the Commission on the Limits of the Continental Shelf (CLCS) (Downer *et al* 2004), thus becoming only the third State after the Russian Federation and Brazil to do so.[10] The Australian claim made under the provisions of Article 76 of the LOS Convention will, if accepted by the CLCS, give Australia a continental shelf of approximately 3.4 million square kilometres, which when combined with its land territories will make it one of the largest States in the world. Two aspects of the Australian claim have particular Antarctic significance. The first is that, if endorsed, the extended continental shelf claim to the south of Heard Island and McDonald Islands will extend into the area south of 60 degrees South and hence fall within the Antarctic Treaty area. The second, is that Australia has sought to assert a claim offshore the AAT. Aspects of the claim – which are reflective of an

---

8   This is to be contrasted with the active enforcement of Australian fisheries law in the waters surrounding Heard Island and McDonald Islands, two sub-Antarctic islands over which Australian sovereignty is uncontested and which lie north of the Antarctic Treaty area's 60 degrees South latitude limit.

9   Part VI, LOS Convention.

10   Neither the Russian nor Brazilian submission to the CLCS concern Antarctica and so will not be discussed here.

Australian assertion of sovereignty – therefore raise issues not only under the law of the sea but particularly under Article IV of the Antarctic Treaty.

In the first case, the Heard Island and McDonald Islands extended continental shelf claim may raise some concerns as to their legitimacy given the islands are uninhabited other than for an occasional visit by research scientists, thereby raising the question as to whether they are truly islands or rocks for the purposes of the LOS Convention, Article 121. Judge Vukas has already expressed his concerns in the International Tribunal for the Law of the Sea (ITLOS) regarding the legitimacy of the Australian exclusive economic zone offshore these islands.[11] However, given the size of the islands and the "economic life" they have generated as a consequence of Australian licensed fishing activities in those waters (principally for Patagonian toothfish) it is difficult to sustain a credible argument that Australia is not entitled to seek to assert an extended continental shelf. That the Australian claim purports to extend south of 60 degrees South into the Antarctic Treaty area is of more significance. For Australia this raises some delicate issues under the Antarctic regime, especially with respect to the prohibition contained in the Antarctic Treaty, Article IV, on the assertion of "any new claim, or the enlargement of an existing claim, to territorial sovereignty in Antarctica" while the Treaty is in force (Kaye 2001: 125-37). Likewise, the claim to an extended continental shelf and the potential that provides for mining in that area seems to conflict with the provisions of the Madrid Protocol which prohibits mining taking place within the Treaty area.[12]

The second Australian claim to an extended continental shelf in Antarctica extends from the continent north of the AAT. The claim seeks to enclose an area of 686,821 square kilometres beyond the limits of the 200 nm exclusive economic zone (Commonwealth of Australia 2004). Not only does the claim raise legal issues under the Antarctic Treaty, but also presents challenges for the CLCS (Jabour 2006).

The role of the CLCS is briefly referred to in the LOS Convention, Article 76(8) where reference is made to the need for coastal States to submit information on their extended continental shelf claims to the Commission. The article then goes on to provide:

> The Commission shall make recommendations to coastal States on matters related to the establishment of the outer limits of their continental shelf. The limits of the shelf established by a coastal State on the basis of these recommendations shall be final and binding.

This rather brief provision in the LOS Convention therefore creates a quasi-judicial process. The role of the CLCS is characterised by McDorman as

---

11   See *The Volga Case* (Russian Federation v Australia) ITLOS Case No 11, 23 December 2002 (2003) 42 ILM 159.

12   Article 7, Protocol on Environmental Protection to the Antarctic Treaty of 4 October 1991 (1991) 30 ILM 1455.

that of "legitimator" (McDorman 2002: 319). It is one in which coastal States seek to justify their continental shelf beyond the limits of 200 nm claims by way of a submission to the CLCS which in turn makes recommendations to those coastal States. The outcome of this process will be the establishment of outer continental shelf limits which are "final and binding" and have implications for the Part XI deep seabed regime.

The work of the CLCS may raise a variety of contentious issues under the LOS Convention. While having sought to already flag that it will not consider applications made with respect to continental shelves claimed offshore disputed territories,[13] the Commission could find itself facing difficulties in making determinations as to whether or not there exists such a territorial "dispute" or likewise whether the baselines upon which the claim is asserted are consistent with the LOS Convention.[14] While given the essentially non-legal and depoliticised character of the Commission's mandate this approach towards disputed claims is justifiable, it has the potential if not handled with caution to raise political tensions in other areas of the law of the sea and within other fora.

In a Note that Australia lodged to accompany its CLCS submission, reference is made to the "principles and objectives shared" by the Antarctic Treaty and the LOS Convention and to the "circumstances" of the area south of 60 degrees South and the "special legal and political status of Antarctica" under the Antarctic Treaty.[15] The Note then observes as follows:

> It is open to the States concerned to submit information to the Commission which would not be examined by it for the time being, or to make a partial submission not including such areas of continental shelf, for which a submission may be made later ... Consistent with the first option, Australia requests the Commission in accordance with its rules not to take any action for the time being with regard to the information in this Submission that relates to continental shelf appurtenant to Antarctica.

At its first substantive consideration of the Australian submission in April 2005, the CLCS referred to the Australian Note and other communications and elected not to consider that part of the submission dealing with region 2 – "Australian Antarctic Territory" (CLCS 2005).

Whilst that would seem for the time being to set aside any controversy over Australia's claim to an extended continental shelf offshore the AAT, the reaction to the Australian claim cannot be ignored. Eight States lodged communications with the Secretary-General of the United Nations in

---

13 See Commission on the Limits of the Continental Shelf – Rules of Procedure, rule 45 and Annex I.

14 Both of these issues are most likely to arise in the context of any claim made by a coastal State with respect to an extended continental shelf asserted offshore Antarctica (Oude Elferink 2002).

15 Attachment to Commonwealth of Australia 2004 "Note from the Permanent Mission of Australia to the Secretary-General of the United Nations accompanying the lodgement of Australia's submission".

relation to the Australian submission, and six of these deal directly with the continental shelf claim in Antarctica (CLCS 2005). The six States – Germany, India, Japan, Netherlands, Russian Federation, and the United States – are all Parties to the Antarctic Treaty and have played prominent roles in Antarctic affairs over the past century. Each of the communications makes direct reference to the provisions of the Antarctic Treaty, particularly Article IV, and denies recognition to rights or claims over the seabed or adjacent offshore surrounding Antarctica. The German communication is representative and states:

> Recalling Article IV of the Antarctic Treaty, Germany does not recognize any State's claim to territory in Antarctica and does not recognize that a State's claim to territorial sovereignty in Antarctica is capable of creating any rights over the seabed and subsoil of the submarine areas beyond and adjacent to the Continent of Antarctica. (Germany 2005)

By contrast, in a communication lodged by France – another Antarctic Treaty Party but also an Antarctic claimant – the AAT extended continental shelf claim is ignored and only those parts of the Australian claim which are adjacent to areas where Australia and France have delimited relevant maritime boundaries in the case of the Kerguelen Plateau and New Caledonia are discussed (France 2005). Whilst for the time being issues relating to an extended continental shelf offshore the AAT have been set aside, the diplomatic communications with the United Nations generated by the Australian claim have only underlined how tenuous Australia's claim to sovereignty over the continent and adjacent offshore areas actually is.

Whaling

Australia has a long history with whaling, first, as an active whaling nation with a vibrant whaling industry littered around southern Australian coastlines. More recently, Australia through its domestic law and policy and international engagement in the International Whaling Commission (IWC) has been an active promoter of whale conservation. Commercial whaling is banned in Australian waters, and in its place whale-watching tourism has flourished in many coastal towns and cities (Gill *et al* 2003).

A principal element to Australia's policy on whales for the past 20 years has been its opposition to all forms of commercial whaling under the International Convention for the Regulation of Whaling (ICRW).[16] Since 1986 a moratorium on commercial whaling has existed under the ICRW as a result of a determination made by the IWC, the body responsible for the Convention's administration. However, Japan has exploited a loophole in the ICRW whereby under Article VIII(1) a Contracting Government may grant to any of its nationals a special permit authorising that national to

---

16   161 UNTS 74.

kill, take, and treat whales for purposes of scientific research. Scientific permits can authorise research only on the high seas, that is beyond the EEZ. The effect of Article 8 is that the killing or taking of whales for scientific purposes is exempt from the operation of the Convention. In the 2005-06 austral season Japan commenced a new program of "scientific" whaling in the Southern Ocean – JARPA II – which itself follows on from a previous scientific program, JARPA, which ran from 1987 to 2005.

Under Article 56 of the LOS Convention, a coastal State has sovereign rights for the purpose of exploring and exploiting, conserving and managing natural resources and all vessels are subject to that country's laws in these matters. In 2000, the Australian Government proclaimed the Australian Whale Sanctuary under the *Environment Protection and Biodiversity Conservation Act* 1999 (EPBC Act). It encompasses all of Australia's EEZ and includes the waters around the AAT and Australia's external territories. Within the Australian Whale Sanctuary it is illegal to kill, injure or interfere with any cetaceans.

Notwithstanding the Australian prohibition on whaling in waters off the AAT, Japan has been able to conduct such activities without fear of prosecution under Australian law. Japan does not recognise Australia's Antarctic claim and hence its authority to legislate with respect to the Zone off the AAT. Yet the Humane Society International (HSI) estimates that since the Sanctuary was established in 2000 nearly a quarter of all the whales killed under JARPA were within the Australian Whale Sanctuary (HSI 2004). This creates a dilemma for not only the Australian Government, but also AAD. The instructions to AAD Voyage Leaders specify that, beyond advising any vessels involved in whaling within Australia's EEZ that they are doing so in contravention of Australian legislation, that their details have been passed on to Australian authorities and that they are asked to leave, no further enforcement action should be taken.[17]

The EPBC Act confers upon an "interested person" the capacity to seek injunctions for contravention of the Act, and is wide enough to include within its ambit environmental and conservation focused non-government organisations.[18] On 19 October 2004 the HSI filed an application in the Australian Federal Court for a case against Kyodo Senpaku Kaisha Ltd, the Japanese company that undertakes the "scientific whaling" program in the Southern Ocean, seeking a declaration of the Court that whaling within the Sanctuary is illegal, as well as a prohibitory injunction restraining Kyodo. The HSI's Wildlife and Habitat Program Manager, Nicola Beynon, said that the aim of the action was to push the Australian Government to prosecute the Japanese whalers (Ocean Conserve 2004). Despite noting what appeared to be a clear *prima facie* case of contravention of Australian municipal law, Justice Allsop at first instance dismissed the application

17 "Extract from instructions to Australian Antarctic Division Voyage Leaders", See Attachment A, Australian Attorney-General 2005.
18 *Environment Protection and Biodiversity Conservation Act* 1999 (Cth), s 475.

(*Humane Society International Inc v Kyodo Senpaku Kaisha Ltd* [2005] FCA 664) citing the lack of means of making any injunction effectual:

> The making of a declaration alone (a course suggested by the applicant) might be seen as tantamount to an empty assertion of domestic law (by the Court), devoid of utility beyond use (by others) as a political statement. (at [34])

This decision appeared to be based primarily on an *amicus curiae* submission of the Federal Attorney-General, which had stated that Japan would consider any attempt to enforce Australian law against Japanese vessels and its nationals in the waters adjacent to the AAT to be a breach of international law on Australia's part, that it could reasonably be expected to prompt a significant adverse reaction from other Antarctic Treaty Parties, and potentially undermine the status quo in the ATS (Australian Attorney-General 2005).

HSI appealed the decision of Justice Allsop to the Full Court of the Federal Court of Australia, and in 2006 by a 2-1 majority the Court ruled in favour of HSI and gave leave to serve the originating process on Kyodo in Japan (*Humane Society International Inc v Kyodo Senpaku Kaisga Ltd* [2006] FCAFC 116). The majority judges, Chief Justice Black and Justice Finkelstein, approached the issues primarily from a procedural perspective focusing more on issues of private international law than public international law questions of Australia's claim to the AAT and enforcement of Australian law. They were of the view that Justice Allsop was "in error in attaching weight to what we would characterise as a political consideration" and concluded that "the political dimension of the dispute is non-justiciable" (at [12]). That there was the potential for the injunction issued by the Court to be disobeyed was not a matter which in their view the Court should contemplate (at [16]). Rather, they were struck by the provisions of the EPBC Act under which "Parliament has determined that it is in the public interest that the enforcement provisions of the EPBC Act should be unusually comprehensive in scope" (at [19]). Whilst Justice Moore in dissent did not disagree with the principal findings of the majority judges, ultimately "the almost certain futility of the litigation which the applicant wishes to pursue" was a decisive factor (at [43]). It was the view of Justice Moore that:

> It is almost certain that the respondent will not submit to the jurisdiction of an Australian court having regard to the broad political context in which it engages in whaling and, in particular, having regard to the fact that it is doing so seemingly lawfully under Japanese law, with the authority of the Japanese Government. (at [45])

Following this judgment it does remain to be seen what action Kyodo will take upon service of the injunction. There is a high probably that given Japan's position towards Australia's AAT claim, let alone issues of the consistency of the operation of the EPBC Act with the Antarctic Treaty, that the injunction will be ignored. If this does occur, it will be something of a mixed blessing for the Australian Government as while on the one hand it sidesteps a diplomatic incident between Australia and Japan, on the other it highlights Australia's limitations in enforcing its law in Antarctica notwithstanding there being an apparently clear infringement of that law.

The Australian Government has yet to publicly respond to the ruling in the HSI case, nor would it be expected to do so given the case is presently at a phase where the onus will rest with Kyodo as to how it may react to the service of an injunction. In the meantime, the Australian Government continues to publicly assert its opposition to Japanese whaling and reaffirm its intention to secure further protection for whales through diplomatic channels (Campbell 2005b).

Concluding Remarks

In case of any possible breakdown of the ATS or other unforeseeable eventuality that could force resolution of the sovereignty issue, the Australian Government has engaged in rhetoric and actions that preserve as best it can, the Australian claim to the AAT. Political judgment has been required in order to assess how far it has been possible to act as a sovereign without forcing the issue to a possibly unfavourable resolution. The LOS Convention has added to Australia's difficulties in maintaining the careful balance between acting in a manner consistent with its claim to 42 per cent of the Antarctic continent and not forcing that issue to the extent that a non-claimant seeks to take the question to an international tribunal. The HSI case also had the impact of publicising Australia's lack of enforcement of its Whale Sanctuary thereby highlighting the seeming contradiction between legislating to preclude an activity and then choosing not to enforce that law.

There remains then an inherent ambiguity in Australia's claim to sovereignty in Antarctica. Whilst it has a long-standing historic basis, the legality of the claim has never been conclusively established internationally. Legally the claim reflects an odd mixture of traditional elements combined with a certain *lex specialis* which has been developed for Antarctica. Reflecting on the Australian Antarctic claim, Greig observed in 1984:

> Australian title did not become definitively established by the application of the rules (viewed in their most favourable light) deduced from the Palmas and Eastern Greenland decisions. Hence, Australia's claim is open to examination in the light of subsequent changes to the law. (Greig 1984: 77-8)

As a result, and despite the apparent assurance given in the Antarctic Treaty as to the *status quo ante* with respect to territorial claims, Australia has continued to seek to assert its sovereignty over the AAT via traditional methods such as enacting new laws and regulations and proclaiming new maritime zones. Yet a certain ambiguity remains. As noted by Bush:

> Australia has communicated mixed messages on the strength of its commitment to its claim. In spite of some bold assertions of Australia's right to control foreigners in the Australian Antarctic Territory including its exclusive economic zone, Australia is not in the camp of those who assert Antarctic sovereignty for its own sake. (Bush 2001: 132)

Whaling has the potential to become a symbolic flashpoint for Australian sovereignty in Antarctica. Japan's JARPA II program will fully commence in the 2007-08 austral season and for the first time will result in the killing of humpback whales for scientific research. Given the iconic status of these whales resulting from their seasonal migration through Australian waters and their economic significance as part of the "whale watching" industry, it must be anticipated there will be considerable public pressure for a robust government response. Whilst the Federal Government's submissions in the HSI litigation reflect a pragmatic assertion of legal realism, and legitimate concerns over the impact upon the Treaty system of a dispute between longstanding Treaty Parties, Australia's Antarctic environmental policy will be seen as fundamentally flawed if it is unable to address concerns over Japanese whaling. The reality is that Australia may fast be approaching the position that it can no longer remain an Antarctic fence sitter but must choose between national interests and international interests. The impact of such a choice for the ATS remains to be seen, however it must be recalled that Australia made such a decision previously when electing to reject CRAMRA and promote the environmental solution which became the Madrid Protocol. Australia's Antarctic policy may once again be at that crossroads.

3

Setting and Implementing the Agenda: Australian Antarctic Policy

Marcus Haward, Rob Hall and Aynsley Kellow

Introduction

Australia has significant national interests in the Southern Ocean and Antarctica. It claims 42 per cent of Antarctica, making the Australian Antarctic Territory (AAT) an important External Territory. Australia also has sovereignty over the sub-Antarctic Territory of Heard Island and McDonald Islands and Macquarie Island with the latter, interestingly, part of the state of Tasmania. Australia is party to key international instruments that apply in the region, including the Antarctic Treaty and its Protocol on Environmental Protection to the Antarctic Treaty 1991 (Madrid Protocol), the Convention on the Conservation of Antarctic Marine Living Resources (CCAMLR) – to which it is the depositary State and host of the CCAMLR Secretariat – and the Law of the Sea Convention (LOS Convention). These instruments, with the exception of LOS Convention, form a regime termed the Antarctic Treaty System (ATS).

Two related drivers influence Australia's Antarctic policy. The first driver is the domestic political agenda. The second, and clearly not mutually exclusive, driver derives from Australia's participation in the development and ratification of international agreements (Davis and Haward 1994), that in turn provide key parameters for Australian Antarctic policy. The domestic agenda is shaped by objectives identified through Australian Government goals for the Australian Antarctic Program. In 1997 the Antarctic Science Advisory Committee (ASAC) received a reference from the Parliamentary Secretary to examine the future uncertainties in the external environment within which science in the future will be conducted (ASAC 1997). The resultant Foresight Review (ASAC 1997) was an important document and shaped the current government goals for the Australian Antarctic Program:

- to maintain the Antarctic Treaty System and enhance Australia's influence within the system;

- to protect the Antarctic environment;
- to understand the role of Antarctica in the global climate system; and
- to undertake scientific work of practical, economic and national significance.

According to the Australian Antarctic Division's "Statement of Purpose and Values", Goal One of the Australian Antarctic Program, to "[m]aintain the Antarctic Treaty System and enhance Australia's influence within it" is to be achieved by:

- maintaining a strong presence at ATS meetings, taking the lead on issues and developing initiatives for international consideration;
- complying with the requirements of the ATS; and
- cooperating with our Antarctic Treaty partners. (AAD 2000)

Australia's Antarctic policy centres on the implementation of its goals and also helps define and operationalise what Richardson and Jordan (1979) termed the policy community – those policy actors that share interest in and concern over this policy area. The policy community includes a number of government agencies (forming what is termed the sub-government) as well as non-government organisations (NGOs) that comprise the attentive public (Pross 1992). The policy community is buttressed by longstanding and bipartisan political support for Australia's Antarctic endeavours since the heroic era expeditions and establishment of the modern Australian Antarctic program in 1947. This support for Australia's involvement within ATS and its commitments to maintaining the AAT underpins Australian policy. Achieving key outcomes within the ATS can advance Australian goals and the link between domestic objectives and international achievements may be a means by which policy effectiveness may also be judged.

This chapter identifies Australia's international and domestic Antarctic policy interests including Australia's relation with and actions within the ATS. The chapter also identifies the key policy actors that form the Antarctic policy community and the network between these actors that contributes to the development and implementation of Australian Antarctic policy. Capacity to develop effective policy towards Antarctica, and the ability to coordinate responses from a range of government and non-government actors is seen as a critical element in the way in which this network operates and represents two ongoing challenges facing future Australian Antarctic policy.

Australian Antarctic Policy and Interests

Australia has a long connection with Antarctica with early British and French voyages leaving from the port of Hobart, Tasmania (Kriwoken and

Williamson 1993). It was Hobart that Roald Amundsen and the *Fram* made port and from where he telegraphed the news that he had been first to the South Pole in December 1911, beating Captain Scott's ill-fated party. The work of Australian scientists and explorers (Louis Bernacchi, Tannant Edgeworth David, Griffith Taylor and, most famously, Douglas Mawson) on a number of expeditions during the period 1890-1914 – the so called "heroic era" of Antarctic exploration – helped reinforce Australia's interests in, and later territorial claims to, Antarctica. While the less well-known (at least in contemporary Australia) Hubert Wilkins pioneered polar aviation, Mawson's continued expeditions and scientific work, along with his influence on government provided the foundation for the Australian Antarctic program. Mawson stands alone in terms of influence on Australian interests in the Antarctic (Haward 2007).

The administration of what became the AAT was transferred to Australia from the United Kingdom in 1933, following a claim made to the territory for Britain and King George V by Douglas Mawson as part of the British, Australian and New Zealand Antarctic Research Expedition (BANZARE) in 1929-31. Mawson raised the Union Jack on Proclamation Island on 13 January 1930 "to assert the sovereign rights of His Majesty over British land discoveries met within Antarctica" and then repeated this proclamation from the cockpit of a Tiger Moth plane that was flown along the coastline, dropping a Union Jack onto the ice on 25 January 1930 (Chester 1986).

The elaboration of territorial claims and the question of sovereignty in Antarctica was the critical element of the "Antarctic problem" in the 1930s and 1940s. The problem was addressed, if not resolved by the development of the Antarctic Treaty in 1958-59. The negotiation of the Antarctic Treaty was a significant diplomatic effort balancing the aspirations and interests of a number of different actors. Formal negotiations lasted 18 months from June 1958 and included 60 preparatory meetings and a formal diplomatic "Conference on Antarctica" that began on 15 October 1959 and ended with the Antarctic Treaty open for signature on 1 December 1959. States like Australia that had territorial claims (in addition to Australia the claimant States are Argentina, Chile, France, New Zealand, Norway and United Kingdom) wished to maintain the status of claims. This position was opposed by the United States and the Soviet Union, both of whom did not recognise any claim but had reserved the right to make claims in the future. The Soviet Union had established research stations in each of the claimant's territory (including the AAT) during the International Geophysical Year (IGY) and the United States had established a station (Amundsen-Scott) at the south geographic pole, effectively within all claimants' territories.

A Chilean initiative provided a *modus vivendi* to resolve the differences between claimants and others through effectively "freezing" existing and any further territorial claims, while allowing States to recognise claims.

Australia played an important brokerage role in the development of the Antarctic Treaty. Australian diplomats had considerable involvement in the drafting of the Treaty, with Casey, the Minister for External Affairs, maintaining an active interest in Antarctic matters. While Casey's direct involvement in the Treaty negotiations was limited he was, nonetheless, instrumental in helping forge relations with the delegates from the Soviet Union that was critical in ensuring their support for the Antarctic Treaty (Hall 2002).

Policy Interests – International

Australia is an original signatory to the Antarctic Treaty and is an active and influential Antarctic Treaty Consultative Party (ATCP). From 2003 to 2006 Australia held the Chair of the Committee for Environment Protection established under the Madrid Protocol. The pursuit of Australia's interests in the ATS depends on an ability to negotiate positions in the various forums of the Treaty system, as well as within numerous working groups and committees including:

- Antarctic Treaty Consultative Meetings (ATCMs);
- Scientific Committee on Antarctic Research (SCAR);
- Committee for Environment Protection (CEP);
- Commission for the Conservation of Antarctic Marine Living Resources (CCAMLR);
- Standing Committee on Antarctic Logistics and Operations (SCALOP); and
- Council of Managers of National Antarctic Programs (COMNAP).

Australia's position within the ATS is buttressed and reinforced by decades of diplomatic and scientific effort. Australia's scientific program is based on over half a century of organised scientific endeavour on the sub-Antarctic islands, the Antarctic continent and the Southern Ocean (AAD 2000; Haward et al 2006).

Policy Interests – Domestic

Antarctica provides powerful and evocative images (Haward 2006). Australia's claim to the AAT, based on heroic era discovery, exploration and science has been supported by significant bipartisan political commitment for over 70 years. As this political commitment has remained, the key interests that drive that commitment have also remained relatively stable, albeit developing and evolving. Brook noted in 1984 that Australia policy interests are summarised as sovereignty; neutrality; protection of the Antarctic environment; Antarctic science; involvement in Antarctica; and benefit (Brook 1984: 256-9). In the 20 years since Brook's analysis certain interests have increased in salience – for example commitment to environmental protection increased in importance as a result of the negotiation and entry into force of the Madrid Protocol. The question of "benefit" from Antarctica was for Brook "immediately qualified, because Australia has an interest also in the protection of Antarctica from unjustifiable or damaging exploitation" (Brook 1984: 259). However, it is important to note the emphasis on "scientific work of practical, economic and national significance" as the current fourth goal for the Australian Antarctic program.

Sovereignty also remains a significant, if sometimes understated interest. The intersection of the LOS Convention and the ATS has recently helped focus attention on sovereignty (see Rothwell and Scott this volume). The declaration of maritime zones off the AAT has been controversial, but resolved by not enforcing territorial sea rights. The question of delimitation of the continental shelf off AAT posed important political and legal challenges to Australia, but also a dilemma in relation to its interests. Failure to include the AAT in survey work and data collection for the extended continental shelf would have indicated a change in attitude to Australia's claims to sovereignty over the AAT (Ruth Baird 2004). The solution to this dilemma was relatively simple, yet fraught with potential difficulties. Australia lodged the data for its claims to an extended continental shelf in accordance with the provisions of the LOS Convention and requested that the Commission on the Limits of the Continental Shelf (CLCS) not examine the data associated with the AAT (Commonwealth of Australia 2004).

Australian involvement in Antarctic politics has, as discussed above, involved a range of activities. Significant recent examples include the support given to Argentina in establishing the Treaty Secretariat and work with Malaysia (2002-05) to facilitate increased interaction between it and the ATS, and ATCPs. The latter initiative indicates how such interests can evolve, as it was Australia that led the debate against Malaysia in the United Nations General Assembly on the Question of Antarctica in 1982 (Woolcott 2003; Tepper and Haward 2005).

Australia's ongoing science program – the Australian Antarctic Program (AAP), initially known as Australian National Antarctic Research Expeditions (ANARE) – was initiated in 1947. The development of ANARE supported the establishment of research stations on Heard Island and Macquarie Island and subsequently the construction of research stations for "wintering over" on the Antarctic continent within the AAT, starting with Mawson in 1954. Australia currently has three year-round continental stations (Casey, Mawson and Davis) and a year-round station on sub-Antarctic Macquarie Island. These stations are supported by a number of summer bases and field camps established for specific research or environmental monitoring purposes (AAD 2000). Influence within the ATS has traditionally been measured by the commitment to and quality of science undertaken in the Antarctic. This criterion is important and is embedded in the Antarctic Treaty and reinforced in the Madrid Protocol. Australia's longstanding commitment to Antarctic science is a further arena of influence, and one that complements its commitment to leadership. The Australian Government's Foresight Review recognised the linkage between Australia's commitment to the ATS and the significance of longstanding scientific programs. Science is a driver of many Antarctic programs, including the AAP. Science is a necessary condition for influence within the ATS but, on its own, will not maximise influence. Influence is also achieved by diplomatic clout as measured through successes in establishment and maintenance of international instruments and through strengthening the system that operates on consensus.

Australia and the Antarctic Treaty System

The first meeting of Antarctic Treaty Parties (the first ATCM) was held in Canberra from 10-14 July 1961. Addressing the first ATCM meeting Prime Minister Menzies noted the intense negotiations that had accompanied the drafting of the Antarctic Treaty and commented on the way in which the Parties had accommodated different views and interests within this instrument for the pursuit of peaceful scientific exploration.

Australia took a central role in the development of CCAMLR in the 1970s and 1980s, hosting the final conference of Parties and, as noted above, becoming depositary State for the Convention, and providing significant support to the Commission secretariat. The negotiations of CCAMLR pioneered innovative approaches to marine resource management, introducing an ecosystem-based approach to managing these resources, an approach that has been incorporated more widely into other international instruments and management organisations in the 1990s.

Despite Australia's commitment to the Antarctic Treaty and the ATS it was also a central player in the most significant challenges to fundamentals of this system. The first of these challenges arose from Malaysia's sponsorship of a United Nations General Assembly (UNGA) debate on the "Question of Antarctica" in 1982. In 1985 the UNGA debate on Antarctica, despite lengthy negotiations, broke down into a standoff between Malaysia and Australia who spoke on behalf of the ATCPs (Woolcott 2003). Richard Woolcott, Australian Ambassador and Permanent Representative to the United Nations, had extensive experience in South-East Asia, including an appointment to the Australian High Commission in Malaysia in the early 1960s (Woolcott 2003). In 1985 the ATCPs led by Australia objected to references in the UN resolutions linking the "common heritage of mankind" concept and law of the sea to Antarctica. These objections led the ATCPs to decide not to participate in passing resolutions on the "Question of Antarctica" (Woolcott 2003). Australia's leadership in the debate on behalf of the ATCPs reflected its clear Antarctic interests, with Woolcott also working to bridge the gap between Malaysia and the ATCPs. The relationship between Prime Minister Mahathir and successive Australian governments had been difficult, reaching its apogee in 1993 when the then Australian Prime Minister Keating labelled Mahathir "recalcitrant" over his refusal to attend a meeting of the Asia Pacific Economic Cooperation forum (Tepper and Haward 2005).

The second and more significant challenge arose from Australia's decision in 1989 not to ratify the Convention on the Regulation of Antarctic Mineral Resource Activities (CRAMRA) (Bergin 1991). The Australian Government's opposition to CRAMRA manifested itself in concerns over environmental protection, although Australia had earlier had concerns about safeguarding Australia's territorial claim and the subsidisation of mineral exploration and extraction. Australia's concerns over CRAMRA, supported by France, were pivotal in scuttling CRAMRA and initiating negotiations that led to the development of the Madrid Protocol. The Protocol was adopted in Madrid on 4 October 1991 and its text and four Annexes entered force on 14 January 1998, with the fifth Annex – that had a separate approval process – not entering force until 24 May 2002.

The Protocol included a commitment to develop rules relating to liability for environmental damage. Australia participated in protracted negotiations over liability that concluded at ATCM XXVIII held in Stockholm in June 2005. ATCM XXVIII supported agreement on the Protocol's Annex VI on Liability Arising From Environmental Emergencies – the first stage in what is expected to become a more comprehensive Antarctic liability regime.

Australian Antarctic Policy: Institutions and Actors

Identification of the drivers of Australian Antarctic policy leads to a consideration of the factors that influence policy and policymakers. It also invites consideration of the conceptual and theoretical bases of public policy. In the mid 1970s Simeon (1976: 570-80) argued that public policy involves interaction between institutions, individuals and ideas. These parameters have been developed and extended by others (Doern and Phidd 1983). Schaffer provides an interesting and no doubt contestable definition of policy as "a committed structure of important resources ... convenient labels given *post hoc* to the mythical precedents of the apparent outcomes of uncertain conflict" (Schaffer 1977: 148). Schaffer's challenging definition highlights the tendency for the term "policy" to be used to order activity and indicate certainty that may mask considerable conflict over the definition of the problem, options, and even the final decision. This emphasises the point made by Parsons that "the student of a particular policy or problems must, above all, be aware of the different frameworks or lenses which may be brought to the interpretation of information and data" (Parsons 1995: 29).

Policymaking is a central activity of government, but government is not the only actor interested or influential in deliberations over policy.

British political scientists Richardson and Jordan (1979) focused on what they identified as limitations in traditional approaches to policy development, or at least the traditional influences on policy making that focused solely on governmental processes. Richardson and Jordan argued that non-government groups were important actors, active in policy development and implementation. Indeed some policies required active help of these groups to implement and to evaluate policy. Richardson and Jordan identified policy as:

> being made (and administered) between a myriad of interconnecting, interpenetrating organisations. It is the relationships involved in committees, *the policy community* of departments and groups, the practices of co-option and the consensual style, that perhaps better account for policy outcomes than do examinations of party stances, of manifestoes or of parliamentary influence. (Richardson and Jordan 1979: 74)

Following Richardson and Jordan's work many others developed the concept and utilised it in a range of areas. Pross, in identifying distinct elements of the policy community – the sub-government and the attentive public – provided further opportunities for analysis. The sub-government includes government agencies and institutionalised interest groups, while the attentive public includes any government agency, private institution pressure groups, specific interests, and individuals – including academics (Pross 1992). Homeshaw, in an analysis of Australian science policy, provided three important additional categories within the policy community – the executive core of key central agencies of ministers, the coordinating sub-government – key agencies within the sub-government and the influence of international actors – for example foreign governments, scientific organisations and individuals (Homeshaw 1995). In terms of the latter Homeshaw argued that the category of the international attentive public needed to be included. Analysis of Australian Antarctic policy reiterates the salience of Homeshaw's categories. The executive core – ministers, the ministerial offices and lead agencies provide important drivers of policy and of the policy process, while international scientific linkages are central to achieving many of Australian government goals for Antarctica. Scientific organisations and individuals form what Haas's termed the epistemic community (Haas 1989), ongoing links developed by shared interests in scientific discovery and, particularly in Antarctic science, international collaborative scientific research.

The Australian Antarctic Policy Community

As Figure 3 illustrates there are a number of actors that comprise the Australian Antarctic policy community. The policy community reflects the increasing sectorisation of policy where policy decisions are dealt with by smaller sub-system arrangements rather than through the full policy or political system, although there will be times where cabinet decisions are

Figure 3: The Australian Antarctic Policy Community

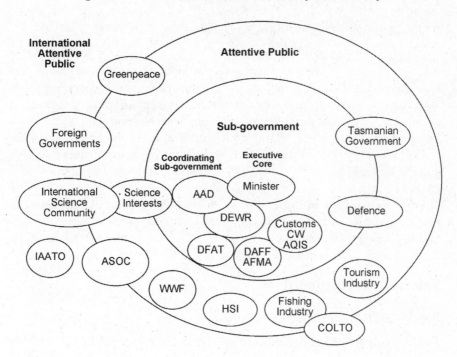

necessary. This enables the close relationship between key groups and the bureaucracy to develop and function – often to the mutual advantage of all actors. Links between different interests within the policy community can enhance discussion, but also indicate the need to ensure coordination as a key element of the policy process (Keating 1996).

The Executive Core: Ministers and Ministerial Offices

Ministers with responsibility for Australian Antarctic policy have played significant roles, from Casey in his commitment for the development of ANARE and the establishment of a continental presence; Prime Minister Menzies at the first ATCM in Canberra 1961; through to strong support from Prime Minister Hawke and Senior Ministers in the proposal not to sign CRAMRA (Woolcott 2003). More recently Australian ministers including Senator Hill have maintained high-level support for Australian Antarctic interests. Senator Hill made two visits to Antarctica in 1996 and 2001. Senator Campbell, Minister of Environment and Heritage between 2004-07, focused on the problems of illegal, unreported and unregulated (IUU) fishing in the Southern Ocean at CCAMLR meetings and took a high profile in condemning Japanese scientific whaling in the Southern Ocean.

The Coordinating Sub-Government

Australian Government Antarctic Division

The Australian Antarctic Division (AAD) is the lead agency for Australian Antarctic policy. A division of the Department of the Environment and Water Resources, AAD combines policy and management responsibilities with science and logistics support for Australia's Antarctic program. It maintains Australia's three Antarctic stations on the continent, a station on sub-Antarctic Macquarie Island and conducts and coordinates scientific research in Antarctica and the Southern Ocean. AAD administers the AAT and the External Territory of Heard Island and McDonald Islands, and provides key advice on advancing Australian interests through the ATS. The link between policy and operations enhances integration of the Antarctic Program but, together with its location in Tasmania, poses some challenges for intra-agency coordination.

The Sub-Government

Foreign Affairs and Trade

The Department of Foreign Affairs and Trade (DFAT) retains a role in Australian Antarctic policy, providing leadership of Australian delegations to ATCMs and support for diplomatic efforts within the ATS. This includes substantial efforts by Australian posts overseas in advancing Australian interests and providing feedback on responses. As Rowe notes, it was DFAT's predecessor, the Department of External Affairs, that was responsible for the development of Australia's Antarctic interests after the Second World War, through the development and operation of ANARE (Rowe 2002: 8).

The Environment and Water Resources

The Department of the Environment and Water Resources (formerly the Department of Environment and Heritage – DEH) is the home department of AAD and advises the Australian Government on policies and programs for the protection and conservation of the environment, including natural, cultural and indigenous heritage (DEH 2004). The Department has responsibility for Australian legislation giving effect to the Antarctic Treaty and related instruments, and it "represents Australia in international environmental agreements and forums ... [including] the Antarctic Treaty System, the International Whaling Commission" (DEH 2004). These functions are undertaken by AAD that, while located in Hobart, acts as any other part of the Department with a central policy role.

Agriculture, Fisheries and Forestry; Australian Fisheries Management Authority

The establishment of Australia's Southern Ocean fishery off Heard Island and McDonald Islands (HIMI) and Macquarie Island was a significant milestone in Australian Antarctic policy. It marked a key element in the evolution of Australian industry moving from a focus on fisheries within the Exclusive Economic Zone (EEZ) towards a distant water capability. Such activities added a new dimension to the "benefit" of Antarctic policy (Brook 1984) and added the fishing industry as actors with clear interests in policy. The development of Australian fisheries in the Southern Ocean, and off HIMI in particular, has increased the involvement of the Department of Agriculture, Fisheries and Forestry and the Australian Fisheries Management Authority in Antarctic policy. Such developments have subtly shifted Australia's interests in CCAMLR.

Defence

While the Antarctic Treaty limits the role of military assets to support for national Antarctic programs, the Australian Defence Force has a role in protecting Australian maritime zones, including those around its sub-Antarctic Territories (Letts 2000: 153). This role is most clearly shown in actions related to protecting the fisheries resources within the Australian EEZ off HIMI and Macquarie Island. Concern over the level and scope of IUU fishing led to Australian enforcement activity using Royal Australian Navy (RAN) vessels beginning in 1997-98. *HMAS Anzac* arrested two vessels for illegal fishing within the Australian HIMI EEZ on 21 October 1997. These vessels were escorted to Fremantle, Western Australia. A second RAN frigate, *HMAS Newcastle*, undertook an arrest of a third vessel on 21 February 1998. Ongoing surveillance activity using RAN vessels were used in the arrest of Russian flagged vessels *Volga* and *Lena* by *HMAS Canberra* supported by *HMAS Westralia* on 7 and 8 February 2002. *HMAS Warramunga* apprehended the Uruguayan flagged vessel the *Maya V* on 23 January 2004.

Customs/ Transport/ Coastwatch/Quarantine

In addition to these RAN actions, Australia has undertaken regular civilian patrols of the HIMI EEZ, most recently with the chartering and commissioning of the *Oceanic Viking* for year-round patrolling in the Southern Ocean. Previous surveillance programs by the civilian patrol vessel *Southern Supporter,* included the hot pursuit of the Togo flagged *South Tomi* in March-April 2001, which was finally apprehended following support from South Africa. In August 2003 a further pursuit took place prior to the apprehension of the Uruguay flagged vessel *Viarsa 1*, again with support from South Africa and the United Kingdom. These hot pursuits occurred after these vessels were suspected of illegal fishing within the HIMI EEZ in contravention of Australian law and tried to evade arrest. Both pursuits were lengthy, with the *Viarsa 1* pursuit lasting 21 days, covering 3900 nautical miles and undertaken in extreme conditions. The *Oceanic Viking* apprehended the Cambodian registered *Taruman* in September 2005 for allegedly fishing within the Macquarie Island EEZ.

The signing of a joint Australia–France cooperative enforcement Treaty on 8 January 2007 enhanced surveillance efforts in and around the HIMI territory and the French Kerguelen Islands. This Treaty, "Agreement on Cooperative Enforcement of Fisheries Laws between the Government of Australia and the Government of the French Republic in the Maritime Areas Adjacent to the French Southern and Antarctic Territories, Heard Island and McDonald Islands", builds on an existing Treaty (signed in 2003) that provides the basis for cooperative surveillance and scientific research. In addition to surveillance, environment security also remains important. The protection of the Antarctic environment has led to the establishment of quarantine protocols affecting movement of people and goods (including food) to and from Antarctic and the sub-Antarctic islands.

State Government – Tasmania and Macquarie Island

The "federal factor" (Chapman 1990) – a term used to highlight the inherently federal character of public policy in Australia, even in areas where jurisdiction is clearly assigned to the Commonwealth – influences and affects Australian Antarctic policy, albeit more limited that in other policy areas. Tasmania's jurisdiction over Macquarie Island provides a "federal factor" to this arena, particularly related to management of the island and regulation of tourism. Given the island's world heritage status, and the significance of Australian Government programs on the island, inter-governmental differences can arise over management. At the same time, however, the Tasmanian Government provides support to the Secretariats of CCAMLR, the Council of Managers of National Antarctic Programs, and the Agreement for the Conservation of Albatrosses and Petrels located in Hobart.

Science

From an initial focus on activities on the sub-Antarctic islands in 1947, ANARE expanded to include activities on the Antarctic continent and the Southern Ocean from the 1950s. The AAP includes contributions from AAD and other government agencies including the Bureau of Meteorology, GeoScience Australia and Commonwealth Scientific and Industrial Research Organisation (CSIRO) (AAD 2000: 5), staff and programs in Australian universities and the Antarctic Climate and Ecosystems Cooperative Research Centre (ACE CRC) based at the University of Tasmania.

The Attentive Public

Non-government Organisations

The traditional model of the policy process gave great emphasis to government and bureaucracy as major actors in the policy process. Non-government organisations have always been seen as important in politicising issues and helping to set the policy agenda, and have had significant impact in Antarctic policy – both internationally and domestically. NGOs have provided important support for Australian interests, most notably during the post-CRAMRA debates that led to the development of the Protocol. Australian initiatives within CCAMLR to combat IUU fishing for toothfish, and the development of ACAP have also been supported by NGOs. The NGO grouping links together a number of different organisations, the umbrella group the Antarctic and Southern Ocean Coalition (ASOC) as well as member organisations such as Greenpeace, the World Wide Fund for Nature (WWF), the Australian Conservation Foundation (ACF) and the Humane Society International (HSI). NGO representatives are on Australian delegations to ATCMs and to CCAMLR meetings, and WWF and HSI are actively involved in forums such as the AAD's CCAMLR Consultative Forum.

Industry

Other actors with interests in Antarctic policy include the tourism industry, represented in ATS forums by its peak industry organisation the International Association of Antarctica Tour Operators (IAATO) and the fishing industry. While Australian Antarctic tourism companies tend to operate on the Antarctic Peninsula they are subject to Australian law and regulations. The fishing industry, while a policy actor in its own right, has supported more traditional NGO activity through ISOFISH – an organisation established to draw attention to the problem of IUU fishing in the Southern Ocean. ISOFISH was established with funding from the Australian fishing industry and News Corporation and provided an effective vehicle for publicising the problems of unregulated toothfish fishing (Fallon and Kriwoken 2004). More recently the individual fishing companies have established the Coalition of Legal Toothfish Operators (COLTO).

Foreign Governments and the International Antarctic Scientific Community – the International Attentive Public

Science has been described as the "currency" of the ATS (Herr and Hall 1989), with the establishment of a scientific program the basis of gaining Consultative Party status. Scientific collaboration established under the IGY, later entrenched within the Antarctic Treaty, also encourages close linkages between scientific programs of different Consultative Parties. This collaboration is facilitated through the linkages fostered through organisations such as SCAR and other international scientific bodies such as the World Meteorological Organisation (WMO) and the International Council for Science (ICSU). ICSU, founded in 1931 is "a non-governmental organization representing a global membership that includes both national scientific bodies (103 members) and international scientific unions (27 members)" (ICSU 2005). ICSU is a major partner in the development of the International Polar Year 2007-08.

SCAR was established during the IGY following a meeting of an ICSU Antarctic meeting held in Stockholm, 9-11 September 1957. ICSU delegates recognised that as the IGY had a major Antarctic component a mechanism to facilitate international cooperation was warranted. This meeting led to the establishment of a Special Committee on Antarctic Research (later renamed the Scientific Committee on Antarctic Research). SCAR is responsible for "initiating, developing and coordinating high quality international scientific research in the Antarctic region, and on the role of the Antarctic region in the Earth system ... and provides objective and independent scientific advice to the Antarctic Treaty Consultative Meetings" (SCAR 2007). Twenty-eight countries are full members of SCAR – with full membership gained through maintaining "an active scientific research programme in Antarctica". There are four associate members "countries without an independent research programme as yet or which are planning a research programme in the future", and seven scientific Unions, members of ICSU that have an interest in Antarctic research (SCAR 2007).

Capacity and Coordination – The Policy Network

Effective international engagement depends on effective coordination of national efforts. The interdependence of international and domestic or national politics has been long recognised and is most evocatively describe by Putnam's image of "the logic of two level games" (Putnam 1988). The ability to exert influence is shaped by the ability to coordinate national objectives and interests as much as it involves coordination of actions with other governments.

> The impact of domestic factors on international policy-making is widely recognized, the mediating influence of co-ordination processes within national government requires careful consideration in its own right. *The internal management of external relationships* has a dual role in ensuring the coherent representation of national interests and in supporting the effective functioning of the international policy process. Poor internal co-ordination not only compromises national interests; it also adversely affects the performance of the system as a whole. (Metcalfe 1994: 276, emphasis added)

The identification of "internal management of external relationships" reinforces the importance of ensuring that institutional arrangements and processes are in place "in order to establish national negotiating objectives and define strategies and tactics" (Metcalfe 1994: 277). Coordination between domestic agencies with interests in Antarctic matters over national objectives is a critical element in ensuring effective influence in international forums. The linkages between members of the sub-government and the attentive public are important in policy development and in advancing Australia's interests. These linkages enhance policy capacity, but also focus on the question of coordination. Policy capacity can be defined as the ability to make decisions and using knowledge to solve policy problems (Peters 1996: 11-12). Peters defines coordination as "an end-state in which the policies and programs of government are characterised by minimal redundancy, incoherence and lacunae" (Peters, 1998: 296). In a similar vein Metcalfe notes that coordination implies that component parts work together such that they do not impede or negate each other's efforts (Metcalfe 1994: 278).

Questions of coordination and policy capacity lead to consideration of the need to manage what Allison termed the "internal components" and "external constituencies" of organisations (Allison 1992: 285). Managing "internal components" either within agencies with differing responsibilities such as the AAD or within the sub-government may be complex, but is a critical element in coordination and in enhancing capacity. Managing the relationships with external constituencies is, by definition, more difficult given that government objectives are not always shared by NGOs or necessarily by other actors within the attentive public. Equally NGOs can be powerful allies in advancing national interests and Australia has been able to work with NGOs in the development of the Protocol, the campaign against IUU fishing, and whaling.

Australian Antarctic Policy – Challenges

Australia faces some important challenges in its future engagement within the ATS. The Antarctic Treaty and its associated instruments and arrangements have been developed to provide a management regime south of 60° South latitude, based on consensus and collaboration. Consensus was tested during the Australian–French initiative to strengthen environmental protection of the Antarctic (and more recently the extraordinarily drawn out process of developing a liability regime, as well as elusive consensus necessarily to establish the Treaty Secretariat). The LOS Convention, negotiated between 1974 and 1982 under the auspices of the United Nations, entered into force 1994. This Convention provides a number of rights for coastal States and establishes a regime of maritime zones. The LOS Convention does not directly address Antarctica but covers the maritime areas within the Treaty Area. The nexus between the two regimes is likely to be a significant driver in the future.

The Antarctic and Southern Ocean also face effects of global climate change, with potential impacts on sea ice and marine ecosystems, as well as on terrestrial Antarctica. Antarctica is providing important data on climate change, and Australia's scientific effort has a major focus on increasing understanding of the role of Antarctica in the global climate system. Australian scientists are drawing on their work in Antarctica and the Southern Ocean in contributions to the Intergovernmental Panel of Climate Change (IPCC) Fourth Assessment Report to be completed in 2007. While Australia is a Party to the United Nations Framework Convention on Climate Change (UNFCC) and has not ratified the Kyoto Protocol to the UNFCC, Australian research from Antarctica and the Southern Ocean will, however, be important in ongoing negotiations on responses to climate change that include the Asia-Pacific Partnership on Clean Development and Climate.

Management of human effects will continue to be a challenge for all Treaty Parties, including Australia. Antarctic tourism is expanding, with increased visitor numbers to a small number of sites (mostly in the Antarctic Peninsula). Antarctic tourism is not intensively regulated under the ATS, but relies instead on national controls by Treaty Parties in their implementation of the Protocol, or the administrative application of hortatory guidelines. Effective management of tourism is also heavily dependent on self-management by tour operators. Antarctic tourism operations are segmented, ship-borne visits are the major component, with smaller numbers of airborne tourists landing on the continent. While there are limited ship-borne tourist operations landing tourists within the AAT, the sub-Antarctic Macquarie Island is a destination for such cruises, with limits on landings and numbers of people (Kriwoken et al 2006). Increasing interest in "adventure tourism" and small expedition-style activities have led to concerns from Treaty Parties related to search and rescue and repatriation of individuals following accidents. The Treaty Parties, with Australia an active player, have moved to address these lacunae, through inter-sessional contact group discussions, a major inter-sessional meeting sponsored by Norway in 2004, and discussion at ATCMs XXVII in 2004 and XXVIII in 2005.

The ATS, through CCAMLR, is continuing to address the problem of IUU fishing. Australia has been active in pursuing this agenda item and has been active since that late 1990s in drawing attention to the problems caused by inadequate controls over high seas fishing in a variety of international forums. Australia faces specific challenges in combating IUU fishing around the Australian EEZ off the external territory of Heard Island and McDonald Islands and to a lesser extent off Macquarie Island.

Conclusion

Australia has largest territorial claim in Antarctica. This claim, based on discovery, exploration and science, has been the centre of Australian policy interests for over 70 years. While the claim to the AAT is important it is not the only driver or policy interest. Australia maintains, too, a major interest in the operation of the ATS and has contributed significantly to the establishment and ongoing development of the instruments and regimes that make up this system. Australian policy and practice towards Antarctica maintains a longstanding domestic bipartisan political commitment, a commitment that is embodied in the first goal of the Australian Antarctic Program – to maintain the ATS and enhance Australia's influence within in this system.

As this chapter has illustrated, success in achieving this goal centres on the relationships between members of the policy community, the ability of the executive core of the policy community to provide direction and enhance coordination of a diverse range of interests. While the development and successful functioning of the ATS is often portrayed as having solved the Antarctic problem, Australia's Antarctic agenda will continue to be shaped by evolving domestic concerns and international engagement over Antarctica.

4

Australian Influence in the Antarctic Treaty System: An End or a Means?

Stephen Powell and Andrew Jackson

Introduction

The Public Servant Perspective

This chapter addresses Australia's Antarctic agenda from the point of view of insiders. We are advisers to the federal Environment Minister primarily responsible for Antarctic policy and delegates to international Antarctic forums. In a sense, we are expected to be custodians of the corporate memory of Australia's policy for Antarctica, in the same way that other contributors to this volume embody the breadth of academic discourse on Antarctic affairs.

We have the privilege of access to government decision-making processes and diplomatic communications, some of which are not, or not yet, in the public domain. At the same time, our perspective is coloured by how conscious we are of the contingencies of daily government business and the limitations of achieving "the possible" in global organisations. Generally speaking, Australia cannot achieve anything for the future of Antarctica until there is international consensus.

The core business of the Policy Coordination Branch at the Australian Antarctic Division (AAD) is to develop and put into effect Australian Antarctic policies and to represent Australia at international forums. The government's first goal for its Antarctic program is to maintain the Antarctic Treaty System (ATS) and to enhance Australia's influence in it (see also Haward *et al* this volume). Our efforts need to be informed by the views of industries (commercial tourism operators and fishing companies), non-government conservation organisations, and academic discourse. Our strategy for protecting Antarctica and preserving Australia's interests in Antarctica needs to be framed by a realistic assessment of how far other countries are willing to walk with Australia towards our goals.

Just as academic commentators have limited opportunities to influence the field of policy development, so too it is only from time to time that public servants have the opportunity to step back and reflect on the broader context of our roles. Twenty years ago Professor Stuart Harris welcomed the "support and encouragement" he received from government officials in the proceedings which led to the publication of *Australia's Antarctic Policy Options* (Harris 1984a: viii). Today, we're grateful for this opportunity to contribute our perspective to this exercise in taking stock of Australia's current Antarctic agenda.

Barely a month elapsed between the 28th Antarctic Treaty Consultative Meeting (ATCM) held in Stockholm June 2005 and the workshop in Hobart which led to this publication. We decided to treat the processes and outcomes of that meeting and other recent ATCMs, the peak forum under the Antarctic Treaty, as a prism through which we might assess how Australian Antarctic policy is developing and how Australia is influencing Antarctic affairs.

Two Decades Since Harris

In the 20 years since *Australia's Antarctic Policy Options* captured the state and the possible directions of Australia's Antarctic agenda, some themes have remained constant. Others have changed. The ATS has also matured over the past two decades.

International relations between the governments signatory to the Treaty have certainly changed since the Harris book, which came in the midst of the (second) Cold War. The world remained divided between eastern and western blocs. President Reagan had suspended Russian flights to the United States in response to Soviet fighters shooting down Korean Airlines flight 007, and the reformist Mikhail Gorbachev was still a year away from taking the reins in Moscow. In this tense context, the continued commitment to setting aside Antarctica for peace and science was a notable achievement. Indeed, as the Soviet Union's representative reminded the 1985 meeting, the Antarctic was "the only demilitarized zone in the world" (ATCM 1985: 160).

Then, ATCMs generally took place every second year (there was no meeting in the year of the publication). Now, they occur annually. A brief comparison of the first meeting following the release of *Australia's Antarctic Policy Options* – the 13th ATCM in 1985 – and the 28th ATCM in 2005 may help set the scene. Interestingly, throughout that entire span of years Australia has not hosted an ATCM (although Australia has hosted related forums and annual Commission for Convention on the Conservation of Antarctic Marine Living Resources (CCAMLR) meetings).

Twenty years ago, 18 countries with the right to take part in decisions of the ATCM – the Consultative Parties – attended the meeting in Brussels. They were joined around the table, for only the second time, by non-Consultative Parties: 11 countries which were beginning to observe

ATCMs, without taking part in decisions, as part of the effort to improve the transparency of the system. One such Party was Sweden, attending its first ATCM in 1985. In 2005, Sweden hosted the meeting in Stockholm – having been duly assessed as maintaining a significant scientific program in Antarctica and therefore obtaining Consultative status. There are ten more Consultative Parties today, bringing the total to 28.[1] Unusually, barely more than half of the non-Consultative Parties (10) turned up to the 2005 ATCM, which could be taken as a sign that there is less concern in the outer perimeter of the Antarctic Treaty about the directions the decision-makers are setting for Antarctic governance.

Administratively, the proceedings of the 13th ATCM were very much the province of the host government. In 2005, for the first time, the hosts had the benefit of a small independent Secretariat of the Antarctic Treaty (established in Buenos Aires, Argentina in September 2004) to organise translation and interpretation, circulate documents and manage other administrative functions. Twenty years ago, Parties were discussing the potential merit of a secretariat along the lines of those handling the administration of other treaties. Now Antarctica has one. In this sense, the Antarctic Treaty has perhaps come of age.

The 13th and 28th ATCMs both lasted two weeks. There were common topics for discussion, including the operation of the ATS, tourism and the inspection provision under the Treaty. But the pace has changed. Twenty years ago, the meeting broke into just two working groups – examining procedural and environmental concerns. In 2005, there were four working groups, focusing on: setting the rules for environmental liability; managing and minimising the environmental impact of tourism; operations; and legal and institutional matters. Moreover, the Committee for Environmental Protection (CEP) met for the eighth time, demanding an entire and quite crammed week on its own, and arguably handling the greatest workload.

A key theme in 1985 was an external challenge to the Antarctic Treaty as non-members, particularly Malaysia, condemned what they saw as the lack of transparency of the ATS. The "Question of Antarctica" had been inscribed on the agenda of United Nations General Assembly for the third consecutive year. Australia's opening statement to the ATCM made our position clear. Although Australia acknowledged that the system could be improved:

> Australia does not accept the criticism a few have recently voiced. On the contrary, we believe that the Antarctic Treaty serves important interests, both national and international, and that the criticisms we have heard are misplaced. (ATCM 1985: 123)

---

1   Argentina, Australia, Belgium, Brazil, Bulgaria, Chile, China, Ecuador, Finland, France, Germany, India, Italy, Japan, the Republic of Korea, the Netherlands, New Zealand, Norway, Peru, Poland, the Russian Federation, South Africa, Spain, Sweden, Ukraine, the United Kingdom of Great Britain and Northern Ireland, the United States of America and Uruguay.

Twenty years on, the system has greatly improved, and although the UN still considers Antarctica every three years or so, there is no sustained attack on the Treaty. In 2005, Sweden addressed the General Assembly on behalf of the States Parties to the Antarctic Treaty, but this was more of an update on work completed under the Treaty than an attempt to combat antagonism towards the current arrangements for the governance and protection of the frozen continent.

Another theme two decades ago was the debate over what rules to place on mineral exploitation in Antarctica. Today, the ATCM has a strong environmental agenda. One of Australia's most telling contributions to the future of Antarctica is the comprehensive 1991 Protocol on Environmental Protection to the Antarctic Treaty (Madrid Protocol), when Australia and others scuttled the proposed minerals regime. What seemed at the time like an audacious proposal by Australia has now been accepted by consensus as the best way to manage the Antarctic. Today the CEP, in place as a result of the Protocol, rivals the Commission for the Conservation of Antarctic Marine Living Resources (the CCAMLR Commission) as the part of the ATS with the greatest volume of business to transact. Australia has generated considerable influence within the CEP, including four years as its Chair.

Australia sent five government officials to Brussels in 1985, including two representatives of the Antarctic Division (previously, the AAD had just one delegate), plus local embassy staff and a delegate from a non-government organisation. In 2005, there were more than twice as many behind the Australian flag. However, the Australians were seldom in one place as we dispersed to the various working groups and the CEP. Seven of the delegation worked for the Division. The delegation was led by Foreign Affairs personnel and joined by staff from the Attorney-General's Department, embassy staff, and a representative of the State governments. The delegation would have been larger, had non-government organisations and commercial tour operators been in a position to send delegates as they did in some previous and subsequent meetings.

Twenty years ago, the ATCM produced 16 Recommendations on actions that member governments should take to further the principles of the Treaty. In 2005, there were 20 such outputs, which nowadays are categorised more precisely as legally binding Measures (of which there were five), hortatory Resolutions (seven) and procedural Decisions (eight).

Clearly, Antarctic Treaty institutions have matured and refined over the past two decades. Has Australia influenced this?

Exercising Influence through the Antarctic Treaty System

Antarctic Treaty Consultative Meeting

Australia is an original signatory to the 1959 Antarctic Treaty. Australia has attended every ATCM and hosted two (the inaugural meeting, in 1961, and again in 1983, the meeting which immediately preceded the Harris book).

It is a truism to say that Australia participates in the ATCM to advance Australia's Antarctic policy interests. However, it is important to acknowledge that in the current formula of the government's goals for Australia's Antarctic program, the Treaty System comes first (DEH 2005: 13). Australia's Antarctic goals are:

- to maintain the ATS and enhance Australia's influence in it;
- to protect the Antarctic environment;
- to understand the role of Antarctica in the global climate system; and
- to undertake scientific work of practical, economic and national significance.

The ATCM is convened specifically to enable representatives of Parties to the Antarctic Treaty to exchange information, hold consultations and consider and recommend to their governments measures to promote the principles of the Treaty. Therefore, it is the primary forum under the Antarctic Treaty umbrella for Australia to seek to influence governance in Antarctica.

The Committee for Environmental Protection meets during the same fortnight as the ATCM, while other groups such as the Council of Managers of National Antarctic Programs (COMNAP) and the Scientific Committee on Antarctic Research (SCAR) are quite separate – they report to and interact with the ATCM. CCAMLR and its Scientific Committee are other important forums for Australia, partly as Australia serves as the depositary government for their Convention, but equally because of CCAMLR's role in managing conservation issues critical to Australia.

The agendas of recent ATCMs have encompassed a broad suite of topics, addressed in 2005 by 72 working papers and 125 information papers, and in 2006 by 44 working papers, 12 Secretariat papers and 120 information papers. The breadth of the items these papers addressed underlined the role the ATCM plays as the key forum for all Antarctic discussions. Themes included the operation of the ATS, the question of liability for environmental damage in Antarctica, safety and operations in Antarctica, developments in the Arctic and in the Antarctic, preparations for the International Polar Year (2007-08), tourism and non-governmental activities in the Antarctic Treaty area, inspections under the Treaty and Madrid Protocol, scientific cooperation and facilitation, operations, education, exchange of information and biological prospecting.

Antarctic Treaty Secretariat

It may be hard to believe, but it took four decades for the Antarctic Treaty to establish a secretariat to support its work. It was the only international agreement of its stature with no permanent address, no web site and no repository of its records. Every ATCM throughout that time was organised independently by the host government. This was very inefficient.

In 2005, the administration of the annual meeting benefited for the first time from the installation of the permanent Antarctic Treaty Secretariat. The Secretariat, an organ of the ATCM, has been set up in Buenos Aires to assist the ATCM and the CEP by handling paperwork, organising the logistics of their meetings, facilitating contact between Parties between sessions, and producing reports and other publications. The Secretariat will also house the definitive records of the Treaty, and set up databases to allow for ready access to key reference materials.

The very existence of this office is something of a measure of Australia's influence. Australia was long a champion of establishing an independent secretariat and, at one point, offered to host the organisation. However, the notion of an independent secretariat could not attract consensus. It was only thanks to several years of delicate negotiations, and a number of Australian initiatives, that final agreement could be reached on the establishment of the office and practical aspects of its operation. The odd-looking contributions formula,[2] for example, was an Australian proposal to break a logjam in the negotiations.

The result, Measure 1 (2003) of the 26th ATCM (Madrid, June 2003), establishing the Secretariat, will formally enter into force when approved by all of the governments that were Consultative Parties at the time of the decision.[3] Meanwhile, Decision 2 (2003) applies the Measure provisionally. This means the Secretariat's operations have commenced, albeit informally, funded by national contributions which are in the interim made on a voluntary basis. Since 2003, Australia has also worked with the interim Executive Secretary to ensure that the institution is fully meeting its obligations and well prepared for its permanent role.

The decision to establish what, on the surface, is merely an administrative convenience took many decades – as good an example as any of the operation of consensus politics in the Antarctic Treaty. That agreement eluded Antarctic Treaty Parties for so many years is explained, for the most part, by some Parties' concerns about the risk of the organisation acquiring a *de facto* identity and decision-making role independent of the

---

2   Decision 1 (2003) established a two-part financial contributions formula: each country is expected to pay annually (1) an equal share of half the Secretariat's budget for the year, plus (2) a variable proportion of the other half of the Secretariat's budget, which is determined by a multiplier. The multiplier is set by which one of five multiplier categories the country elects itself to. The system is similar to calculations other international organisations use that include an element of the "capacity to pay" concept, but rather than being determined by a measure like the country's GDP, membership of categories is entirely in the hands of the individual governments.

3   At January 2007, 16 of the 27 relevant Consultative Parties had approved Measure 1 (2003).

ATCM. The fear was that issues fundamental to the effectiveness of the Treaty, such as the protection of the status quo on sovereignty issues, would be undermined by a non-independent body purporting to represent the Parties. Australia's approach was to argue for absolute objectivity in the Secretariat, completely free of the influence of any particular Treaty Party, along with absolute subordination to the ATCM so that there could be no threat of the Secretariat acting other than in strict accordance with the wishes of its parent. Whether or not this is achieved remains to be seen, but Australia's contribution to the debate at the 29th ATCM concerning the budget, work priorities, reporting and representational roles of the Secretariat illustrates Australia's commitment to ensuring this outcome.

Liability Annex

The 28th ATCM adopted a new Annex VI to the Madrid Protocol, on "Liability Arising from Environmental Emergencies". This is the most significant instrument to be added to the ATS since the 1991 adoption of the Protocol. It is also arguably the best example of consensus politics.

The story goes back many years (but, unlike the Secretariat issue, not to the start of the Treaty). In the negotiations leading to the Protocol, Australia argued successfully for the inclusion of an environmental liability provision. This reflected the importance that had been given to liability in the defeated minerals regime, and the desire to ensure that the environmental regime included some "teeth" that would create an incentive to comply with the obligations. It was not possible to include the liability rules in the Protocol – the complexity of the issue and the time available for negotiations precluded this, just as they had in the minerals negotiations.[4] The result was Article 16 of the Protocol, which obliged the Parties to devise, in one or more annexes, rules relating to liability for environmental damage.

Negotiations commenced in 1993 within a group of legal experts. Biannual discussions failed to reach any conclusion, other than to identify the issues on which there was no agreement and for which the ATCM would have to provide policy direction. The matter was referred to the ATCM in 1998, whereupon negotiations continued until 2005, when Annex VI was adopted. But the Annex falls well short of what was originally proposed by Australia, and what was envisaged in the Protocol. In fact, many argue that Annex VI barely addresses the Article 16 requirement – it establishes obligations relating to compliance with the response action obligations of Article 15. Thus, to put this in a positive light, what has been

---

4   See Article 8 of the Convention on the Regulation of Antarctic Minerals Resource Activities: no mining could have taken place until the liability regime had been concluded and was in force. Given the complexity of environmental liability issues in other regimes, no less so in the Antarctic, some would argue that even had the minerals convention been ratified, Article 8 would have prevented mining for many years.

achieved was seen as the first step toward the more elaborate regime that would underpin the "comprehensive" scope of the Protocol.

Consensus eluded the ATCM on the question of environmental liability for some 13 years because of the complex legal issues involved and the significant policy differences between Parties. Put bluntly, to simplify the narrative, the more ambitious position of countries such as Australia was subjected to attrition until there was no option but to accept the lowest common denominator – the last resort of consensus. Some might point to the acceptance of very low liability limits in a very narrow range of circumstances as complete capitulation. However, Australian negotiators took a more optimistic and pragmatic view – something is better than nothing – and this represents the first step towards a comprehensive regime, by addressing what is currently the most likely cause of environmental harm (ie maritime casualties). Importantly, the other Parties accepted Australia's view that there must be a commitment to further work and decided at Stockholm to review progress in five years, and to set a timeframe for the resumption of negotiations to elaborate further rules and procedures.

Treaty Parties will now implement the Annex under their respective domestic legislation. Parties will require their operators to take preventative measures, establish contingency plans and take response action to environmental emergencies arising from their activities, or pay the costs of emergency response action taken by others. It is a good start.

Antarctic Continental Shelf

We will step out of the Antarctic Treaty for a moment to examine another Antarctic policy issue on which Australia has taken a lead. Article 76 of the Law of the Sea Convention (LOS Convention) requires a coastal State to delineate the continental shelf beyond the limits of the Exclusive Economic Zone (EEZ) where a physical continental shelf can be shown to exist.[5] To define this so-called "extended continental shelf" a coastal State must submit data to the Commission on the Limits of the Continental Shelf (CLCS) within 10 years of the entry into force of the convention for that State – by 16 November 2004 in Australia's case (see also Rothwell and Scott this volume).

As an early signatory to the Convention, Australia was among the first coastal States having an extended continental shelf to which such a deadline would apply. Furthermore, Australia had the earliest deadline of any Antarctic coastal State. Thus, Australia was in the position of having to "test the waters" on addressing the application of Article 76 to Antarctic

---

5   Within the exclusive economic zone a coastal State has exclusive rights to the resources of the water column and the sea floor – the EEZ cannot extend beyond 200 nautical miles (nm) from the territorial sea base line. Where there is a physical continental shelf extending beyond the EEZ, a coastal State may have exclusive rights to the sea floor resources, generally up to a maximum limit of 350 nm.

waters. However, the impact of such action on the operation of Article IV of the Antarctic Treaty needed careful handling. On one hand, Australia, as a champion of the Antarctic Treaty, was committed to protecting the status quo of how, through Article IV, Antarctic Treaty Parties set aside their differences of opinion over territorial sovereignty, and would not wish to provoke objections. On the other, Australia as an Antarctic claimant is a coastal State for the purposes of the LOS Convention and is entitled to assert an extended continental shelf in Antarctic waters. Furthermore, Australia had entered the Antarctic Treaty having already proclaimed a continental shelf and was now entitled to delimit its previously undefined limits in accordance with its obligations under international law.

In 1999, having unsuccessfully tried to amend LOS Convention practices with respect to application of Article 76 in Antarctica, the Australian Government decided that it had no option but to proceed with the collection of Antarctic data, with a view to submission to the CLCS if that would be necessary to protect Australian interests. Simultaneously, Australia engaged in intense diplomatic action to find a mechanism by which Australia could avoid argument or misunderstanding about its intentions. This involved sustained high-level discussions between 1999 and 2004 with a number of other Antarctic Treaty Parties sharing a close interest in the question. The common interest was protection of the fundamentals of the Treaty, including its respect for the status quo on the sovereignty issues addressed by Article IV. The outcome defused the issue – Australia submitted its Antarctic data to the CLCS, but accompanied its submission with a request that the Commission not consider the data for the time being. Thus, Australia had met its obligations under LOS Convention, protected its national interest and preserved the balance within the Antarctic Treaty. Subsequent representations to the CLCS by other States welcomed Australia's approach to sidestepping this problem. It was also acclaimed by an academic commentator.[6]

The outcome for Australia was that the national position was protected, while Australia had also complied with its international legal obligations, maintained its relationships with key other players, and preserved the integrity of the Antarctic Treaty. Significantly, and unusually, an issue which was critical to the stability of the Treaty was resolved without being canvassed in the ATCM.

Management of Antarctic Tourism

It is critical that the agendas of the peak forum of the Antarctic Treaty keep pace with the changing trends of human activity in the Antarctic. In the time of the Harris book, for instance, those visiting Antarctica on national scientific expeditions far outnumbered those travelling for pleasure. It was understandable that in 1984-85, when only two or three commercial ships

---

6   The approach was described as a "masterstroke" in Jabour (2006: 197-8).

plied Antarctic waters per year, carrying 500 or so passengers, tourism was not the ATCM's most prominent concern. By 2005-06 however, 35 ships (retired polar research vessels and, increasingly, mainstream cruise ships) plus perhaps a dozen commercial yachts visited Antarctica. They carried 29,797 tourists, of whom over 25,000 stepped ashore (Figure 4). For every three tourists, two crew members, guides or lecturers were onboard.

Figure 4: Ship-borne Antarctic Tourists, 1969-70 to 2005-06[7]

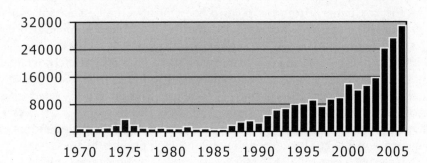

Higher numbers of tourists do not in themselves indicate greater environmental effects. Indeed, commercial operators have set excellent standards of low-impact tourism, and have contributed to greater scrutiny of the environmental practices of national programs. Nonetheless, the remarkable growth is a measure of a pressure on the Antarctic wilderness and governments would be negligent not to monitor the trends and respond.

Conservation organisations have called for limits "before Antarctic tourism reaches such numbers that it is effectively out of control" (ASOC 2006a: 2). One of the most experienced Australian operators has acknowledged that "there is a strong feeling within the Antarctic community that we may be approaching critical levels of visitation which will require careful management in the not too distant future" (Mortimer 2004: 6). However, the International Association of Antarctica Tour Operators (IAATO), representing almost all Antarctic tour companies – which has a good relationship with most Treaty Parties – cautions against jumping to conclusions on the basis of numbers alone. The industry group frequently reminds regulators of the positives from tourism, and that firsthand experience can be "a driving force in Antarctic conservation" (IAATO 2005: 2).

---

7   Source: Data provided to Antarctic Treaty Consultative Meetings in recent years courtesy of the International Association of Antarctica Tour Operators.

Australia views tourism management as a key challenge, but – like other Treaty Parties – has worked with the industry, rather than seeking to impose a simple limit on overall numbers. The Australian Government's policy (AAD 2004a) accepts tourism as a legitimate activity – provided it upholds the principles of the Antarctic Treaty, is ecologically sustainable and socially responsible.[8] Australia has consistently argued for the ATCM to address the environmental, safety and self-sufficiency aspects of commercial ship and aviation tourism, as well as one-off adventure activities, private scientific and heritage-based expeditions and has been willing to do this through prescriptions developed over time, rather than a package.

The key pattern from the point of view of governments is that, when the tour ships put passengers ashore, they tend to follow the pack. In the past 15 seasons, while the number of passengers has increased roughly eight-fold, the number of sites visited each season has only risen by a factor of 3.5 (Crosbie 2005: 8). Consistently half of all landings in any season were at just ten sites on the Antarctic Peninsula. The 20 most visited sites account for roughly three-quarters of all visits (Naveen et al 2001). Regulators, therefore, can make great strides by working with the operators to develop sensible guidelines for a relatively small number of sites.

In recent years, the ATCM has adopted specific site use guidelines, which identified the sensitivities of frequently visited Antarctic Peninsula sites and recommended practical controls to protect their values. While Australia did not introduce this latest initiative, site-specific management is a goal of Australia's policy and it has influenced the nature of both the guidelines and the process by which they are negotiated. Guidelines were discussed at the 28th ATCM and resulted in on-site reviews in early 2006 by a team comprising five nations (Argentina, Australia, Norway, the United Kingdom and the United States) and the tourism industry (through IAATO). This group refined guidelines which set restrictions on the number of visits, suggested a code of conduct and contained the information a tour guide should need to manage tourists through a landing (Powell 2006). The guidelines are succinct and user friendly (more detailed descriptions are available elsewhere, for example Naveen 2003).[9]

The guidelines confine landings to ships with a maximum of 200 or 500 passengers, depending on the sensitivity of the site. Ship visits are limited to one to three per day. In most cases there is an overnight closure or rest

---

8   In 2005-06, Australian-based operators carried one in 10 (3211) passengers to Antarctica. Four Australian-based or Australian-connected companies operated cruise ships, two yachts, one landed aircraft on the continent and one chartered overflights.

9   The *Compendium of Antarctic Peninsula Visitor Sites* has for over two decades censused four penguin species (gentoo, Adélie, chinstrap and macaroni) and four species of flying birds (blue-eyed shags, southern giant petrels, kelp gulls and skuas), to determine "whether any detected changes are naturally occurring or anthropogenic, perhaps caused by tourism or other human activities" (Naveen 2003: 8).

period for wildlife. Each site is zoned into "closed areas", "guided walking" and "free walking", depending on the likelihood of visitors encroaching on vegetation or wildlife. There is a 50-metre precautionary approach distance from nesting seabirds. Other recommendations are specific to each site.

The 12 sets of guidelines tabled at the June 2006 ATCM and CEP, with Australia's co-sponsorship, achieved the unanimous support of all 28 Consultative Parties. As a result, from the 2006-07 tourist season, all but one of the 15 most visited sites in Antarctica will be covered by some form of site-specific visitor management. Formal management plans for Antarctic Specially Managed Areas or national station visits cover some of these sites; site guidelines fill the gaps.

Site use guidelines by no means answer all the questions the growing Antarctic tourism sector poses. More speculative and controversial topics remain under debate, including whether to ban very large passenger ships, how to accredit operators and what to do about the ever-present rumour that developers are planning an Antarctic hotel. However, the new site guidelines established a successful process, which brought together governments and industry and the best available information, to address specific localised concerns. This approach may well offer a constructive model for years to come.

Influencing the Antarctic Future

Influencing the Health of the Antarctic Treaty System

Australia has long championed the ATS as the most appropriate governance framework for the Antarctic region, and has been keen to maintain consensus. But that is not to say that Australia has not taken actions that have, at least for a time, unsettled the Treaty. A vivid example of this was the 1989 decision of the Australian Government not to sign the Antarctic minerals regime. That said, Australia was eager to re-establish consensus quickly, and achieved it. That action established Australia as a Party to take very seriously. Australia has subsequently maintained a high level of engagement in Treaty forums with a strong delegation well prepared to engage in most issues.

Australia is now involved in every forum of the ATS and seeks to lead and influence discussions. Australia's efforts have been directed at strengthening the support mechanisms (the Secretariat and the information exchange processes), the compliance mechanisms (such as inspections) and the environmental protection mechanisms (including the Protocol and CCAMLR), while protecting the fundamentals of peaceful use of Antarctica and scientific cooperation. Australia also works within the ancillary and related bodies such as SCAR and COMNAP to ensure harmonious and productive relations. The significance of these efforts has been reflected in the priority Australia's Antarctic program gives to maintaining the Treaty System and enhancing Australia's influence.

Australia has also sought to advance the interests of the Antarctic Treaty within other regimes that have addressed Antarctic issues (such as the World Heritage Convention, the Ramsar Convention and the LOS Convention), with a view to ensuring the primacy of the Treaty with respect to governance in the Antarctic. This has extended to defending the Treaty from external threats and criticisms, such as occurred during the many years of proposals that the UN should manage Antarctica as the "common heritage of mankind". This campaign essentially argued that the Antarctic was locked up by an exclusive club of wealthy western nations.

Malaysia has been particularly associated with the UN campaign and Australia led the defence of the Antarctic Treaty for many years, dating back to the debates in the time of the Harris book (see Haward *et al* this volume). Malaysia's attitude has moderated in recent years, with softened rhetoric paralleling increasing interest in involvement in Antarctic research. Recognising this change in attitude, the Treaty Parties have for the last five years invited Malaysia to observe the ATCM. Australia has hosted visits to Antarctica by Malaysian scientists (to demonstrate the advantages of cooperation under the Treaty) and strongly encouraged Malaysia to accede to the Treaty. Australia's support for Malaysian activities in Antarctica has been predicated on Malaysia's positive movement towards accession – cooperation will be limited if positive progress is not maintained. Positive signs emerged in 2004 when Dr Mahatir (the past Prime Minister and architect of Malaysia's Antarctic policy) observed that the common heritage of mankind position had been unsuccessful, that the Treaty Parties had resolved the minerals issue, claimants appeared less strident, and the Treaty was no longer the closed club it may have seemed – even inviting Malaysia to observe its proceedings.

Australian Air Link with Antarctica

It is worth noting that Australia is also entering a new era in its Antarctic operations with the implementation of an air link between Hobart, Tasmania and Casey station. The air link will enhance Australia's ability to support scientific research by reducing reliance on ships for passenger movement and the concomitant cultural change presents an opportunity for the AAD to reappraise its priorities.

Funding for the air link was announced in the 2005 Federal Budget, committing A$46.3 million to the project over four years. Regular flights on a long-range passenger jet are planned for the summer months, starting in 2007-08. Twenty to 30 flights may be conducted per season once the system is fully operational, landing on a snow-capped blue ice runway and linking with the existing ski equipped CASA 212 aircraft within Antarctica.

Through the air link, Australia is creating a new entry point into the Antarctic. The major facility in East Antarctica for intercontinental flights creates prospects of connections to other scientific facilities at, for example, Dome C, South Pole and McMurdo (all to the east of Casey) and Mirny,

Molodezhnaya, Syowa and others (to the west). Over time this could lead to the establishment of a reliable circum-Antarctic logistics network.

Another International Polar Year

Science continues to be a key currency of the ATS and one of the most important reasons for the presence of Australia and other countries on the frozen continent. Coordinated research will take centre stage during the International Polar Year 2007-08 (IPY: sponsored by the International Council for Science and the World Meteorological Organisation), which promises to become the world's largest internationally coordinated and interdisciplinary research program. More than 60 countries and tens of thousands of participants, from March 2007 to March 2009, will address six themes:

- the environmental status of polar regions;
- change in the polar regions;
- connections between the poles and the rest of the globe;
- the frontiers of science in the polar regions;
- from the Earth's inner core to the sun and the cosmos beyond; and
- cultural, historical, and social processes of circumpolar human societies.

The IPY Joint Committee (co-chaired by Dr Ian Allison of AAD) has endorsed over two hundred projects, typically sponsored by national funding agencies: 42 are directed at the Antarctic, 105 are Arctic focused, and 66 will operate in both poles or connect global processes to polar regions. There is also an outreach program to inform the public and encourage "the next generation of polar researchers" (IPY 2004).

Australia is leading eight of the major IPY projects, co-leading three, and there are a further 46 projects with Australian involvement. In particular, Australia is leading the "Census of Antarctic Marine Life", a five-year study of the evolution of life in Antarctic waters, examining the diversity of biota and how it might respond to future climate and environmental change.

This burst of concerted polar research follows the international polar years of 1882-83 and 1932-33, and the International Geophysical Year 1957-58 (IGY). The IGY, in demonstrating that scientists, even from nations on different sides of the Cold War, could work together amicably, led the 12 founding countries to set aside the entire continent as a zone of peace and science under the Antarctic Treaty. Therefore, it is to be hoped that the intense scientific activity in the coming years will in turn renew political enthusiasm for the special status of the Antarctic and its unique governance structure.

Conclusion

In the decades since Harris, there have been significant and unpredicted changes in Australia's policy approach to the Antarctic, embodied in our role in the ATCM. Australia has shifted from a resources view (characterised by the then preoccupation with the Antarctic mining question) to a view based on environmental protection. In the Southern Ocean, CCAMLR has matured from a nascent regime into a well-established ecosystem management body which, in many ways, leads the world in its approach to marine conservation and its response to activities outside the regime's conservation approach. The Antarctic Treaty has matured with the establishment of a permanent Secretariat. The Madrid Protocol has been negotiated and entered into force, tourism has multiplied and management responses are being developed. The Treaty has successfully defeated strident criticism, new nations have acceded and the critics, such as Malaysia, are warming to it.

Throughout this period, Australia has sought to lead many of the debates. In many cases Australia has been successful. Australia has not been afraid to go out on a limb (witness the rejection of CRAMRA – Convention on the Regulation of Antarctic Mineral Resource Activities – and the approach to the extended continental shelf), but at all times the overriding objective has been to preserve the fundamentals of the Treaty and to allow consensus to prevail.

Looking ahead, the air link and the International Polar Year will be catalysts for Australia to examine new ways of doing business in Antarctica. The Australian Antarctic program has been looking at such developments, to define how Australia will engage with the Antarctic in 2020 and beyond. The initial findings indicate that the reasons for Australia's involvement in Antarctica will remain unchanged in the foreseeable future, but the way business is undertaken in the Antarctic will continue to evolve. Australia's place in Antarctica will increasingly be defined by better international collaboration in science and logistics and significantly enhanced flexibility in its planning and operations.

Australia has considerable influence in many aspects of Antarctic policy and law, especially within the ATS, and in the future Australia will use its influence to strengthen the Treaty and its associated instruments and institutions. In the Antarctic business, this remains wholly sensible and it is the most effective way to protect the fundamentals and, at the same time, to achieve progress. Collaboration in science and logistics will match the longstanding cooperation that has characterised Australia's approach to the policy and legal issues. Importantly, Australia's Antarctic future will not be bound up exclusively in what happens on the ice or on the water. It will be equally focused on what can be achieved within the governance forums which, we argue, must remain centred on the Antarctic Treaty.

Australians involved in the execution of our Antarctic policy may well celebrate the fact that we have achieved and maintained considerable influence within the Antarctic as a result of the efforts over the past 20 years or so. We would argue that Australia's contribution and influence is now substantially greater than it was at the time of the Harris book (recognising that the goal of "influence" was introduced to the program in that period). However, we consider that influence is not an end in itself – influence is directed at strengthening the ATS as the most effective framework to govern the Antarctic. We seek to strengthen the Treaty not only because it is a fine example of what people can achieve when they set aside their differences, but because it remains the best way to achieve Australia's policy interests in the region. Hence, pursuing and achieving influence within the ATS is the indirect mechanism for satisfying our sovereign, scientific, environmental, strategic and other interests in the Antarctic. Without the Treaty, and without our influence in it, Australia (and Antarctica) could be significantly disadvantaged.

5

Enforcement and Compliance in the Australian Antarctic Territory: Legal and Policy Dilemmas

Tim Stephens and Ben Boer

Introduction

The Australian Antarctic Territory (AAT) is an area of immense propor-
tions, situated in a highly remote and demanding physical environment.
The AAT covers almost six million square kilometres, or around 42 per
cent, of Antarctica. Australia's maritime zones in the Southern Ocean are of
even greater dimensions, comprising around nine million square kilometres of ocean space. Taken together, these terrestrial and marine areas
represent an area more than twice the size of the Australian continent, and
are of strategic, scientific and environmental significance for the Australian
nation. They are also of critical ecological importance in a global context.

Successive Australian governments have regarded the exercise of legislative jurisdiction in the AAT as vital to preserving Australian sovereignty
over the territory and adjacent offshore areas (House of Representatives
1992). Consequently the AAT is subject to a considerable body of Commonwealth legislation in a range of subject areas. Australia has also
recognised the importance of maintaining the unique international legal
regime applicable to the Antarctic, and the delicate compromise concerning territorial sovereignty on which it is built (see Rothwell and Scott this
volume). For this reason Australia has not asserted the full range of enforcement rights that attach to its territorial claim. This posture is coming
under increasing pressure with the intensification of commercial and other
activities in the AAT, some of which pose a threat to the Antarctic environment. How Australia responds to this challenge is pivotal to the articulation and implementation of an effective Antarctic policy agenda.

The first section of this chapter reviews the key features of the Antarctic Treaty System (ATS) that establishes the international legal framework
for enforcement and compliance in Antarctica. It is seen that although the
ATS contains mechanisms for promoting compliance with its provisions, it

falls far short of an internationalised system of management. Instead member States are relied upon to give the ATS regime effect within their jurisdictional competence. As a consequence Australia enjoys considerable capacity to assert legislative and enforcement jurisdiction in the AAT. The second section of the chapter investigates how this capacity has been exercised. This is done through an analysis of the legislative regime devised by successive Australian governments for the AAT and the Southern Ocean. In recent years, Australia has become more forthright in the assertion of prescriptive jurisdiction, most notably through the application of environmental laws in the Exclusive Economic Zone (EEZ) proclaimed by Australia offshore the AAT. This has raised expectations on the part of elements of the Australian non-government organisation (NGO) environmental community that extensive and often innovative laws will be fully enforced on the continent and in the seas, especially where the environment is threatened. However, rather than meeting these expectations, the Australian government has adhered to a longstanding policy of maintaining the stability of the ATS. Arguably this has come at some cost to Australian claims to sovereignty in the AAT.

Enforcement and Compliance in Antarctica: The Antarctic Treaty System

Antarctica occupies a unique position in international law by virtue of its deliberately ambiguous status. This is clearly demonstrated by Article IV of the Antarctic Treaty,[1] under which claims to territorial sovereignty in the Antarctic remain in abeyance (Triggs 1986). Pre-existing claims are not renounced, but neither are they recognised, and the position of other States seeking to assert an Antarctic claim is not prejudiced.[2] Moreover, while the Treaty remains in force, no activities in Antarctica may constitute a basis for asserting, supporting or denying a claim to territorial sovereignty.[3]

In many respects Antarctica represents part of the global commons (Triggs 1984). The Antarctic Treaty declares that the continent should be used for peaceful purposes only,[4] that it should be an area of scientific investigation and cooperation,[5] and under no circumstances the scene of international discord.[6] Subsequent instruments, most notably the Protocol on Environmental Protection to the Antarctic Treaty[7] (Madrid Protocol) have tended to reinforce the importance of protecting the environment for

---

1   402 UNTS 71.
2   Article IV(1).
3 · Article IV(2).
4   Article I(1).
5   Articles II, III. See also Preamble, 3rd recital.
6   Preamble, 2nd recital.
7   30 ILM 1461.

all humanity and for future generations. However, despite arguments made over the years for the Antarctic continent to be declared as a world park (Mosley 1984), the seven claimant States continue to assert an entitlement to sovereignty over the continent. These claims are, for the foreseeable future, an insuperable impediment to the establishment of Antarctica as part of the "common heritage of humankind" in a manner akin to the deep seabed regime under Part XI of the United Nations Convention on the Law of the Sea[8] (LOS Convention). Moreover, even if the claimant States agreed that the continent should be listed as a World Heritage area under the Convention Concerning the Protection of the World Cultural and Natural Heritage,[9] the contentious nature of the claims, combined with the requirements of the Convention, would make it unlikely that such a nomination would succeed.

The Antarctic Treaty's compromise on the issue of sovereignty is pivotal to international and national legal regimes applicable to Antarctica (Scott 1997). All activities must be viewed through the sovereignty lens, and the ATS mechanisms for compliance control and enforcement are no exception. The ATS contains several tools designed to ensure that members and non-members comply with its stipulations. However, they are far from comprehensive and, for reasons of political and practical necessity, the ATS permits member States to further the aims of the ATS through the exercise of prescriptive and enforcement jurisdiction.

The ATS Enforcement Regime

The enforcement and compliance regime under the Antarctic Treaty has three main components. First and foremost, the Parties are responsible for ensuring the activities in which they are themselves involved take place in conformity with the Treaty. They are answerable for the activities undertaken by their own expeditioners, scientists and other personnel. They must also seek to ensure that third Parties do not engage in "any activity in Antarctica contrary to the principles or purposes" of the Antarctic Treaty (Article X).

The second main feature of the compliance system is information sharing. Under Article VII(5) each Party must give notice of expeditions to Antarctica, the occupation of stations, and the introduction into Antarctica of military personnel or equipment. By reporting information of this type, the Parties may be made aware of possible infractions of the Treaty, permitting diplomatic pressure to be brought to bear in response, if this is necessary.

The third component is the inspection system established by Article VII(1) that promotes observance by exposing potential breaches of the Antarctic Treaty. As with the requirement to provide notice of expeditions

8   1833 UNTS 397.
9   1037 UNTS 151.

and other activities, the inspection system is designed to improve the transparency of the regime so that breaches may be identified, and draw an appropriate response. Under Article VII, the Parties may designate observers to undertake inspections anywhere on the continent without notice. This was seen as important for ensuring that the Antarctic remained demilitarised and it was a major innovation given the Cold War context in which it was agreed (Watts 1992). By operation of Article VIII(1) these observers, together with scientific personnel exchanged between Parties, enjoy immunity from jurisdiction from all States except their own State of nationality. However, this proviso operates "without prejudice to the respective positions of the Contracting Parties relating to jurisdiction over all other persons in Antarctica". It must be emphasised that these observers enjoy immunity on the basis of their nationality – they are not given independent inspection functions by a Treaty body.

The three components of the Antarctic Treaty compliance system have been replicated, with some variation in emphasis, in other ATS instruments. For example, the Convention for the Conservation of Antarctic Seals[10] (CCAS) relies primarily on the first tool for enforcement and compliance, namely national jurisdiction and control. To this end Article 2(2) provides that each Party shall "adopt for its nationals and for vessels under its flag such laws, regulations and other measures ... as may be necessary to implement this Convention".

The Convention on the Conservation of Antarctic Marine Living Resources[11] (CCAMLR) similarly provides in Article XXI(1) that each Party must "take appropriate measures within its competence to ensure compliance with the provisions of this Convention and with conservation measures adopted by the Commission". CCAMLR has proven to be one of the most important elements of the ATS. It regulates an expansive area (not only south of 60 degrees South latitude, but also northwards to the Antarctic Convergence) and is one of the most developed and sophisticated regional fisheries management organisations (Molenaar 2001). It has faced both internal and external compliance challenges. The traditional methods of compliance control have been used to respond to problems of compliance by CCAMLR members, including through observation and inspection as provided by Article XXIV. However, it has been necessary to adopt a more innovative approach to deal with illegal, unreported, and unregulated fishing activities by non-members. Hence, the CCAMLR Commission has sought to further the objectives of CCAMLR through adopting "conservation measures" including vessel monitoring and catch documentation schemes. The CCAMLR regime therefore illustrates the potential for the compliance and enforcement regime of the ATS to develop and adapt to new challenges.

---

10   11 ILM 251.
11   19 ILM 841.

The most recent, and significant, addition to the ATS is the Madrid Protocol, which establishes a comprehensive regime for environmental protection in Antarctica based upon the ecosystem approach. It was a major advance in international environmental law, and as a consequence has been viewed as a template for subsequent multilateral environmental agreements (Rothwell 2000). However, in relation to enforcement and compliance the Madrid Protocol relies upon the basic three-part formula adopted over 30 years earlier in the Antarctic Treaty. Article 13(1) provides that each Party must "take appropriate measures within its competence, including the adoption of laws and regulations, administrative actions and enforcement measures, to ensure compliance with this Protocol". Secondly, under Article 13(4), the Parties must draw to the attention of all other Parties any activity that may affect the implementation of the objectives and principles of the Protocol. Thirdly, Article 14 creates a system of inspection, the purpose of which is to "promote the protection of the Antarctic environment and dependent and associated ecosystems, and to ensure compliance with [the] Protocol".

The Exercise of Jurisdiction

Although the ATS does establish international systems for enforcement and compliance, these are built upon a basic structure that allows ATS Parties to exercise jurisdiction in certain circumstances. The exercise of jurisdiction on a nationality basis is, for instance, central to the efficacy of the regime. However, the ambiguous formulation of the jurisdiction provisions of ATS instruments would appear to allow Australia and the other territorial claimants to exercise jurisdiction on other bases.

The issue of jurisdiction was one of the major unresolved problems for the founding members of the Antarctic Treaty (Auburn 1982), and remains so today. The matter was referred to in Article IX(1)(e) of the Antarctic Treaty as a question to be addressed by Antarctic Treaty Consultative Meetings (ATCMs). However, no measures on jurisdiction have been adopted. In addition all subsequent ATS agreements omit to deal with the issue of jurisdiction in anything other than highly uncertain and incomplete terms. For instance, CCAS relies on national and flag State enforcement,[12] but does not preclude the exercise of jurisdiction on a territorial basis (Watts 1992: 173). A similar interpretation of Article XXI(1) CCAMLR is possible. That provision states that members "shall take *appropriate* measures within its competence to ensure compliance with the provisions of this Convention" (emphasis added). Watts (1992: 174) has observed that the language of this provision was left deliberately obscure:

> It is the underlying territorial, and thus jurisdictional, difference which explains the judgmental flexibility inherent in the requirement to take "appropriate" measures, and, even more so, the knowingly ambiguous

---

12   Article 2(2).

phrase requiring the State to be acting "within its competence". Nothing is said about what that competence is; claimant States are free to say that it allows them to take measures on both a territorial and nationality basis, while it is equally open to non-claimant States to deny that any competence exists.

In lieu of the resolution of such questions relating to jurisdiction, the Antarctic Treaty seeks to ensure that there is an amicable solution to any disputes that might arise. Hence, Article VIII(2) requires "Contracting Parties concerned in any case of dispute with regard to the exercise of jurisdiction in Antarctica" to "immediately consult together with a view to reaching a mutually acceptable solution".

In sum, the ATS provides an uncertain framework for the exercise by States of enforcement jurisdiction, whether this is to implement the ATS instruments themselves or unilateral measures adopted by States going beyond basic ATS stipulations. Having regard to the significant development of international environmental law in other contexts, particularly in relation to the establishment of sophisticated supervisory regimes and non-compliance procedures (Boyle 1991; Birnie and Boyle 2002: 586), it must be asked whether the parameters of the ATS regime for compliance and enforcement need to be updated to respond to increased activities in the Antarctic. Is the model, the basics of which were agreed in the late 1950s, now the most appropriate and effective one for advancing the central concerns of the ATS, including the protection of the Antarctic environment? The preferable alternative, drawing on contemporary practice in international environmental law, would be a more comprehensive and internationalised management regime. However, a significant impediment to such a system is the posture of Australia and other territorial claimants that wish to continue to project their influence upon the continent. In this context the only realistic option appears to be to improve processes of international management that can operate synergistically within the existing sovereignty and jurisdictional framework provided by the ATS.

Law Enforcement and Compliance in Antarctica: Australian Legal and Policy Dilemmas

Writing in 1984, Brook identified Australia's six main policy interests in Antarctica as being: the maintenance of its claim to the AAT, the continued non-militarisation of the continent, effective environmental protection, the advancement of science, ongoing Australian involvement and influence in the ATS and a share in any economic benefits flowing from the exploitation of resources.

The exercise of legislative and enforcement jurisdiction in the AAT is designed to serve several of these policy goals, foremost among them Australia's claim to sovereignty (Triggs 1986: 130, 241). In achieving this objective Australia does not need to demonstrate the same level of activities and influence in Antarctica as might be necessary in more accessible territory with a temperate climate. It was accepted in the *Island of Palmas Case* that "sovereignty cannot be exercised in fact at every moment on every point of a territory".[13] Moreover the decision of the Permanent Court of International Justice in the *Eastern Greenland Case*[14] suggests that occupation may be a good basis for title to territory so long as there is an adequate display of an intention to act as sovereign, as evinced by legislative enactment and some minimal level of administration.

Australia relies on these general principles to bolster its position that notwithstanding its limited physical presence it effectively exercises sovereignty over the AAT, principally through the enactment of legislation (Crawford and Rothwell 1992: 323). However, there remain questions as to whether this is sufficient (Triggs 1986: 323), and such doubts are amplified to the extent that Australia enacts legislation in relation to which it has neither the capacity nor the intention to enforce.

Twenty years ago Triggs (1986: 242-3) examined Australian legislative and administrative activities applicable to the AAT to determine whether Australia had manifested a clear intention to claim and exercise sovereignty over the area. That examination revealed several weaknesses and inconsistencies in the legislative framework that were subsequently the subject of inquiry, and criticism, by a Federal Parliamentary committee (House of Representatives 1992). Are these conclusions applicable today?

Australian Legislation Applicable in the AAT

Australia's claim to territorial sovereignty over the AAT, and attendant offshore maritime zones, is supported by a complex, wide-ranging and distinctive legislative regime.

Government of the AAT: The Basic Law

The AAT was accepted from the United Kingdom as a Commonwealth territory under s 2 of the *Australian Antarctic Territory Acceptance Act 1933* (Cth). The Act in its current form does no more than accept the assignment of authority. As originally enacted it provided in s 3(1) that "the Governor-General may make Ordinances having the force of law in and in relation to" the AAT. However, no such ordinances were ever made and this section was repealed by the *Australian Antarctic Territory Act 1954* (Cth) (AAT Act) which established the basic law for government in the AAT.

Under the AAT Act, the basic law governing the AAT is an amalgam of the laws of the Australian Capital Territory (ACT) and the Jervis Bay Territory. The civil laws of the ACT are in force in the AAT insofar as they are "applicable to the territory" (s 6(1)), while AAT criminal laws are

---

13　*Island of Palmas Case (Netherlands/US)* (1928) 2 RIAA 829, 840.

14　*Legal Status of Eastern Greenland (Denmark v Norway)* [1933] PCIJ Ser A/B No 53, 48.

imported from the Jervis Bay Territory (s 6(2)). It is not clear how much of the ACT legal system is in fact "applicable" (it has been estimated that up to 80 per cent is irrelevant to the AAT), and in practice ACT laws have not been applied in the AAT (Crawford and Rothwell 1992: 76). Regarding enforcement, special arrangements may be made for vesting powers and functions in a specified authority or person under s 7(2). In addition, s 10 gives ACT courts jurisdiction in and in relation to the AAT. Importantly, s 8 of the AAT Act provides that other Commonwealth Acts do not operate in the AAT unless they are expressed to extend to the territory.

The Commonwealth has not sought to extend all federal legislation to the AAT, but instead has applied specific Acts, many of which relate to environmental matters. This selective approach could be interpreted as a failure by Australia to exercise sovereignty completely and effectively (Triggs 1986: 252). However, a more favourable view is that the Common-wealth has enacted only those laws necessary and appropriate for Antarc-tica, having regard to the nature of activities in the AAT, the geographic and climatic obstacles to routine enforcement, and the principles of international law relating to effective maintenance of territorial claims. An additional consideration is the propriety of a broad-ranging legislative regime that is not capable of being enforced. Even with the existing regime there is considerable disparity between the scope of the applicable laws and the willingness and capacity of the Australian Government to enforce them.

The laws of ACT and the Jervis Bay Territory that extend to the AAT may be repealed, amended or supplemented by Ordinances made under ss 9 and 11 of the AAT Act by the Governor-General for the peace, order and good government of the AAT. Only three such Ordinances have been passed: the *Migratory Birds Ordinance* 1980 (Cth), the *Criminal Procedure Ordinance* 1993 (Cth) and the *Weapons Ordinance* 2001 (Cth). An important aspect of all these Ordinances is that they operate on a territorial basis. They apply to all persons within the AAT, to nationals and non-nationals alike. Yet although the *Criminal Procedure Ordinance* invests Australian voyage and station leaders with substantial coercive powers to enforce the law against all present within the AAT there is no demonstrated intention by the Australian Government to apply these against foreign interests.

Jurisdictional Immunities Under the Antarctic Treaty Act 1960

This basic law for Australian governance of the AAT must be read in con-junction with additional legislation. Among the most important is the *Antarctic Treaty Act* 1960 (Cth), which gives effect to the Antarctic Treaty in Australian law by providing for the jurisdictional immunities conferred by Article VIII. It will be recalled that under that provision designated observers, and scientific personnel who have been exchanged between expeditions or stations, are to be subject to the exclusive jurisdiction of the State of their nationality. The *Antarctic Treaty Act* mirrors this in providing at s 4(1) that foreign nationals are not subject to the laws applicable in the

AAT "in respect of any act or omission occurring while he is in Antarctica for the purpose of exercising his functions". Read in conjunction with s 3 of the Act, which provides that the only persons to whom the legislation applies are observers, scientific personnel exchanged and members of the staff accompanying any such persons being nationals of a State Party of the Antarctic Treaty, it is evident that the *Antarctic Treaty Act* creates a very narrow jurisdictional exemption. The conclusion must therefore be that Australian law may be given a very broad application to the activities of foreign nationals within the AAT, both as a matter of domestic law and international law (House of Representatives 1992: 15).

Jurisdiction and Enforcement in Relation to Environmental Matters

The Commonwealth has introduced a substantial body of legislation to address a range of matters concerning the protection of the Antarctic environment. The *Antarctic Treaty (Environment Protection) Act* 1980 (Cth) (AT(EP) Act) is the central enactment and was originally passed to implement the *Agreed Measures for the Conservation of Antarctic Fauna and Flora* adopted in 1964 at the Third Antarctic Treaty Consultative Meeting (Rothwell 1996: 113-21). It has since been augmented by the *Environment Protection and Biodiversity Conservation Act* 1999 (Cth) (EPBC Act) that is also applicable to the AAT.

The AT(EP) Act has been substantially amended over time as the ATS has expanded. Amendments have been made to give effect to CCAS, CCAMLR and Madrid Protocol and to consolidate other legislation such as the now repealed *Antarctic Mining Prohibition Act* 1991 (Cth), which made it an offence for any person to engage in mining activity in the AAT or the adjacent continental shelf,[15] or for an Australian national to engage in mining activity in Antarctica outside the AAT.[16] The AT(EP) Act deals with three main issues, namely the conservation of Antarctic biota through a system of protected areas and a permit system, requirements for environmental impact assessment, and inspections and offences. The legislation applies not only to Australian nationals but also to "any persons and property, including foreign persons and property" in the AAT.[17] However, under s 7(1) no action or proceeding lies against any person in relation to anything done by that person under the authorisation of "recognised foreign authority" namely a permit issued by another Party to the Madrid Protocol. This is an important exemption, and indicates the willingness of Australia to forego jurisdiction if this will facilitate international cooperation to protect the Antarctic environment.

The suite of Australian environmental legislation and regulations applicable in the AAT is now considerably bolstered by the EPBC Act. This

---

15   *Antarctic Mining Prohibition Act* 1990 (Cth), s 6. See now the AT(EP) Act, s 19A(1).

16   *Antarctic Mining Prohibition Act* 1990 (Cth), s 7. See now the AT(EP) Act, s 19A(2).

17   AT(EP) Act, s 4(1)(a). This is subject to s 4(1) of the *Antarctic Treaty Act* 1960 (Cth).

Act seeks primarily to safeguard features of the environment that are of national significance. It applies to all activities concerning Commonwealth terrestrial and marine environments, including the AAT, Australia's sub-Antarctic possessions and the Southern Ocean.[18] In relation to Antarctica, the EPBC Act has two main functions. The first is to prohibit direct or indirect actions which are likely to have a significant impact on the environment. The second is to establish the Australian Whale Sanctuary (AWS)[19] in all areas of the Australian EEZ, including the EEZ offshore the AAT.

Jurisdiction and Enforcement in AAT Maritime Zones

Putting aside some narrow exceptions carved out by the *Antarctic Treaty Act* 1960 (Cth) and the AT(EP) Act, the Commonwealth has asserted a general territorial jurisdiction in legislation extending to the AAT. The same cannot be said for the legislative regime applicable to adjacent maritime zones claimed by Australia.

As with claims to the continent, assertions of jurisdiction over maritime areas in Antarctica must be understood in the context of Article IV of the Antarctic Treaty. There has been much debate regarding the effect of the provision in relation to maritime zones, as Article IV(2) stipulates that "[N]o new claim, or enlargement of an existing claim, to territorial sovereignty in Antarctica shall be asserted while the present Treaty is in force". Australia claims several maritime zones offshore the AAT and, with the possible exception of the EEZ (which is an innovation of the LOS Convention that postdates the Antarctic Treaty), it appears that these comply with the Antarctic Treaty as they amount to the assertion of an existing claim (Kaye and Rothwell 1995: 201-2).

With the enactment of the *Seas and Submerged Lands Act* 1973 (Cth), Australia proclaimed a 3 nautical mile (nm) territorial sea around Australia and the external territories, including the AAT (Harry 1981). This was subsequently extended to 12 nm in November 1990 (Opeskin and Rothwell 1991). Australia's claim to an Antarctic continental shelf was made much earlier as part of a general claim from the mainland (Commonwealth of Australia 1953). The limits of Australia's claim were only clearly revealed in November 2004 when Australia submitted its claim to an extended continental shelf under Article 76 of the LOS Convention to the Commission for the Limits of the Continental Shelf (Downer *et al* 2004).

As regards the EEZ, Australia initially asserted a 200 nm Australian Fishing Zone (AFZ) offshore the mainland and external territories in 1979 but shortly afterwards issued a proclamation that excepted AAT waters. While Australian fishing vessels continued to be governed by relevant fisheries legislation,[20] all waters seawards of the territorial sea were opened

---

18   EPBC Act, s 5(1).

19   EPBC Act, s 225.

20   *Fisheries Act* 1952 (Cth).

to foreign fishing interests (Kaye and Rothwell 1995). This exemption has been retained in the contemporary fisheries legislation, the *Fisheries Management Act* 1991 (Cth).[21] Subsequently, in 1994, Australia declared an EEZ in relation to the mainland and the AAT (Commonwealth of Australia 1994). This did not result in any change to the fisheries arrangements as the EEZ offshore the AAT was exempted from the AFZ. However, the now repealed *Whale Protection Act* 1980 (Cth) was extended in operation to all EEZ areas.[22] This is continued under the EPBC Act which advances the conservation of cetaceans under Australian law. The Act establishes the AWS and makes it an offence to kill or injure whales and marine mammals. The extent of the AWS is coterminous with the outer limits of Australia's EEZ and therefore includes the seas adjacent to the AAT out to a distance of 200 nm.

The key reason for exempting foreign persons and vessels from Australian fisheries legislation applicable to the AAT EEZ was to avoid upsetting the negotiation of CCAMLR, which Australia has implemented by the *Antarctic Marine Living Resources Conservation Act* 1981 (Cth). In terms of the jurisdictional reach it is less expansive than the AT(EP) Act. It applies to Australian citizens and Australian flagged vessels and their crew (of whatever nationality). It also applies to all foreign nationals and foreign vessels "in and in relation to Australia or the Australian fishing zone" (s 4(2)(b)). But as the AFZ does not include Australia's EEZ offshore the AAT, the Act does not operate upon foreign nationals within these waters.

The legislative stance that the Australian Government has adopted in relation to Antarctic fisheries is a clear example of the dilemma that is confronted when asserting Antarctic jurisdiction. While it may be essential for maintaining and consolidating Australian sovereign claims, on the other hand the projection of a jurisdiction perceived to be exorbitant, or against the spirit of Article VIII of the Antarctic Treaty, may in fact defeat Australia's policy objective to promote cooperative arrangements to protect the Antarctic marine environment. On one view Australia may be seen to have relinquished its sovereign claims in the broader interests of an effective ATS. However, a more positive view is that this decision is a clear demonstration of Australia's sovereignty to determine the extent to which its laws are operative. Moreover, Australia may rely upon Article IV(1) of CCAMLR which provides that no acts or activities taking place while the Convention is in force shall be interpreted as a renunciation or diminution of any right or claim.

---

21 The Australian Fishing Zone is defined in the *Fisheries Management Act* 1991 (Cth), s 3. The EEZ adjacent to the AAT are "excepted waters" by Proclamation made under s 11.

22 *Maritime Legislation Amendment Act* 1994 (Cth), Sch 1.

Increasing Jurisdictional Consistency

The AAT legislative regime is generally consistent in terms of its juris-dictional assertions, although there are some exceptions. Examining the legislation then operative, Triggs (1986: 262) argued that "the persistent failure to assert jurisdiction on a territorial basis ... raises the implication that Australia has not acted as sovereign within the Australian Antarctic Territory". It is not possible to draw this conclusion today. Whereas earlier enactments relied principally on a nationality basis of jurisdiction, and included broad exemptions for foreign nationals of ATS members and third States, more recent legislation has tended to assert a general territorial basis of jurisdiction. This trend is most evident in the EPBC Act. However, while greater legislative consistency might appear, on its face, to have served Australia's sovereignty interests in Antarctica, there remains the perennial issue of enforcement. A power asserted, but not acted upon, is problematic from the perspective of maintaining the authority of Australian claims over Antarctic territorial and maritime areas (Crawford and Rothwell 1992: 78).

Enforcement and Australia's Antarctic Agenda: Contemporary and Future Challenges

There has been no objection by claimant States to the Australian exercise of prescriptive jurisdiction over Antarctica, with Antarctic Treaty Parties aware that under its Article IV(2) national legislation cannot be a basis for a new territorial claim, or the enlargement of an existing claim. Similarly, the prospect of enforcing Australian law against Australian nationals in the AAT, and elsewhere on the continent, has not generated international con-cern. The instances in which the enforcement machinery has been activated in relation to Australian nationals is extremely rare, and even when utili-sed is has generally not led to prosecution.

Any attempt by Australia to enforce domestic law against non-nationals would be highly controversial. For this reason the Australian Government has to date maintained that while entitled to enforce Austra-lian law on a territorial basis, it refrains from doing so in the interests of maintaining good relations among and between claimant and non-claimant States. In practical terms Australia has been relieved of any need to contem-plate enforcement over non-nationals by virtue of the low levels of human activity in the AAT. However, as many States look south and the intensity of governmental and commercial activities in the AAT increases, Australia is under pressure to revisit the delicate policy balance that it seeks to maintain.

Contemporary and Future Challenges for Australia

The growing presence of foreign interests in an increasingly regulated AAT poses two policy dilemmas for Australia – one external and one internal.

allenge is maintaining the plausibility of Australia's territo-
he exercise of legislative jurisdiction is important for retain-
y then both the value of the legislation and the strength of
im may be questioned if the law is not in fact enforced on the
nternal policy dilemma is satisfying domestic constituencies,
such as environmental non-government organisations, who legitimately
seek to ensure that the Executive carries through the will of the Parliament
by implementing Australian environmental laws. The obvious, and seemingly intractable, difficulty faced by Australia in seeking aggressively to
enforce such laws is that it may destabilise the ATS, or at the very least give
rise to frictions, and potentially lessen Australia's influence in ATS fora.
This would clearly be contrary to Australia's interests in Antarctica.

Japanese Whaling Case

The ongoing litigation in the Federal Court of Australia in *Humane Society
International Inc v Kyodo Senpaku Kaisha Ltd*[23] (*Japanese Whaling Case*) has
raised dramatically the visibility of these internal and external challenges
and throws light on the ways in which the Australian Government is seeking to address them (see also Rothwell and Scott, and Jabour *et al* this
volume).

There is a long history of interaction between Australia and Japan on
Antarctic whaling issues. Like Australia, Japan is a Consultative Party to
the Antarctic Treaty and both States are Parties to the International Convention for the Regulation of Whaling.[24] When the *Whaling Act* 1935 (Cth)
was proclaimed in 1936, Japan was the only State to issue a protest and this
remains a rare example where a State has sought to reject the exercise by
Australia of prescriptive jurisdiction in Antarctica (Triggs 1986: 246). Japan
has for many years engaged in whaling activities within 12 nm of the AAT,
apparently in breach of Australian legislation.

In recent years these whaling activities have substantially increased.
Japan introduced the Japanese Whale Research Program under Special
Permit in the Antarctic (JARPA) in the 1987-88 season and continued this
program until the 2004-05 season. The principal focus of JARPA was the
taking of Antarctic minke whales. More than 6800 minke whales were
killed in Antarctic waters in the 18 years over which JARPA was conducted. In 2005 Japan announced its intention to conduct the Second Phase
of the Japanese Whale Research Program under Special Permit in the
Antarctic (JARPA II). The program commenced with a feasibility study for
the 2005-06 and 2006-07 seasons, and the full-scale program is scheduled to
commence as from the 2007-08 season. Projected catches for the full-scale
JARPA II program are 850 plus or minus 10 per cent minke whales, 50
humpback whales, and 50 fin whales.

---

23 *Humane Society International Inc v Kyodo Senpaku Kaisha Ltd* [2005] FCA 664.
24 161 UNTS 72.

Against this background, the *Japanese Whaling Case* involves efforts by a non-government environmental organisation to enforce the EPBC Act against a Japanese company undertaking whaling operations in Australia's AAT AWS. While it is a matter for the Commonwealth Director of Public Prosecutions to decide whether to pursue criminal proceedings for breaches of the EPBC Act, the legislation also allows, under s 475, an "interested person" to apply to the Federal Court for an injunction restraining the Commission of illegal conduct. If the litigation is successful it will effectively result in the judicial arm of government applying Commonwealth law in the Australian EEZ offshore the AAT against foreign nationals, contrary to the wishes of the Executive. It is no surprise, therefore, that the case has generated considerable controversy as regards its implications for Australia's Antarctic interests and the stability of the ATS.

In its application and statement of claim, filed on 19 October 2004, Humane Society International Inc (HSI) sought a declaration that Japanese whaling activities contravene provisions of the EPBC Act that make it an offence to kill, injure, take or interfere with any Antarctic minke whale in the AWS.[25] HSI identifies a total of 428 minke whales killed in the AWS since 2001 by five vessels owned and operated by Kyodo Senpaku Kaisha (KSK). HSI also seeks injunctive relief, restraining KSK from engaging in further whaling. In so far as the EPBC Act is concerned, the HSI possesses a strong claim. The evidence of past and proposed whaling activities by the KSK in the Antarctic AWS is not disputed and the provisions of the EPBC Act are clear. The fact that Japan does not recognise Australian territorial sovereignty in the AAT and consequently an entitlement to assert an EEZ does not detract from this (but see Blay and Bubna-Litic 2006). What has complicated the litigation in Australian law is the fact that KSK has no presence in Australia and under *Federal Court Rules* the HSI requires leave from the court to serve the application and statement of claim upon KSK in Japan.[26]

The decision whether or not to grant such leave is a discretionary one. The judge at first instance, Justice Allsop, declined to grant leave after taking submissions from the Commonwealth Attorney-General on the international legal and diplomatic implications of the proceedings. On the basis of the Attorney's submissions, Justice Allsop concluded that prosecuting the case "may upset the diplomatic status quo under the Antarctic Treaty and be contrary to Australia's long-term national interests, including its interests connected with its claim to territorial sovereignty to the Antarctic".[27]

An appeal against this decision was allowed by the Full Federal Court, which held that the initial judge's discretion miscarried.[28] In their joint

---

25 EPBC Act, Ch 5, Pt 13, Div 3 (ss 224-247).

26 *Federal Court Rules* (Cth), O 8, r 2.

27 *Humane Society International Inc v Kyodo Senpaku Kaisha Ltd* [2005] FCA 664 at [27].

28 *Humane Society International Inc v Kyodo Senpaku Kaisha Ltd* [2006] FCAFC 116.

judgment Chief Justice Black and Justice Finkelstein noted that the EPBC Act established the AWS which applied in the waters 200 nm seawards of the AAT and that the legislation applied to non-Australian citizens and non-Australian vessels. They took at face value the intent of Parliament in enacting the EPBC Act:

> The Parliament may be taken to know about the remoteness and general conditions pertaining to the [Australian Whale] Sanctuary which its legislation has established. It may also be taken to have appreciated the circumstances under which its laws may be enforced in relation to the Sanctuary are quite exceptional. It nevertheless made no provision for the exclusion of the general enforcement provisions of the EPBC Act to matters occurring within the Sanctuary, even where those matters related to conduct by foreign persons aboard foreign vessels.[29]

They concluded that Justice Allsop was in error in refusing to grant leave even if the continuation of the case was contrary to Australia's foreign relations. It was said that it would be anomalous if matters concerning Australia's diplomatic relations could not be raised in answer to HSI's claim if the defendant were present in Australia, but were relevant if service out of Australia was in issue. Furthermore, it was held that Justice Allsop erred "in attaching weight to what we would characterise as a political consideration".[30] The third member of the Court, Justice Moore, agreed, stating that "courts must be prepared to hear and determine matters whatever their political sensitivity domestically or internationally".[31] However, he dissented in the result, holding that the appeal should be dismissed because it was highly unlikely that the defendant would obey any order of the Court.

While the majority justices dismissed as irrelevant the Attorney-General's submissions on the political sensitivity of the proceedings they provide key insights into the Australian government's attitude to Antarctic sovereignty issues. Many aspects of the submissions are uncontroversial, repeating longstanding Australian policy stances. They reaffirm Australia's claim to the AAT and offshore areas, and assert that these are consistent with Article IV of the Antarctic Treaty. They also highlight the importance attached by the government to the exercise of legislative jurisdiction in the AAT. It is observed that as a matter of Australian law the EPBC Act applies to foreign nationals and foreign vessels in the AWS. However, it is also noted that Japan does not recognise the AAT and would regard enforcement action against its vessels as contrary to international law. To avoid

---

29 *Humane Society International Inc v Kyodo Senpaku Kaisha Ltd* [2006] FCAFC 116 at [7].

30 *Humane Society International Inc v Kyodo Senpaku Kaisha Ltd* [2006] FCAFC 116 at [11].

31 *Humane Society International Inc v Kyodo Senpaku Kaisha Ltd* [2006] FCAFC 116 at [38].

disputes concerning such matters, the submissions observe, all territorial claimants have generally refrained from enforcing national laws again foreign citizens.

This much accords with the position of previous governments. However, where there is a departure is in the suggestion that non-enforcement against non-nationals is not a restraint borne out of Realpolitik but is in fact a requirement of international law.[32] This view is not one that is supported by the language of Article VIII and it is a stance that has not previously been adopted by government. In this respect the *Japanese Whaling Case* may mark something of a retreat from Australia's generally assertive stance as regards the enforcement jurisdiction it claims to enjoy over the AAT.

The reticence to enforce Australian law in Antarctica also contrasts with the muscular response to illegal fishing in the sub-Antarctic AFZ surrounding Heard Island and McDonald Islands. The applicable legislative framework, that includes automatic forfeiture of foreign vessels engaged in illegal fishing, appears in open conflict with the LOS Convention. Australia has also engaged in the pursuit and interdiction of vessels that may arguably go beyond the rights it enjoys under the law of the sea (Stephens 2004: 12). Ultimately the major point of difference between handling the issue of illegal fishing and Japanese Antarctic whaling is that Australia may deal with the former issue, as least as regards Heard Island and McDonald Islands, confident not only as to its sovereignty but also that enforcement is unlikely to create tensions that undermine a broader international legal regime. Moreover, the Australian Government's willingness to adopt measures that go beyond those prescribed by CCAMLR confirms that Australia's sub-Antarctic agenda does not always involve a wholesale deference to applicable international legal regimes as the means by which Australia's environmental interests in Antarctica are to be protected.

Conclusion

The legal and political geography of Antarctica continues to present formidable legal and policy challenges for effective enforcement of Australian and international law. This chapter has sought to examine the enforcement and compliance regime established by the ATS and to explore the policy dynamics within which Australian domestic law must operate. As has been seen, the relationship between the two has not been straightforward. The essential tension has been between, on the one hand, a broad exercise of legislative jurisdiction in order to preserve the credibility of Australia's sovereign claim and, on the other, an anxiety that any enforcement of such laws on a territorial basis will weaken Australia's influence in the ATS or undermine cooperative efforts to achieve important continental outcomes

---

32   *Humane Society International v Kyodo Senpaku Kaisha, Outline of Submissions of the Attorney-General (Cth) as Amicus Curiae,* [16], [22].

such as effective environmental protection and the conservation of biological diversity.

In this respect Australia is on the horns of a dilemma. As regards other Parties to the ATS, its acts carry no lasting implications in terms of sovereignty by virtue of Article IV of the Antarctic Treaty. Australia may therefore seek to adapt its legislative and enforcement position to achieve outcomes that maintain Australian influence in the ATS and also enhance the efficacy of the now environment-focused ATS regime. Regarding non-Parties however, who are not bound by Article IV, such modifications may be regarded as a weakening of sovereign claims. This dilemma can only intensify as a result both of the increasing range of activities in the AAT that come within the purview of an increasingly comprehensive Australian Antarctic law and as the ATS system matures and develops features of an international supervisory regime. The temptation will then be to refrain from enforcement, or to confer additional authority upon ATS institutions. This may be considered legitimate if it achieves positive conservation outcomes for the continent, but Australia will not wish to be in a position where, having granted such authority, the regime proves ineffective or collapses. That would be to the very clear detriment of Australia's Antarctic agenda.

6

Antarctic Science in a Changing Climate: Challenges and Future Directions for Australia's Antarctic Science and Policy

Rosemary A Sandford

The early years of the 21st century are significant ones for Australia's Antarctic science programs. They benchmark where Antarctic science has come from and the directions it is likely to take over the next 20 years in an increasingly complex scientific and policy environment, nationally and internationally.

In 2006, the Australian Antarctic Division (AAD) marked the twenty-fifth anniversary of its relocation from Melbourne to Hobart in Tasmania and the consolidation of its operations in Hobart as Australia's Antarctic scientific and operational hub.

The period 2006-07 marks a turning point in international recognition of the significance of Antarctica and the Southern Ocean as key drivers of the global climate system. National and international scientists and decision makers now acknowledge that many climatic and oceanic changes in the region are being driven by the rapid rise in atmospheric carbon dioxide (CO_2) and its effects on these Antarctic systems (IPCC 2007).

In 2007-08 the celebration of the International Polar Year (IPY) is a time when the eyes of the world are on the Earth's polar regions and on Australia's Antarctic programs (Stoddart 2007: 25). It also marks the 50th anniversary of the International Geophysical Year (IGY).

Australia's Antarctic science programs cannot, however, be considered in isolation from other significant developments in national and international politics and public policy. For example, the release of the Inter-governmental Panel on Climate Change (IPCC) Fourth Assessment Report in February 2007, its enthusiastic uptake by the media and the response of senior Australian politicians, signalled to the Australian public that climate variability and change (referred to interchangeably in the popular press as "global warming" or "climate change"), has come of age politically in Australia.

The release of the IPCC Report followed hard on the heels of several significant events in 2006. In June 2006, the Oscar award-winning film *An Inconvenient Truth* by the former US Vice-President, Al Gore, opened in the USA; the British government released the Stern Review Report on the Economics of Climate Change in October 2006; and in Australia, the Lowy Institute published the results of its 2006 public opinion poll on attitudes to climate change. The poll demonstrated that concern about the likely impacts of climate change was registering as a potential national election issue in the minds of a significant number of Australians (Lowy Institute 2007). By early 2007, the combination of these factors and vivid media images of severe drought in rural areas, water shortages in the major capital cities and catastrophic bushfires across south-east Australia, appeared to be having an impact on the Australian psyche and on the Australian government's policy position.

It is thus timely to consider what Australia's Antarctic science programs and their supporting institutions might look like in a changing science-policy climate, and to address the underlying questions: What are some of the key domestic and international challenges facing Australia's Antarctic science program as it reviews the way it does business in a changing global climate, and how might or should it respond to these?

Background

Australia operates three stations on Antarctica – Casey, Davis and Mawson and a sub-Antarctic station on Macquarie Island. All stations operate year round. In addition, temporary field camps and bases are established in other locations inland on the Antarctic icecap or on the coast, as required for scientific research and logistical purposes (Stoddart 2007: 25-6).

As Stoddart further comments: "Australia's programme of research in Antarctica and the Southern Ocean is tightly focused on fields of study which are of strategic importance to the work of the government department of which it is a part – the Department of Environment and Heritage (DEH)" (2007: 30). The department was recently reconfigured as the Department of the Environment and Water Resources. It seems however, that its broad objectives remain unaltered: environmental protection, marine ecosystem sustainability, and understanding the role of Antarctica in the Earth's climate system (Stoddart 2007: 30).

The history and practice of scientific research in the Antarctic are embedded in international law and convention. The Preamble of the 1959 Antarctic Treaty recognises that it is in the "interest of all mankind" for Antarctica to continue forever to be used exclusively for peaceful purposes; and it acknowledges the value and contributions of scientific knowledge resulting from international cooperation in scientific investigations such as those undertaken during the 1957-58 IGY. Peace and science have been, and continue to be, hallmarks of the Antarctic Treaty, which Australia joined as one of the original signatories and a claimant of 42 per cent of Antarctica, upon its entry into force in 1961.

Although the Cold War was underway at the time the Treaty was adopted, both the geopolitical and scientific environments have changed markedly since then. The Cold War standoff between the two super powers of that era, the USSR and the USA, no longer dominates world politics. Following the collapse of the former USSR and a unilateral surge in the economic and military power of the USA, the USA now dominates the geopolitical order and the rapid rise to economic prominence of nations such as China and India is the focus of growing global concern about the implications of this growth for CO_2 emissions and climate change.

Australia's Antarctic scientific initiatives and directions in 2007 bear little resemblance to those of 1959 as they have evolved to mirror changes in domestic and international politics and Australian government priorities. No doubt they will continue to change as they respond to external factors, including climate change. When Antarctica is viewed through the prism of 2007, globalisation and the environmental challenges ahead make for a vastly more complex and potentially more uncertain landscape than that faced by Antarctica and the world in 1959.

Australia's Antarctic Science in the Making

Since 1974, regular reviews of the Antarctic science program by scientific committees such as the Advisory Committee on Antarctic Programs (ACAP), the Antarctic Research Advisory Committee (ARAC) and the Antarctic Scientific Advisory Committee (ASAC), have shaped the nature, practice and strategic directions of Australia's Antarctic scientific research. These reviews have usually been instigated by the government of the day, so any changes in scientific research direction or emphasis tend to reflect the policy directions and priorities of the national government, be it Labor or Liberal. Perhaps no review has been more significant in terms of reshaping the strategic directions of Australia's Antarctic science and policy efforts than the Foresight Review (ASAC 1997), driven by the policy and the national research priorities of the conservative Howard Liberal government.

The 1997 ASAC report, "Australia's Antarctic Program Beyond 2000: A Framework for the Future" (known as the "Foresight Review"), was a watershed in framing contemporary Antarctic science-policy strategic directions. The focus of the "Foresight Review" was on future strategic directions for Australia's Antarctic science research. This approach contrasted with previous reviews which had largely been science-based analyses of the progress and success of past research activities. Using the technique of foresight analysis, ASAC identified four goals for Australia's Antarctic science program. These were then slightly modified by the Australian Government in 1998 following a period of public consultation (Australian Government 1998). The goals were to:

- maintain the Antarctic Treaty System (ATS) and enhance Australia's influence within the system;

- protect the Antarctic environment;

- understand the role of Antarctica in the global climate system; and

- undertake scientific research work of practical, economic and national significance (Stoddart 2001).

In 2003, ASAC completed yet another evaluation of Australia's Antarctic program as part of a rolling series of reviews and evaluations of the extent to which Australia's Antarctic program was meeting its scientific objectives. The 2003 ASAC report resulted in the development of the Australian Antarctic Science Program, Science Strategy 2004/05–2008/09 (AAD 2003).

The strategy is a five-year plan that determines the strategic directions for Australia's current scientific program in Antarctica. It heralds a distinct shift from discipline-based programs to four, multidisciplinary theme/priority areas: ice, ocean, atmosphere and climate; Southern Ocean eco-systems; adaptation to environmental change; and impacts of human activities in Antarctica. The last two programs have now been amalgamated to form the Environmental Protection and Change program (Riddle 2006: 28). These themes support three of Australia's National Research Priorities: (i) building an environmentally sustainable Australia; (ii) frontier technologies for building and transforming Australian industries; and (iii) safeguarding Australia (AAD 2003).

This science strategy is very different from its predecessors in that it goes beyond detailed descriptions of the relative successes of past individual research programs, most of which appeared to have complimented rather than criticised, progress made. It consists of a brief description of the major issues in each of the four priority research areas, focusing on the relevance of issues to Australia's future. Detailed work plans are drawn up annually for the priority areas and for fundamental research against which progress is accounted (AAD 2003: 1). The four priority areas also determine priorities for the allocation of financial and human resources (Australian Government 1998: 4; Stoddart 2001: 62)

Resources are allocated to those topics that underpin the government's commitment to the ATS, its policy objectives for its Antarctic program, and its more general policies on science and the environment as embodied in its national research priorities (AAD 2003: 2). While AAD budgets are outlined in general terms in their annual reports, it was not possible to obtain or analyse details of recent science program budgets for this chapter, partly because the AAD's internal accounting methods have varied considerably over the years. In this respect, it has proved difficult to separate with any precision the actual costs of undertaking individual research programs from the costs of the logistical support and infrastructure required to support each research program.

Stoddart argues that Australia runs a large, comprehensive and productive scientific program as evidenced by the number of scientific papers produced per annum when compared with the output from the UK's program and its considerably larger number of scientists over the period 1995-2001 (Stoddart 2001: 63). In 2005, Dastidar and Persson (2005) commented that interest in Antarctica was on the rise and that there has been a distinct upward trend in the number of publications over the years: from 169 papers in 1980 to 735 papers in 2002. They further comment that four countries generated 60 per cent of the output in Antarctic science: USA, UK, Australia and Germany (Dastidar and Persson 2005: 1552-4).

In 1999-2000, the Australian Antarctic Division undertook a Priority-Based Budgeting exercise to assist in the allocation of resources according to 1998 goals (Stoddart 2001: 62) and the Government's Budget papers for 2001-02 show clearly where the emphasis of the budget allocation lies relative to its goals (Stoddart 2001: 63-4). These are outlined in Table 2. It should also be noted that figures include the attributed costs of logistics and do not reflect the direct costs of the outputs (Jackson 2007 pers.comm).

Table 2: Priority-Based Budget for AAD, 1999-2000

Goal	Allocation (million $AU)
To maintain the Antarctic Treaty System and increase Australia's influence in the system	15.93
To protect the Antarctic environment	40.70
To understand the role of Antarctic[a] in the global climate system	23.34
To undertake scientific work of practical, economic and national significance	19.78
Total	99.75

(Source: Stoddart 2001)

Stoddart then breaks down these funding allocations against the discipline programs (Table 3, *see over*), noting that "these are accrual figures and therefore represent the true cost of maintaining a particular activity. People on stations and days of ship time are major cost drivers" (Stoddart 2001: 64). It must be noted that this is only AAD expenditure as it was in 2001-02 and does not include expenditure of other agencies in these disciplines.

Unfortunately, figures for 2000-07 were not available at the time of writing. In their absence, one can only speculate that figures from this period might indicate if, or how, subsequent budgets have been constructed to reflect and evaluate the merits and costs of the shift from discipline-based programs to multidisciplinary, themed research, including an increased emphasis on marine research and oceanography. The apparent change in budgetary emphasis over the years from the physical sciences to

Table 3: Discipline-based Budget for AAD

Program	Allocation (million $AU)
Antarctic Marine Living Resources	7.21
Atmospheric Science	24.25
Biology	32.41
Geoscience	6.64
Glaciology	10.66
Human Impacts	12.38
Human Biology and Medicine	0.41
Oceanography	1.84
Antarctic Data Centre (including mapping activities)	3.27

(Source: Stoddart 2001)

biological sciences and environmental impacts, appears to coincide with growing concern in both scientific and policy circles about the impacts of global warming on the Southern Ocean and on marine ecosystems, and recognition of the need for greater scientific investigation in these areas.

Science-Policy Changes in Australia's Antarctic Science Program 1967-2007

Australian Antarctic science and policy have a long history of co-dependency. Science has been used to support Australia's sovereignty and policy interests on the continent (see Rothwell and Scott this volume) and government policy priorities have, in turn, been used to justify the need for continued scientific research and the expansion of scientific programs. The interdependence of policy and science is enshrined in the text of the Antarctic Treaty and cemented by relations among the Treaty Parties in their pursuit of peace and science. International scientific collaborations are perhaps the centrepiece of the science-policy relationship. The symbiotic relationship between science and policy in Australia's Antarctic program is almost certainly mirrored within other national Antarctic programs, including those of the UK and the USA.

Australia's Antarctic research program has undergone a number of transformations since 1967. Arguably, the most significant change in recent years has been from one of science as a primary driver of Australia's national and international Antarctic policies, to one of government policy as the major determinant of scientific research priorities and resource allocation. In relation to climate change, the policy has lagged well behind the science, although this now appears to be on the cusp of a change. In fact the challenge posed by climate change could well be the primary focus of the Antarctic science and policy programs in the 21st century. This will be addressed in subsequent sections.

At the domestic level, the Antarctic science program has experienced a number of structural changes. These have generally resulted from organisational changes in national government agencies. Haward (2006) argues that there has been a shift from centralisation to decentralisation in the administration and operation of Australia's Antarctic programs. For example, the Antarctic Division as the sole driver and the "command and control centre" of Antarctic science has been replaced by a more decentralised approach involving organisations such as universities, the Antarctic Climate and Ecosystems Cooperative Research Centre (ACE CRC) and other national and state government agencies as formal partners and/or scientific collaborators.

The ACE CRC is a partnership of university, state and the national government bodies, including the Department of the Environment and Water Resources, of which AAD is a division. Other ACE CRC partners include: scientific organisations such as the Bureau of Meteorology (BOM) and the Commonwealth Scientific and Industrial Research Organisation (CSIRO). With the ACE CRC as the lynch pin organisation of Australia's broader Antarctic research network, scientific and policy teams are working cooperatively on issues of national and international significance. The role of Antarctica and the Southern Ocean as drivers of global climate change and the likely effects of climate change on Southern Ocean ecosystems and fisheries are key research foci.

Other notable changes in Antarctic research are shifts in program emphasis, priorities and composition, including the shift from disciplinary-based research with its roots in the heroic era of exploration and logistics to a more multidisciplinary and themed approach. Until the early 1970s, Australia's science effort in the Antarctic was driven primarily by the physical sciences and by logistical operations to support the science program and the maintenance of fixed bases on the Antarctic continent. Since then, the research focus has shifted from an emphasis on the physical sciences to be more inclusive of a greater range of ecological and social scientists. The dominance of discipline-based programs in the physical sciences has now been overtaken by an increased number of more inclusive, multidisciplinary approaches to scientific investigation which incorporate atmospheric, marine, environmental, and social scientists. This should enable the science program to respond more appropriately to a rapidly changing policy climate where the issues that need to be considered by policymakers extend beyond the relatively narrow confines of scientific disciplines.

Another noticeable change since the late 1970s is that the gender imbalance in science programs has been substantially redressed so that women are now better represented in what has traditionally been a male-dominated science program.

Irrespective of these moves to modernise the practice of science, the strategic directions of Australia's Antarctic science programs remain driven largely by the policy priorities of the government of the day and the extent to which scientists are able to influence these. Opportunities to influence government policy priorities lie with the accumulated scientific capital built up by Australian scientists under the auspices of scientific advisory committees of the ATS, particularly the Scientific Committee on Antarctic Research (SCAR), and at a national level through the Advisory Committee on Antarctic Programs and ASAC. Professional collaborations and networks among scientists have existed for decades. Although national governments come and go, international scientific networks span the globe, work to longer time horizons than do politicians, and often outlast them. Scientists are thus potentially able to influence policy outcomes.

The need for effective integration of climate science and public policy is a prime illustration of how scientists and policymakers might cooperate in the public interest and how, in so doing, they can help shape the future of the planet. Global warming is probably the major challenge facing the Antarctic in 2007 and beyond. Climate change is scientifically and politically complex and it affects virtually every aspect of life on earth. As confirmed by the IPCC Fourth Assessment Report (IPCC 2007), global warming is occurring more rapidly than was anticipated when the current Science Strategy 2004/05–2008/09 was compiled. This is a major challenge for both Antarctic science and policy.

Antarctic Science and Policy: Present and Future Challenges

Many of the science-policy changes in Australia's Antarctic science program between 1967 and 2007 have occurred and/or are occurring in response to changes in international politics. Some of these changes were foreshadowed previously and include: the end of the Cold War, the emergence of a new world order dominated by the USA and the ascendancy of the Chinese and Indian economies.

The usual issues of national and international concern that are identified in Antarctic literature, include the waxing and waning of the fortunes and spheres of influence of the Antarctic Treaty, its Parties and potential Parties, and related international conventions and infrastructures such as those of the Commission for the Conservation of Antarctic Marine Living Resources (CCAMLR; see Lugten this volume), Convention for the Conservation of Antarctic Seals (CCAS), the International Whaling Commission (IWC; see Jabour *et al* this volume) and the Agreement on the Conservation of Albatrosses and Petrels (ACAP; see Hall this volume). It is fair to say that historically, the ATS has been rather inward looking and focused more on the exclusivity of its sphere of operation than on apparently more tangential external factors/issues beyond the Treaty system itself, even though the issues might impinge on ATS operations.

In contrast, recent acknowledgement of the significant role of Antarctica and the Southern Ocean in the global climate system, lends weight to the argument that Australian Antarctic science and policy need to think beyond their traditional boundaries. For policy and decision makers, this means investigating the ways in which scientific knowledge gained from Antarctic systems can contribute to an understanding of the global impacts of climate change beyond Antarctica. For example, how might the impacts of climate change on the Southern Ocean affect the movement of populations such as environmental refugees adapting to – or fleeing from – sea level rise in low-lying countries of south east Asia and the South Pacific?

Other issues that will impinge on Antarctic scientific and policy priorities include resource availability and resource security, including the depletion of global oil reserves and the approach of a peak oil crisis (Bakhtiari 2006: 10). An oil crisis will have an impact globally. Australian or other deployments in the region, ship and airlink travel and the running of stations on the continent will not be immune from global effects. Tourism in Antarctica will be similarly affected. Fear of a global oil crisis in the 1980s resulted in the emergence of the Convention on the Regulation of Antarctic Mineral Resource Activities (CRAMRA) as a response to that crisis. The CRAMRA negotiations eventually collapsed, in part as a result of pressure exerted by key member nations and a well-organised, international environmental movement (see Powell and Jackson this volume). In the 1991 Protocol on Environmental Protection to the Antarctic Treaty (Madrid Protocol), Article 7, Prohibition of Mineral Resource Activities states: "Any activity relating to mineral resources, other than scientific research, shall be prohibited". In response, Bakhtiari comments that despite the difficulties of drilling in Antarctica and tragic environmental consequences, public opinion could change as the domino effect of reduced oil supply increases (Bakhtiari 2006: 10).

Should global oil reserves dwindle to a level incompatible with globalisation, continued economic growth and the growing energy needs of developed and developing nations, what then will become of the Madrid Protocol's mining prohibition and the Treaty's commitment to peace and science? In that scenario, might not the ATS experience difficulties similar to those of the International Whaling Commission where whaling for commercial gain is pursued by some countries in the name of scientific research? What would this mean for Australia's Antarctic science program and priorities? If faced with an energy crisis, would Australia, a claimant to 42 per cent of Antarctica and an Antarctic continental shelf, reject the opportunity for geological prospecting (even if under the guise of scientific research) for new energy sources including oil?

Global warming is already having an effect on terrestrial and marine ecosystems including those of the Southern Ocean and the Antarctic Peninsula as ice melts and the ocean warms and becomes increasingly acidic (ACE CRC 2007). Not only are these changes of concern for ecosystem survival and productivity, but they are directly relevant to ensuring food security for a growing world population. Conflicts over food and resource security for an expanding population can be expected to increase. Can Antarctica expect to remain aloof from such pressures?

The potential movement of exotic pests and diseases into the Antarctic and sub-Antarctic regions is already causing concern. These pests and diseases may arrive (and survive) naturally in response to climate change or they may be borne by scientists and other visitors arriving on ships and from 2007 on the Antarctic air link from Hobart (Riddle 2006).

Population growth, globalisation, economic development and resource scarcity do not exist in isolation from one another. They are interdependent and their individual and combined interactions need to be addressed at international, national and sub-national levels as their effects are felt at all three levels of governance. All of these issues will be aggravated by the predicted impacts of climate change on human communities, terrestrial and marine ecosystems.

It is anticipated that conflicts over resource security compounded by the predicted impacts of climate change, will increase. Antarctica and the Southern Ocean will not remain immune from resource security conflicts as competition grows for the energy and food resources that lie or might lie in this region. It is also conceivable that there may well be a revisiting of the CRAMRA negotiations of the 1980s (Sandford 2006). Nor is Australia likely to take a back seat in such a scenario. "Scientific work of practical, economic and national significance" (Australian Government 1998) such as scientific investigation of mineral accessibility and extraction on the continent and the expansion of Southern Ocean fisheries in the name of scientific research, may well take precedence over public good "blue sky" research. In an intensely competitive international environment such as that portrayed above, the national interest of each country will almost certainly win out over the planetary public interest. Australia will be no exception. All these issues will pose challenges to, and require responses from, Australia's Antarctic Program.

International issues are not however, the only issues with which a national government has to contend. Governments have to consider and make decisions about competing policy and budgetary objectives and priorities, domestic and international. In the 2007 Federal election year, the Australian government and opposition will have to weigh up a host of potentially competing environmental, economic and social priorities. As well as the usual range of domestic issues, additional causes of political concern and public interest will include providing drought relief in rural Australia and ensuring adequate water supplies to all Australians including those in capital cities with dwindling water resources. Dealing with extreme events such as bushfires, cyclones and floods in most states and planning for much-publicised sea level rise along our densely populated coastal regions are other issues competing for policy and budgetary priority. All these matters require decisions in the immediate, short and medium term. In contrast, Antarctic science operates in longer time frames.

How then can it hold its own in the near-sighted world of domestic politics? This is, arguably, the key domestic challenge facing the Australian Antarctic science program.

So, how should Australia meet this suite of challenges and how might Antarctic science and policy make a positive contribution in this regard?

Future Directions for Australia's Antarctic Science and Policy

At the time of writing, AAD has just completed its Antarctic Futures Project to define Australia's role in Antarctica to 2020. As Andrew Jackson, Antarctic Futures Project Manager, notes:

> [The Antarctic Futures Project] looks beyond the Division's current scientific and operational planning; beyond the introduction and consolidation of the air transport system; beyond the life of the Antarctic Climate and Ecosystems Cooperative Research Centre; and beyond the point at which some pundits say that 'peak oil' will have materialised. (Jackson 2006: 34)

Jackson then raises the question: how can we plan ahead when there are so many uncertainties? He suggests that we can start with what we know and that "the project will present an agreed '2020 vision'" of Australia's engagement with Antarctica – but whose "agreed" vision will this be and to what extent will it look to the wider picture beyond Australia's direct self-interest in maintaining its position in the ATS? These questions will presumably remain unanswered until the Antarctic Futures Project Report is made available to the public.

So what might Australia's Antarctic future look like in 10, 20, 50 years time and what can scientific research in one of the planet's last relatively unspoiled wildernesses tell us about what we might expect into the future? Global climate change is the most pervasive and complex challenge facing Australian science and policy. It is "the issue of the century" (Frith 2007: 12) and an emphasis on the role of Antarctica and the Southern Ocean in climate change could well hold the key to future directions for Antarctic science and policy – providing that scientists and decision makers are prepared to consider the interdependence of issues beyond the immediate confines of the ATS. This will require active cooperation across disciplines and across all levels of government. A grand plan no doubt, but as Jackson (2006) suggests, we start with what we know which, in the case of Australia's Antarctic science and policy programs, is substantial.

In my opinion, Australia's Antarctic program to 2020 should include two key objectives. The first is to increase political and public understanding of the domestic relevance of Antarctic and Southern Ocean science in developing Australia's response to climate change.

While the value of international and national scientific research is appreciated among scientists, the direct audience for research outputs tends to be limited. Traditionally, research findings have been published in scientific, peer-reviewed journals and less specialised publications targeted at what can best be described as the informed general public. The general media is, however, starting to ask questions about the wider implications of this research and government has a responsibility to make the science more accessible and transparent. It is a measure of the seriousness with which the media is now taking climate change as a driver of the nation's economic, social and environmental future, that *The Weekend Australian* recently commenced publication of the first of a series of major special reports on Business and the Environment (*The Weekend Australian* 24-25 March 2007: 1-12).

One of the goals of the Antarctic Science Strategy is that it should focus, *inter alia*, on science of national significance. Perhaps this goal should now be rephrased to consider how knowledge gained from Antarctic science might be better integrated in a national coordinated approach to addressing climate change at a regional level and in ways that overcome the competition among government agencies for scientific supremacy and resources? As David Crombie, President of the National Farmers' Federation, comments, "what we really need is accurate regional data ... there is a plethora of information at the global and national levels but that's useless to the 130,000 farmers who manage 60% of Australia's landmass" (Parker 2007: 3).

For the insurance industry, "looking down the road to see what is coming" is second nature (Parker 2007: 3). For some years now, the insurance industry has been a keen proponent of the need for government and communities to understand the causes and consequences of climate change. To quote Sam Mostyn, Insurance Australia Group (IAG): "[A]s an insurance company we [IAG] would very much like to be able to see the big picture of climate change and the impact on Australia. That is a role that only the Commonwealth Government can play" (Parker 2007: 3).

Corporations with an eye on the future realise that we cannot afford to wait for scientific precision in order to act, as the cost of not acting will exceed the costs of acting now. The influential Australian Business Round-table on Climate Change which includes big companies such as IAG, Origin, Swiss Re and Visy, has already voiced this concern (Henry 2007: 4).

Each of AAD's science programs provide valuable insights into what Australians might expect from global warming. We already know that the ice is melting in the world's polar regions, including in parts of Antarctica; that the Southern Ocean is warming and becoming more acidic; that sea levels are rising; and extreme events including storm surges and cyclones are becoming more frequent and more intense. We also know that Antarctic and Southern Ocean research has helped explain how rainfall patterns are changing across southern Australia, the source of much of the country's wheat production. More alarming news comes from research into the impacts of ocean warming and acidification on marine ecosystems and the living resources of Antarctica and the Southern Ocean, those resources on which much of the world's population depends. Taken collectively, these findings have implications for all Australians and for our Pacific neighbours, as well as for other countries.

Policy and decision makers cannot wait until the science is considered "without error" before they act. Public policy is a social science; its focus is on that most unpredictable of creatures, the human being. By nature and necessity, public policy development and decision making is less exact than its physical science counterparts. Some of our low-lying Pacific neighbours, including those in the Carteret Islands, are already facing the threat of evacuation from their island homes and the potential collapse of their cultural identity, family and social structures, as a result of relocation to other destinations (ABC 2007b). They cannot afford to wait until science tells them precisely what level of sea rise they might expect and when exactly they might expect it, as already their terrestrial food and freshwater sources are diminishing as the sea encroaches on their islands. Closer to home, what will ocean warming, acidification, coral reef destruction and the possible collapse of marine ecosystems mean for Australia's domestic fisheries and the tourism-dependent economy of North Queensland?

The fundamental question here is: how might Antarctic science and policy be better integrated and delivered in ways that improve political and public understanding of the domestic relevance of Antarctic and Southern Ocean science to climate policy decisions?

The second key objective of Australia's Antarctic program in this century relates to the interdependence of the issues facing Australia in a world where rapid change and the unexpected, rather than the expected, have almost become the norm (see Hemmings this volume). There is a risk that international cooperation and the peaceful pursuit of science may become less of a cornerstone of the ATS than has been the case in the past. The impacts of global warming on, and growing resource disparities among, nations, will become more apparent during this century. This will increase the risk of conflicts over resources. In such a scenario, environmental protection and conservation – presently major goals of Australia's Antarctic science strategy – are likely to become of secondary importance to national resource security.

In this context, the Antarctic Program to 2020 should be to use Australia's high standing and positive profile in the ATS to leverage its position in other treaties and conventions such as the United Nations Framework Convention on Climate Change. In so doing, it could seek to address the interdependence of issues related to climate change – its impacts, the development of mitigation measures and the need for adaptation strategies. Diplomatic and scientific capital are transferable and, in this respect, Australia is well placed as a middle power to act as an honest broker of environmental and resource security issues both within the ATS and between the ATS and resource management conventions such as those relating to fisheries and resource extraction (Sandford 2006).

This is not a new concept. Australia's ability and preparedness to perform "above its weight" in the global arena and to act creatively as an impartial third party in international trade negotiations, regional conflict resolution and coalition building among Treaty Parties, has long been recognised (Evans and Grant 1991; Calvert 2000). By adopting a lynch pin role as an honest broker, Australia could to some extent use its combined Antarctic science-policy expertise to anticipate and buffer itself against the likely impacts of conflicts arising from global and regional changes. It is hoped that Australia will also take its Pacific island neighbours and other nations into consideration as it seeks to protect its own national interests.

Conclusion

This chapter poses two questions: what are some of the key domestic and international challenges facing Australia's Antarctic Science Program as it reviews the way it does business in a changing global climate, and how might it, or should it, respond to these? It then traces the emergence of Australia's Antarctic science programs, identifies the major internal and external challenges experienced since 1967 and the responses of Australia's Antarctic science program to changes in national political and policy priorities.

The chapter suggests that climate variability and change are the most important research priorities and the most complex challenges facing Antarctic science and policy in the 21st century and that any science-policy response must consider the relationship between Antarctica and the Southern Ocean as a key driver of the global climate system and less obvious issues such as globalisation, population growth, depletion of the global energy reserves and environmental and resource security. The ATS can no longer remain aloof from the interdependence of these issues.

Finally, this chapter recommends two objectives that should be incorporated into planning for Australia's future in Antarctica and the Southern Ocean. They are: to increase political and public understanding of the domestic relevance of Antarctic and Southern Ocean science in developing Australia's response to climate change; and to use Australia's high standing and positive profile within the ATS to leverage its position as an honest broker both within the ATS and in other conventions such as the Framework Convention on Climate Change and in so doing, seek to address the interdependence of issues related to climate change – its impacts, the development of mitigation measures and the need for adaptation strategies.

7

Emerging Issues of Australian Antarctic Tourism: Legal and Policy Directions

Murray P Johnson and Lorne K Kriwoken

Introduction

Antarctic tourism activity presents legal and policy challenges for the Antarctic Treaty System (ATS). Bastmeijer (2003) argues that the Protocol on Environmental Protection to the Antarctic Treaty 1991 (Madrid Protocol) and domestic legislation do not effectively question the legitimacy of the many forms of Antarctic tourism. States Parties have only partially used the Protocol's environmental impact assessment (EIA) provisions for tourism proposals (Richardson 2000). The majority of domestic implementing legislation of state Parties has the role of authorising tourism activity (Bastmeijer 2003). Since 2001, there has been increased recognition at Antarctic Treaty Consultative Meetings (ATCM) of the need for additional measures to regulate Antarctic tourism. In March 2004, an Antarctic Treaty Meeting of Experts on Tourism and Non-Governmental Activities in Antarctica (ATME) was convened[1] to examine tourism issues, including "jurisdiction, industry self-regulation; and an analysis of the existing legal framework and identification of gaps" (ATCM XXVI 2003). Subsequent ATCMs have extended the examination of emerging tourism issues and the associated regulatory directions.

Australia's national legislation and administration of the region responds to obligations under the Antarctic Treaty 1959. Despite the relatively low demand for tourism regulation in the Australian Antarctic Territory (AAT),[2] Australia has consistently worked with the Antarctic Treaty Con-

---

1   Convened at Tromso-Trondheim on 22-25 March 2004, in accordance with Decision 5 of ATCM XXVI.

2   The Australian Antarctic Territory is subject to significantly less tourism activity when compared with the Antarctic Peninsula and the Ross Sea Region, due largely to the more challenging access constraints. Also, there are relatively few tourism companies or vessels operating from Australia.

sultative Parties (ATCPs) to achieve integrated management of Antarctic tourism. In response to emerging tourism issues, Australia has developed a tourism policy and argued for the implementation of schemes for industry accreditation and onboard observers, an Antarctic shipping code and site-specific visitor guidelines (AAD 2004b). Australia (2005a) has also sought to establish ATCP policy on the development of land-based non-government infrastructure.

This chapter considers the emerging issues of Australian Antarctic tourism, through a critique of its legal and policy approach. An introduction of Australia's legal and policy framework precedes the analysis of increasing tourism activity, technological developments and land-based tourism facilities. This is followed by an examination of non-members of the International Association of Antarctica Tour Operators (IAATO) operating tourism companies or vessels from Third Party States. The chapter concludes with an outline of how Australia can adopt suitable legal and policy directions for tourism within the ATS.

Australia's Legal and Policy Framework

Section 8(1) of the *Antarctic Treaty Act* 1960 (Cth) (AT Act) gives effect to the Treaty in Australian law and s 3(2) gives effect to the agreement made under Article VIII of the Treaty that designated persons[3] should only be subject to the laws of their own country, wherever they are in Antarctica (Rothwell and Davis 1997). The cornerstone of Australia's Antarctic environmental protection legislation is the *Antarctic Treaty (Environment Protection) Act* 1980 (Cth) (ATEP Act), which implements Australia's international obligations. The ATEP Act has been amended to give effect to the Madrid Protocol and its Annexes. Expressions used in the ATEP Act are intended to be interpreted in a manner consistent with the Protocol (and/ or Treaty) and the ATEP Act operates with a series of associated Regulations, including those concerned with EIA. The EIA process supports a three-tiered evaluation consisting of Preliminary Assessment (PA), Initial Environmental Evaluation (IEE) and Comprehensive Environmental Evaluation (CEE) (Kriwoken and Rootes 2000).

Australia's view is that policy interests are best served by maintaining and strengthening the ATS (Brook 1984). This view is supported by Australia's current policy on Antarctic tourism (Australia 2004a):

Australian Policy on Antarctic Tourism

Recognising the pre-eminent role of the Antarctic Treaty and the Protocol on Environmental Protection to the Antarctic Treaty in the management of Antarctica, and recognising also Australia's obligations as a signatory to these instruments, the following policy has been adopted by the Australian Government in relation to tourism activities in Antarctica.

---

3   'Designated persons' are designated observers (Treaty, Article VII(1)) or scientific personnel (Treaty, Article III(1)(b)) and their accompanying staff.

The Australian Government recognizes the legitimacy of tourism activities in Antarctica provided they further the principles and objectives of the Antarctic Treaty and their conduct is ecologically sustainable and socially responsible.

Tourist activities that further the Antarctic Treaty are those that are undertaken in accordance with the Antarctic Treaty and its associated instruments.

Tourism in Antarctica will be considered ecologically sustainable if it is assessed in accordance with the Madrid Protocol as having no more than a minor or transitory impact on the Antarctic environment and the intrinsic values of Antarctica.

Socially responsible activities are activities that (a) are of a peaceful nature; (b) do not degrade, or pose a substantial risk to, areas of biological, scientific, historic, aesthetic or wilderness significance; (c) will not detrimentally affect any other activity in the Antarctic Treaty area, in particular scientific research activities and their associated support activities; and (d) have the capacity to respond promptly and effectively to accidents and emergencies.

Increasing Tourism Activity, Technological Developments and Land-Based Tourism Infrastructure

While the scale of Antarctic tourism is small when compared with the industry in other parts of the world (Stonehouse 2000), the high growth rate is remarkable (Mason and Legg 2000). Antarctic tourist numbers have increased more than 13-fold in the past 16 years, from 2460 in 1990 to 32,042 in 2005-06 (IAATO 2006a). Australian nationals accounted for 8.4 per cent (2515) of 2005-06 tourists (IAATO 2006c). Antarctic tourist numbers are influenced by the increasing number of tour operators and the use of larger capacity passenger ships. The seven original IAATO members in 1991 have now grown to 80 parties. There are 16 recognised Australian-based companies, or companies with Australian offices, that offer Antarctic tourism services (AAD 2006), 11 of which are IAATO members. Australian-based operators carried one tenth (3211 persons) of all tourism-related passengers in 2005-06 (Powell 2006).

The geographic reach of Antarctic tourism expanded in response to the industry's search to offer untouched or pristine areas, as tourism pressure on well-known sites increases (Richardson 2000). Technological developments and sophisticated logistics enable further geographic expansion to the extent that virtually any location within Antarctica can be made accessible to tourists (Press 2001). The majority of tourism is sea-based, with operators landing on the coastal zone. If sea and land conditions are difficult, helicopters are increasingly available and reliable. Aircraft runways on the Antarctic continent have the potential to facilitate new tourism activity (Traavik 2004). Whilst Australia's Antarctic Air Link Project is intended to deliver improved and more flexible access to the continent for scientific research (AAD 2005a), such technological developments are also of interest to the tourism industry.

The regulation of land-based infrastructure to support tourism has been an issue of considerable ATS examination since it was raised at the 2004 ATME (ATCM XXVIII 2005a). Even its notional definition being "the creation of permanent or semi-permanent infrastructure ashore, in order to promote and support tourism activities" (New Zealand and Australia 2006: 3) has been subject to interpretive examination (IAATO 2006d). Examples of such infrastructure would include jetties, wharves, airstrips/runways, footpaths, roads, accommodation facilities (from tented camps to scientific stations to hotels) and logistics centres. ATCPs share concerns regarding the potential for undesirable consequences to eventuate from such infrastructure development, including potential environmental impacts, the need for Parties to protect aesthetic and wilderness values and the potential for legal jurisdictional complexities to arise (Australia 2005a; New Zealand 2005; ATCM XXIX 2006; New Zealand and Australia 2006).

Whilst recognising the merits of IAATO setting and maintaining industry standards, ATME emphasised that it remained the responsibility of Parties to establish the regulatory basis for the tourism industry. Despite acknowledging that the Protocol lacks provisions for regulating the development of land-based infrastructure to support tourism, the ATCP considerations toward identifying a suitable regulatory approach have been wide-ranging but inconclusive to date (ATCM XXIX 2006). A binding ATS Measure would deliver the strongest regulatory effect and a preceding Resolution of interim protection would be appropriate, due to the time it takes for the ATS to institute Measures (New Zealand and Australia 2006). This approach would assist many Parties to implement their domestic legislation, as many currently do not prohibit such facilities without recourse to an appropriate ATCM statement. Australia prepared a draft Measure for consideration by the Parties at ATCM XXVIII, which implied that "Parties shall not authorise the development of any new permanent or semi-permanent infrastructure for the conduct or support of tourism or non-government activities in Antarctica" (Australia 2005a: 4). However, several ATCPs emphasised that their domestic legislation would not accommodate such prohibition of tourism-related development and there was broader support for an approach that involved Parties voluntarily declining to authorise such development proposals (ATCM XXVIII 2005a). This non-mandatory interim approach was further supported at ATCM XXIX (2006).

Many ATCPs accept tourism as a legitimate activity, providing it is undertaken in a manner consistent with the Article 3 principles of the Madrid Protocol. However, regulatory limitations have been identified with respect to insufficiencies within the Protocol's EIA process, variations/inadequacies of domestic legislation and the inability of the Treaty to deal with private property rights or usufructuary rights (ATCM XXVII

2004; ATCM XXVIII 2005a; ATCM XXIX 2006). While the range of technical developments associated with tourism access to the region continues to increase, State Party EIA is currently the only means of regulating proposals involving new technological developments. In considering the regulation of land-based infrastructure to support tourism, the ATCPs have not yet reached consensus on the extent of Party involvement.

Section 7A of the ATEP Act requires the Minister to act in a manner consistent with Article 3 environmental principles. In the case of Comprehensive Environmental Evaluation (CEE), the Minister must not authorise activities that cannot be carried out in a manner consistent with the environmental principles (ATEP Act s 12L(5)). Yet provision is made for conditional authorisation of proposed tourism activities, regardless of the level of EIA conducted (ATEP Act ss 12F(2), 12J(2)-(4), 12L(3) and 12P). Furthermore, the Minister must authorise the carrying out of proposed tourism activity if a PA establishes it is likely to have no more than negligible impact on the environment (ATEP Act s 12F); or if an IEE establishes the activity is likely to have a minor or transitory impact on the environment (ATEP Act s 12J). Bastmeijer (2003) argues that such legislative provisioning obliges national authorities to authorise all tourism activities that are not subject to a CEE.

It is arguable whether Australia's existing regulatory approach to controlling tourism activity and technology will prove effective in meeting its policy aspirations in the longer term, particularly in light of the emerging tourism issues under consideration. For example, there are no specific national regulatory controls placed on tourist numbers, vessel type or size, activity type or scale, or technological developments. Such inadequacies fail to account for the experience that certain conservation values can only be sustainably realised if tourism activity is constrained in size and frequency (Wearing & Neil 1999). There are no specific provisions that seek to regulate land-based tourism facilities or technical developments that enhance access capabilities (Johnson 2002). Albeit activity authorisations under the ATEP Act provide for conditions to be applied to individual tourism proposals (ATEP Act ss 12F(2), 12J(2)-(4), 12L(3), 12P).

Setting a benchmark of no more than a minor or transitory impact for development of land-based infrastructure to support tourism has been promoted by New Zealand and Australia (ATCM XXVIII 2005a). Whilst the ATCPs have been unable to reach consensus on regulatory approaches, IAATO adopted a by-law (Bylaws Article II, Section E) that requires their members to subscribe to the principle that their planned activities will have no more than a minor or transitory impact on the Antarctic environment (IAATO 2006d). IAATO (2006d) argue that this by-law will ensure appropriate impact minimisation and is in keeping with IAATO's support of land-based tourism provided it conforms to the requirements of the Madrid Protocol. However, the reach of this industry self-regulatory initiative does not extend to non-IAATO members.

The Antarctic tourism industry's role in support of national science programs continues to increase and many existing land-based infrastructure facilities support tourism, albeit they are not specifically for tourism (for example aircraft runways and national stations). This poses the question as to whether such a role could be used as a means to avoid direct regulation of land-based infrastructure development to support tourism. There is also some potential for tourism entities to claim property rights over the use of such infrastructure facilities. Antarctic and Southern Ocean Coalition (ASOC) (2005a) have recommended that ATCPs not lease, transfer or grant title of existing and future national program stations to these tourism entities. Interestingly, IAATO (2006d) argue that infrastructure shared with national programs, where tourism is used as a means to support science, should be seen in a separate light.

Given the extent of uncertainty surrounding potential impacts (that is direct, indirect and/or cumulative) associated with the emerging tourism issues, it is relevant to consider whether Australia should adopt a precautionary response to Antarctic tourism. Scott (2001) has argued that "the current management of tourism by the ATS is incompatible with the strong application of the precautionary principle demanded by the 'comprehensive' level of environmental protection to which the regime is committed". Bastmeijer's (2004) assessment illustrates the reasons and benefits of applying the precautionary principle to tourism and argues that the ATS applies the precautionary principle to a limited extent. Bastmeijer also considers that applying the precautionary principle may become necessary to act in accordance with the objectives of the Protocol. Outside of permit systems, the Australian regime provides very limited provision for the exercise of precautionary regulation. However, the regulation-making provisions of the ATEP Act s 29(2) give broad ranging capability to Australia to legislate precautionary measures for the future control of tourism activity (Johnson 2002). Australia (2004a) considers that ATCPs must take the lead on key management initiatives and ensure that national regulatory mechanisms are based on (or at least consistent with) ATCM decisions. Hence, the ATEP Act should be amended to allow the progressive inclusion of ATCM judgments in the Australian legal regime.

ASOC (2004a) argue that for a tourism policy to be effective, it must set limits on absolute tourism levels, affect the shape of the industry and prevent land-based developments. Australia's tourism policy does not meet ASOC's expectation, particularly in comparison to the New Zealand Government policy statement on Antarctic tourism which maintains that it will work with the ATS to limit tourism, where necessary control tourism, avoid promoting expansion of tourism, support limits on site visitation and oppose any expansion of land-based tourism (New Zealand 2004a). The New Zealand policy approach may well reflect broader sovereignty interests over the Ross Dependency. The relatively low tourism activity in the AAT has allowed Australia to take a more technical policy approach without risking its sovereignty interests.

The likelihood of future proposals for the development of land-based infrastructure to support tourism is well recognised (ATCM XXVIII 2005a). Australia has made significant contributions to the examination of regulating land-based infrastructure to support tourism in Antarctica. Australia (2005a) has argued that IAATO and the Parties cannot rely on new industry entrants to make environmental considerations a priority, particularly in respect of the development of land-based infrastructure to support tourism. In spite of Australia's opinions being expressed within the ATS, the existing Australian policy on Antarctic tourism makes no specific account of refining and/or applying domestic legislation to more effectively regulate increasing tourism activity, technological developments and development of land-based tourism infrastructure. Policy amendment in this regard would assist Australia's ability to avoid future jurisdictional complexities arising from claims of property or use rights within the Australian Antarctic Territory.

Tourism Operations by Non-IAATO Members

The role of industry self-regulation has proven of particular importance for encouraging implementation of ATCM standards (Richardson 2000). However, the arguable success of industry self-regulation has prevented ATCM consensus to adopt additional legal instruments (Bastmeijer 2003). The prevailing self-regulatory regime does not judge or prohibit any type of Antarctic tourism activity and the demands of the industry continue to change, such as a growing reluctance of large-vessel operators to seek IAATO membership (United Kingdom 2004; IAATO 2004a). Analysis of the 2005-06 season reveals that non-IAATO member large vessels accounted for 64 per cent of all large vessel voyages to Antarctica. Furthermore, an estimated 47 per cent of all large vessel tourists travelled with non-IAATO member operators.

IAATO's by-laws place stringent passenger landing restrictions on vessels carrying more than 200 passengers and prohibit passenger landings for vessels carrying more than 500 passengers (IAATO 2006a). This may represent an obstacle to IAATO membership, as the tourism market increasingly demands a land-based passenger experience. ATCPs are concerned with the growing number of large tourist ships operating in Antarctica and continue to question how the tourism activities of large ships might be regulated (ATCM XXIX 2006).

ASOC (2001a) has argued that ATS confidence in IAATO depends on it representing a large proportion of tourism operators (ASOC 2004b), with such confidence becoming unstable as the industry expands, particularly if IAATO alters or abandons long-held standards in order to retain ATS confidence and consequent industry support. In June 2001, IAATO voted to widen its membership ranks, in recognition of the steady growth in large ship and adventure-based tourism. Essentially, the membership threshold level for ships was increased from 400 to no more than 500 passengers.

ATME (2004) recognised the merit of a strong tourism industry association but noted the prevailing regulatory gaps associated with tourism companies that are not members of IAATO (Traavik 2004) and stressed that State Parties have primary responsibility for establishing the regulatory basis for the industry. The collaborative development of site guidelines illustrates recent ATCP efforts in this regard. ATCM XXVIII adopted Resolution 5(2005) "Resolution on Site Guidelines for Visitors" which recommends that ATCPs urge all those intending to visit sites be fully conversant and adhere to the relevant Site Guidelines (ATCM XXVIII 2005b). The 12 Site Guidelines developed gained unanimous support at the June 2006 ATCM (Powell 2006). However, ATCM XXIX (2006) stressed the importance of implementation albeit as non-binding guidelines. In absence of any current means by which the Site Guidelines can be made legally binding and enforceable (ASOC 2006b), it appears their implementation will not address the ATME regulatory findings.

State Party justification for industry self-regulation has been threatened both by the relaxation of IAATO operating standards (Richardson 2000), and the continuing growth in tourism activity, particularly that conducted by non-IAATO members. Molenaar (2005) argues that the applicability of self-regulation is dependent upon IAATO membership and that the future extent of non-IAATO membership has the potential to become a very significant regulatory problem, particularly if ATCPs continue to rely on industry self-regulation. Even IAATO acknowledge the limitations of industry self-regulation, in spite of their ongoing efforts to manage and improve operating standards (such as improvements to the standard Post Visit Site Report Form, revision of Site Specific Guidelines and development of an accreditation scheme) (IAATO 2006b). In 2006, IAATO (2006b) advised the ATCPs that several non-IAATO member vessels did not submit an EIA, file advance notifications or submit post-visit site reports.

In responding to these threats to regulatory effectiveness, Australia may be expected to take a more active role when assessing non-IAATO operator proposals. It could be argued that this is a less pressing concern for Australia at present, due to the low percentage of tourists being conveyed by non-IAATO member operators registered in Australia. Nevertheless, in the interests of responding to ATME's concerns, Australia should ensure non-IAATO members are aware of ATCM measures and monitor the conditions of tourism activity approvals with an onboard observer. In an effort to close this expanding regulatory gap, Australia should consider distinguishing non-IAATO operator EIAs and approvals under the ATEP Act. Essentially, the ATEP Act could draw upon IAATO's existing operating standards and procedures as they relate to each tourism proposal, as well as adopting relevant IAATO suggestions for regulatory improvement.

Harris (1984b: 11) argued that "policies and objectives are determined on the basis of perceptions of facts and not on the basis of facts". Despite the small scale of non-IAATO member Australian operator tourism activity, any future trend toward increasing non-IAATO membership will prove difficult for Australian policymakers to ignore, particularly as the Australian access and activity regime is conducive to industry self-regulation. The implementation of Australia's Antarctic Tourism Policy has demonstrated ongoing efforts to improve the management of all visitors, regardless of IAATO affiliation. However, it is not apparent how such policy implementation would specifically respond to a future trend of increasing non-IAATO membership. For example, Australia's involvement in a joint review of Site Guidelines for Visitors raised numerous broader policy issues of guideline implementation (United Kingdom *et al* 2006) but failed to recognise or address how non-IAATO tourism activities at the subject sites would be regulated. To improve effectiveness, Australia's Antarctic Tourism Policy requires refinement to clarify how its implementation will ensure all visitors are aware of and able to comply with the Treaty, the Protocol and the tourism-related management measures developed by ATS. The policy would benefit from articulating its implementation from both self-regulatory and ATCP regulatory frameworks.

The United Kingdom (2004) has argued that the ATCPs should ensure the IAATO position is maintained or strengthened in the ATS, on the basis that, in the absence of self-regulation, the Treaty Parties would need to make a greater contribution to industry regulation. Such resource considerations are unlikely to be overlooked by Australian policymakers, given the well established knowledge that active Antarctic environmental protection demands greater government resources than reliance on the constructive ambiguity provided by a framework agreement (Harris 1984b). Australia's Antarctic Tourism Policy notes that implementation will be achieved within the ATS. In order to deal more effectively with the issue of non-IAATO membership, Australia should collaborate with ATCPs to establish the future context of self-regulation. Particular emphasis should be given to identifying the means by which tourism activities of large ships can be regulated, how to make Site Guidelines for Visitors legally binding and enforceable and whether to enhance IAATO's position on industry regulation.

Operating Tourism Companies of Vessels from Third-Party States

Third Party State regulation remains an unresolved jurisdictional issue, most pronounced with respect to flag State jurisdiction (Bush 2000). In the context of Antarctic tourism, a significant proportion of tourist vessels are flagged with States which are either non-Treaty Parties or non-Consultative Parties (Richardson 2000). Vicuña (2000: 65) notes that "almost 50 per cent of tourist vessels operating in the Antarctic are registered with non-Treaty Parties, mainly flying flags of convenience". These vessels are not bound by the terms of the Treaty or the Protocol, due to general rules of international law. Yet the majority of companies organising Antarctic tourism activities that require the use of these vessels are based in Treaty Party countries. In light of such regulatory complexities, there is a potentially significant role for national policy in meeting the increasing proportion of Third Party tourism activity.

ATME (2004) reiterated the prevailing regulatory gaps associated with tourism companies that choose to operate their company or vessels from Third Party States. ATME deferred the consideration of questions relating to the regulatory framework for tourism, leaving only suggestions of a possible industry accreditation scheme, options for establishing an onboard observer scheme and the progression of guidelines relating to Antarctic shipping as tasks for elaboration to the ATCM XXVII (ATME 2004).

The ability of regulation to account for third Party tourism operations is essential to comprehensive tourism enforcement (Tracey 2001). Chia (2000) noted that whilst Australia's participation in the Treaty has rendered its claims irrelevant in terms of Treaty Parties, its claims could still potentially be applied to Third Party States. The ATEP Act s 3(1) interprets 'foreign' as pertaining to a country other than Australia. Accordingly, application of the ATEP Act is not limited to foreign nationals of other ATCPs. This provides Australia with some scope to regulate the activities of Third Party tourist vessels and nationals involved in tourist activities. To date, this has not been a pressing matter for Australia, given the greater proportion of Treaty Party nationals accessing the Antarctic. Nevertheless, a significant increase in Third Party operations may necessitate refinement of the Australian regime, particularly in respect of clarifying a means to exercise the national regime against Third Party breaches. Such legislative reform should draw upon the existing provisions of the *Environment Protection and Biodiversity Conservation* Act 1999 (Cth) (EPBC Act). The EPBC Act s 5(1) applies to the activities of foreign nationals, operators and vessels within the AAT. Litigation associated with Japanese whaling in the Australian Whale Sanctuary[4] confirmed that foreign nationals or companies involved in activities that contravene Australian legislation could be made subject to proceedings under the EPBC Act (see Rothwell and Scott, Stephens and Boer, and Jabour *et al* this volume).

Industry Accreditation Scheme

Australia has proposed accreditation of tour operators as a means to assist closing gaps in the current regulatory regime, whereby a common set of standards could be applied to companies and/or vessels operated from Third Party States (Australia 2004b). The accreditation framework proposed by Australia sought to achieve an agreed minimum standard of

---

4   *Humane Society International Inc v Kyodo Senpaku Kaisha Ltd* [2005] FCA 664.

operation by all tourism operators, under the direction of the ATCM (Australia 2004c).

An Intersessional Contact Group (ICG) on accreditation recognised the need for an accreditation scheme that avoids conflict and duplication with existing national legislation (United Kingdom 2005). The ICG noted that the role of ATCPs would be to ensure the accreditation scheme is compatible with national legislation, take measures to encourage uptake and amend legislation to only authorise accredited tourism companies.

IAATO subsequently drafted an alternative accreditation scheme centred upon self-regulatory by-laws, guidelines, and practices (IAATO 2005b). The means of applying IAATO's proposed accreditation scheme to non-IAATO members/operators and government-supported tourism has not been resolved (IAATO 2005b; IAATO 2006e) and ATCPs have since noted their desire for the accreditation scheme to be mandated and vetted by the ATCM (ATCM XXIX 2006).

The ICG on accreditation recognised the need for policy discussion of the issues associated with accreditation. With an updated version of the accreditation scheme scheduled for presentation at IAATO's June 2007 Annual General Meeting in Hobart, Australia (IAATO 2006e), it appears timely that Australia seek to re-engage the ATCPs considerations over the regulatory and policy issues.

Onboard Observer Scheme

ATME identified two regulatory means for establishing an onboard observer scheme: using either the Antarctic Treaty or national legislation that implements the Protocol (ATME 2004). New Zealand advised ATCM XXVII that the observer framework already exists within the ATS (New Zealand 2004c), as the responsibility rests with individual Parties to "take appropriate measures … to ensure compliance with the Protocol".[5] However, there are constraints involved with performing inspections of tourist vessels under Article VII of the Treaty (ATME 2004), with only six tourism-focused inspections having been conducted in the last 16 years (ASOC 2004c; ATCM XXVIII 2005a). While the initiative of establishing an ATS onboard observer scheme is no longer a priority on the ATCM agenda, the ICG on accreditation highlighted observers as a means to address loopholes in the national implementation of Protocol obligations with respect to tourism regulation (United Kingdom 2005).

IAATO has run an observer program for 16 years, with observers placed onboard vessels operated by provisional and probational members (New Zealand 2004b; IAATO 2006b). IAATO believes an observer scheme provides a system that allows infringements to be dealt with under relevant national legislation (IAATO 2004c). IAATO prefer to appoint National

---

5   Madrid Protocol, Article 13.

Program observers from the country in which the tourism company is registered (IAATO 2004b; IAATO 2006b). New Zealand has been running an observer scheme (National Representative Scheme) since the 1970s, whereby National Representatives accompany tourist expeditions to the Ross Sea region (New Zealand 2004b). By contrast, Australia's use of onboard observers has been intermittent.

Consistent with Article VII of the Antarctic Treaty and Article 14 of the Madrid Protocol, the ATEP Act ss 13 and 14 provide for the appointment of Australian inspectors with a range of inspection powers. Appointed inspectors have powers to arrest (ATEP Act s 16(1) (a)) and bring before an authority of justice (ATEP Act s 16(3)) any persons believed to have committed an offence against the ATEP Act. Whilst inspectors have powers to search vessels (ATEP Act s 17(1)), some constraints apply with respect to foreign vessels. In particular, searches of foreign vessels require the prior approval of the person in control of the vessel (ATEP Act s 17(2)(b)). The effectiveness of Australia's inspection provisions is further constrained by jurisdictional and geographical limitations. Loopholes in national implementation of the Madrid Protocol for tourism regulation warrant refinement to Australia's legal regime. Regime refinements should concentrate on establishing a framework for cooperative and educational measures of inspection and observation. The ATEP Act should be amended to provide for the appointment of inspectors that have been endorsed through ATCM forums.[6] Such an approach would suppress sovereignty concerns, particularly if supported by ATEP Act requirements to distribute inspection findings amongst ATCPs and industry stakeholders (such as IAATO). Provisions for the allocation of onboard observers should clearly distinguish between the self-regulatory and Australian regime components of inspection and reporting.

Antarctic Shipping Guidelines

Despite long-standing Australian and ATCM recognition of the need for vessel design, operation and manning standards appropriate for Antarctica (House of Representatives Standing Committee on Environment 1989; ATCM XXIII 1999), there are no existing international conventions relating to ship design and operation, which provide specific provision for Antarctic conditions. The absence of universal vessel standards has influenced the introduction and operation of a wide range of vessels used in ship-based Antarctic tourism. Currently tourist vessels are not required to be ice-rated or registered, nor do any seasonal restrictions apply in recognition of sea ice risks to navigation. The future application of Antarctic shipping standards would present opportunities of application to third parties (Vidas 2000), and prove crucial to any substantial increase in tourism-related

---

6   For example, CCAMLR "special inspectors" are provided for under s 13 of the *Antarctic Marine Living Resources Conservation Act* 1981 (Cth).

shipping in Antarctic waters (Richardson 2000). By extending the application of such shipping standards to members of the International Maritime Organization (IMO), Scovazzi (2000) considers how non-binding guidelines could be argued to apply to Third Party States.

The Council of Managers of National Antarctic Programs (COMNAP) have concluded that the IMO *Guidelines for ships operating in Arctic ice-covered waters* provide a good basis for an Antarctic shipping code, subject to a few editorial modifications (ATCM XXVII 2004; COMNAP 2004). ATCM XXVII (2004) endorsed the guidelines and conveyed them to the IMO for adoption,[7] subject to further ATCM consideration of two issues, namely the use of heavy oils south of 60° South latitude and the introduction of non-native organisms through the discharge of ballast water. The IMO is scheduled to consider the Guidelines in late 2007, pending the IMO Antarctic sub-committee's prior review. COMNAP (2006) has advised that all vessels operating in the Antarctic Treaty area must follow the IMO *Guidelines for the control and management of ships ballast water, to minimise the transfer of harmful aquatic organisms and pathogens*.[8] Furthermore, COMNAP has emphasised the regulatory significance of the International Convention for the Control and Management of Ships Ballast Water and Sediments[9] which will require ships to implement ballast water management plans, maintain records of ballast water operations and conduct ballast water management in accordance with prescribed standards (COMNAP and IAATO 2005; COMNAP 2006).

Australia's regulation of Antarctic shipping centres on the *Protection of the Sea (Prevention of Pollution from Ships) Act* 1983 (Cth) (PS(PPS) Act), which provides for the prevention of pollution for ship discharges of oil, sewage and garbage. The standards provided for in the PS(PPS) Act essentially relate to the vessel pollution prevention standards established and regulated under the marine pollution convention, MARPOL.[10] Whilst amendments have been made to give effect to Annex IV of the Protocol (Rothwell and Davis 1997), the PS(PPS) Act does not provide for ATCM vessel standard recommendations to be incorporated into the Australian regime for Antarctic tourism regulation. In fact, the Australian regime makes no provision to regulate the type, size or capacity of vessels involved in tourism activity. The above discussion of ATS consideration of Antarctic shipping guidelines provides considerable insights for national regulatory refinement. This would be in keeping with Australia's (2005b)

---

7   ATCM XXVII, Decision 4 (2004) – Guidelines for ships operating in Arctic and Antarctic ice-covered waters.

8   Adopted by the IMO assembly in 1997, by resolution A.868(20).

9   Adopted by the diplomatic conference at the IMO in London on 13 February 2004. The Convention does not come into force until 12 months after ratification by 30 States.

10   The role of MARPOL 73/78 is recognised as a mechanism to prevent certain types of marine pollution.

promotion of proactive and precautionary quarantine measures. The Australian legal regime could be enhanced by extending the coverage of the PS(PPS) Act to account for IMO resolutions, agreements and/or guidelines on Antarctic shipping. Broader application would be achieved through extension to the relatively larger membership base of IMO Agreements. The PS(PPS) Act or ATEP Act should be amended to recognise relevant ATCM recommendations relating to Antarctic shipping standards or other vessel standards recommendations (Johnson 2002).

Conclusion

Australia is well positioned to meet the emerging issues discussed in this chapter, given its history of active participation in the ATS. Australia would do well to utilise ATS institutions as a means of progressing regulatory and policy directions, thereby minimising potential concerns arising from perceptions of unilateral responses to tourism issues.

In considering increasing tourism activity, technological developments and the development of land-based infrastructure to support tourism, it is apparent that Australia currently authorises all tourism activity that is not subject to a CEE. Australia's legal regime would benefit from the inclusion of strategic and precautionary provisions to deal with, amongst other matters, future tourism interests toward aircraft runways on the Antarctic continent. The Australian legal regime should also be amended to allow for the progressive inclusion of ATCM judgments on tourism. Australia's policy does not aim to more effectively apply domestic legislation nor set limits on tourism activity, technology development or land-based infrastructure development. Policy refinement is necessary to better respond to such emerging issues.

Increasing tourism operations by non-IAATO members would threaten Australia's preference for industry self-regulation and would prove difficult for Australian policymakers to ignore, particularly in light of the potential resource implications. It is anticipated that Australia may be expected to take a more active regulatory role when assessing non-IAATO operator proposals. Consideration should be given to incorporating IAATO operating standards and procedures into the Australian legal framework. Australia should also collaborate with ATCPs to establish the future ATS context of self-regulation, particularly for the issues raised in this chapter.

Any significant increase in the operation of tourism companies or vessels from third Party States would demand refinement to Australia's legal and policy framework. ATCM efforts to close third Party regulatory loopholes relate to schemes for tourism operator accreditation and onboard observers, as well as an Antarctic shipping code. ATCP consensus has not yet been reached on the framework or regulatory status of accreditation and there remains a need for ATS policy discussion of the associated implications. Australia should seek to ensure that the resultant accreditation scheme is compatible with domestic legislation. The Australian regime for inspections would benefit by amendments that provide for cooperative and educational onboard observers, including recognition of ATCM endorsed observers. The Australian legal regime could be further enhanced to account for the substantial insights gained from recent ATS reviews of Antarctic shipping codes. Australian legislation should account for ATCM judgments, as well as IMO resolutions and guidelines related to Antarctic shipping. The assessment of third Party tourism trends highlights the need for Australia to respond by extending its policy effort beyond States Parties and into a more global context. Whilst Australia has made effective policy realisation through ATS cooperative institutions, there looms a need to strengthen coalitions with Third Party States.

8

Net Gain or Net Loss?
Australia and Southern Ocean Fishing

Gail L Lugten

Introduction

The marine life of the Southern Ocean has long been a lure to industry. Within 30 years of Captain Cook's 1770s discoveries, commercial exploitation of living marine resources began, with the sealing industry financing further exploration of the Southern Ocean and sub-Antarctic islands. This was followed in the late 19th and early 20th centuries by an intense whaling effort. The Southern Ocean also provides a habitat for about 100 different species of fish. Their slow growth and longevity means that Antarctic fish species are susceptible to over-exploitation and, as with seals and whales, overexploitation has been common. Throughout the 20th century, and particularly in the early 1970s, international fishing fleets targeted Antarctic cods and icefish. A subsequent decline in levels of Antarctic fish populations led to fishing interest in species lower down the food chain, including that living marine resource that underpins the whole Antarctic ecosystem – krill (Fothergill 1994: 32).

The concept of a 200 nautical mile (nm) Exclusive Economic Zone (EEZ) emerged during the 1970s. As an increasing number of coastal States declared their own EEZ, many fishing fleets lost their traditional in-shore fishing grounds and headed south in search of prolific and profitable Antarctic fish stocks. During the 1980s, Southern Ocean commercial fishing targeted mackerel icefish and harvested it to near extinction. By 1992 marbled rock cod stocks were also threatened. In the late 1990s, commercial fishing interests then turned to Patagonian toothfish and it is this species that remains the most valuable of all Southern Ocean fish.

This chapter will submit that the primary fishing priority of Australia's Antarctic fishing agenda must be to stop the historical cycle of environmental pillage. Accordingly, Australia must act to ensure the sustainability of Patagonian toothfish so that it does not suffer the fate of previous target species. Further, for the current Australian Government, this priority is as much about sovereignty and border protection, as about environmental protection (Kimpton 2004: 537). The chapter addresses the jurisdictional difficulties presented by national, regional and international laws which cover oceanic areas that include the high seas, zones of national jurisdiction and the management area of a regional fishery body. In addition, the chapter also addresses both legal fishing activity and Australia's attempts to address Southern Ocean illegal, unreported and unregulated (IUU) fishing. It will be submitted that Australia's approaches to IUU fishing have shown themselves to be dynamic, innovative and flexible, but more needs to be done.

The Patagonian Toothfish and IUU Fishing

There are two species of toothfish in the Southern Ocean: the Patagonian toothfish (*Dissostichus eleginoides*) and the Antarctic toothfish (*Dissostichus mawsoni*). The latter is found closer to the Antarctic continent where sea ice forms and for this reason it has not yet been subjected to the harvesting levels of the Patagonian toothfish (Agnew 2000: 361). The Patagonian toothfish is a large fish reaching more than 2 metres in length. They reach maturity later than most fish (between 10-12 years) and they have low fecundity. These biological factors make stocks of the Patagonian toothfish extremely susceptible to overfishing. As the Patagonian toothfish is the most valuable fishery in both Antarctic and sub-Antarctic waters, and its population status and stock dispersal are still uncertain, there is a clear need for precaution in its management (Williams 2002). Yet, in the contemporary period, effective management is undermined by a proliferation of IUU vessels which fish without authorisation, fail to report their catches or misreport their catches (IPOA-IUU Article 3; UN FAO 2001).

Illegal fishing is the term applied to foreign vessels fishing without authorisation in the waters of a coastal State, or vessels which fish without authorisation in an area and for a species governed by a (multilateral) regional fishery body (IPOA–IUU Article 3). Illegal fishing may also go unreported and be unregulated. The first appearance of the term IUU fishing was in relation to Patagonian toothfish fishing in the Southern Ocean, and it occurred at the 1997 Convention on the Conservation of Antarctic Marine Living Resources (CCAMLR) Commission meeting.[1] Today, IUU fishing is a major problem worldwide, and is considered by the United Nations to be the single major obstacle to achieving sustainable fisheries in both areas under national jurisdiction and on the high seas (UN 2004). Put simply, how can governments legislate, or regional fishery bodies regulate, to sustainably manage their fish stocks if their management plans are constantly being undermined by an increasing number of operators who fish outside the legal regime and with no respect for quotas?

---

1   Report of the Sixteenth Meeting of the CCAMLR Commission (CCAMLR-XVI) (1997), paras 8.7-8.13.

IUU fishers appeared in the Atlantic and Indian Ocean sectors of the Southern Ocean in the mid 1990s. Over the next few years, the IUU fleet moved eastward and found rich pickings around the South African Prince Edward Islands, the French sub-Antarctic Kerguelen Islands and Australia's sub-Antarctic Heard Island and McDonald Islands (HIMI). IUU fishing is a global phenomenon, and in the Southern Ocean it exists in both the high seas and in coastal zones. For the purposes of Australia's Antarctic agenda, it is the IUU fishing in the HIMI and Macquarie Island EEZs that is the most immediate priority (Williams 2005).

There is no real way of knowing the quantity of the catch taken by IUU vessels, however one report has estimated that the catch of toothfish by IUU operators is almost equal to the catch by legal fishers which, in the six year period to 2005, was 80,960 tonnes of IUU catch compared with 83,696 tonnes of legal catch (AAD 2005b). The total IUU toothfish catch was valued at AUD$1 billion wholesale (Davis 2000). The trend has not abated and, if anything, IUU fishing in the Southern Ocean has increased. There are significantly more IUU sightings than seizures in the Australian Fishing Zone (AFZ), a consequence of the sheer size of the zone, which is the third largest in the world, and a lack of Australian response resources in the vicinity of the sightings.

Regional Management Through the Commission for the Conservation of Antarctic Marine Living Resources

In the 1970s, the history of overexploitation of Antarctic marine life, combined with the new potential to exploit krill, provided the impetus for negotiation by the Antarctic Treaty Consultative Parties of a comprehensive conservation regime for the Southern Ocean. Accordingly, in 1977, the Ninth Antarctic Treaty Consultative Meeting formulated the main components of a new Antarctic living marine resources convention. Recommendation IX-2 of this meeting contained the basic features of a new regime and many principles contained in it were eventually placed in the new Convention (Couratier 1983: 145). These principles included the geographical area covered by the Convention (that is south of the Antarctic Convergence (see Figure 5)) and the need for an ecosystem approach to resource management. The CCAMLR came into force on 7 April 1982.[2] There are 24 CCAMLR Commission Members: Argentina, Australia, Belgium, Brazil, Chile, European Community, France, Germany, India, Italy, Japan, Republic of Korea, Namibia, New Zealand, Norway, Poland, Russia, South Africa, Spain, Sweden, Ukraine, United Kingdom, United States of America and Uruguay; and a further 10 Contracting Parties: Bulgaria, Canada, People's Republic of China, Cook Islands, Finland, Greece, Mauritius, Netherlands, Peru and Vanuatu.

---

2   19 ILM 837.

CCAMLR Commission may adopt Conservation Measures (hereafter CMs), binding on all members within 180 days of notification (Article IX(6)(b)). In practice, a member can avoid being bound by notifying the Commission that it is unable to accept the measure (Article IX(6)(c)), however, that mechanism has only ever been utilised for practical reasons. CCAMLR manages fish stocks (such as the Patagonian toothfish) and annually sets Total Allowable Catches (TACs) based on precautionary scientific evidence. These are published and distributed to member States. Australia is a party to the calculating of the CCAMLR TAC. It then records how the CCAMLR TAC is to be applied in the AFZ.

Figure 5: CCAMLR Area of Application

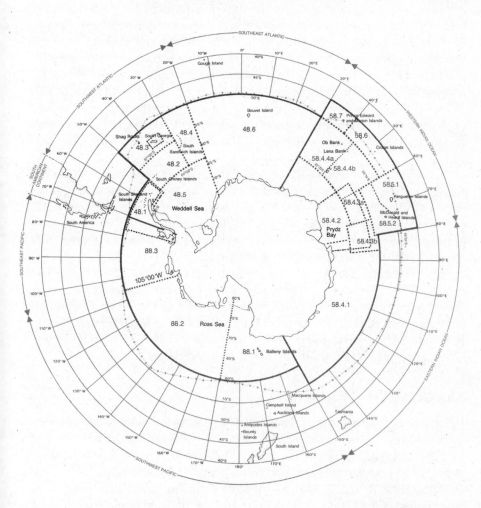

Source: CCAMLR 2007

CCAMLR can be acceded to by any State interested in research or the harvesting of marine living resources in the geographic area covered by the Convention (Article XXIX). Therefore, it is appropriate to consider the impact of CCAMLR conservation measures on States which are actively fishing in the Southern Ocean, but which are non-members of CCAMLR. Here, a distinction needs to be drawn between the capacity north of the Antarctic Treaty area, and inside the area. The situation in the sub-Antarctic is that there are no legal obligations imposed on non-members except that sub-Antarctic claimant States can enforce the Convention against non-members in the coastal jurisdictions claimed by them (for example, Australia can enforce the terms of the Convention against non-members in the AFZ that surrounds Heard Island and McDonald Islands). In fact, the Convention requires that the attention of non-Party States be drawn to any activities by them that might affect its objectives (Article X). In international law, if non-members are not bound by the Convention they can ignore CCAMLR conservation and management measures and thereby prevent the effective implementation of a comprehensive ecosystem approach. In contrast, within the Antarctic Treaty area, the standing of a claimant is no different to any other Party to either the Antarctic Treaty or CCAMLR. All Parties have a duty to address actions that undermine the treaties. The fact that a particular offending State might not be a Party to CCAMLR or the Antarctic Treaty in no way affects the likelihood that they will not recognise a coastal State in Antarctica.

CCAMLR is undoubtedly amongst the most progressive of regional fishery bodies, using a truly interdisciplinary approach to combating IUU fishing and taking action at the legal, political, scientific, technological, economic and education levels. CCAMLR is renowned for its ecosystem approach to management (which provides for the need to protect the ecosystem of the seas surrounding Antarctica and to increase knowledge of its component parts); application of the precautionary principle (for example TACs); use of vessel monitoring and electronic surveillance (CM 10-04); promotion of trade-based measures such as the Catch Documentation Scheme (CM 10-05); and commitment to educating Member States, fishers and the general public (for example the "Fish the Sea and Not the Sky" campaign for seabird mitigation fishing practices).

The CCAMLR Conundrum

Undoubtedly two major weaknesses in the CCAMLR regime are surveillance and enforcement. Ultimately, these are left up to the Member States such as Australia (Article XXI). At the same time, Member States are frequently too busy addressing surveillance and enforcement in their own fishing zones to make any meaningful contribution to the high seas zone within CCAMLR's jurisdiction. The result is a weak surveillance and enforcement system that is unable to preclude over-harvesting.

Accordingly, if Australia is serious about enforcement in the CCAMLR zone, it must be prepared to take a more active, physical role in law enforcement. Two particular issues need to be addressed:

- the question of how to provide adequate surveillance in 35 million square kilometres of ocean; and

- where surveillance does reveal a suspicious high seas vessel, under what law can that vessel by inspected and apprehended?

The subjects of surveillance and inspection are a part of law enforcement and both points are elaborated below (see also Stephens and Boer this volume).

Surveillance

On 24 November 2003, the Australian Foreign Minister and the French Secretary of State for Foreign Affairs, signed in Canberra the Treaty on Co-operation in the Maritime Areas Adjacent to the French Southern and Antarctic Territories, Heard Island and the McDonald Islands (Kimpton 2003: 541-2). The Treaty came into effect in February 2005. The aim of this Treaty is to enhance cooperative surveillance in the French and Australian sub-Antarctic fishing zones by allowing the two countries to collaborate in patrol missions, exchange of information and hot pursuit. At the time of negotiating this Treaty Molenaar concluded that in future years the Eastern Antarctic States would be likely to create a web of relevant bilateral and/or regional agreements which would make an important contribution to State practice (Molenaar 2004: 34). So far, this has not occurred. In fact, a similar Treaty under negotiation with South Africa since the late 1990s has still not eventuated. Australia has both a moral and legal duty to pursue such multilateral surveillance mechanisms. First, it will be recalled that the South African navy was good enough to support Australia in the hot pursuit of the *South Tomi* and the *Viarsa 1*. However, Australia has only bothered to conclude a cooperative Treaty with the one State in the region that is clearly wealthier than we are: France. This behaviour suggests that Australia is a "taker" in the region, not a "contributor" to it. Secondly, apart from the moral duty to cooperate, a legal duty clearly exists in the wording of those international instruments that require States to cooperate at the regional, subregional and global levels. Central to these provisions is the need to establish and contribute to regional fishery bodies such as CCAMLR.

Australia must pursue multilateral surveillance mechanisms with other regional States. Furthermore, any political diplomatic mechanism will be ineffective unless it is accompanied by a genuine willingness on the part of all Member States to make financial and resource commitments (although it is acknowledged that Norway is in a unique position due to the fact that it does not claim an EEZ over its sub-Antarctic Bouvetøya).

The financial costs of Southern Ocean physical surveillance are exorbitant, and it will be additionally necessary for CCAMLR Member States to cooperate in technological surveillance (including satellites and/or the proposed Committee on Fisheries global list of fishing vessels), for a more comprehensive surveillance network.

Inspection

Having surveyed and detected an IUU vessel on the high seas, further difficulties arise with the policing enforcement of CCAMLR conservation measures. That is, under what law can a suspicious vessel at sea be inspected?

If the suspicious vessel and any enforcement vessel are both flagged to CCAMLR Member States, CCAMLR rules relating to the System of Inspection allow for Member-flagged vessels to be inspected (CCAMLR 1989a). This is an on-the-spot system for inspection at sea. The purposes of inspection are to verify commercial harvesting activities and compliance with CMs and TACs. Commission Membership is open to States which show an interest in the research or harvest of living marine resources in the area. Therefore, it might be assumed that vessels fishing in the CCAMLR area will be legal vessels from Member States, or illegal vessels from non-Member States. But reality is not that simple. Recent IUU abuses have occurred by both CCAMLR Member and non-Member States (for example, the *South Tomi* was flagged to Togo, a non-CCAMLR Member. However, the *Lena* and the *Volga* were both flagged to Russia, and the *Maya V* was flagged to Uruguay. Both Russia and Uruguay are CCAMLR Commission Members). Furthermore, CCAMLR's consensus based decision-making process frequently leads to slow or negligible decision making, particularly where the decision is aimed at controlling the performance of a Commission Member (Hemmings 2004: 202-3).

The second (and most promising) option for inspection at sea is provided by the 1995 Agreement for the Implementation of the Provisions of the United Nations Convention on the Law of the Sea of 10 December 1982 Relating to the Conservation and Management of Straddling Fish Stocks and Highly Migratory Fish Stocks (UN Fish Stocks Agreement).[3] The Fish Stocks Agreement is open to all States. Central to its provisions is the need for all States to establish and participate in regional fisheries management organisations (RFMOs) that share information and cooperate in scientific research. Specific provisions that would aid in enforcing CCAMLR conservation measures on the high seas include the following:

- Article 18(2) provides that States are not permitted to authorise the use of their flag to vessels fishing on the high seas unless they are able to effectively exercise responsibility over such vessels.

---

3   34 ILM 1542.

- Article 19(1) provides that the flag State must ensure compliance by its vessels with regional conservation and management measures. Such measures are further reinforced by the controversial, watershed provision of Article 21.

- Article 21 provides that a State which is Party to the Fish Stocks Agreement and a member of a relevant RFMO, has the right to board and inspect fishing vessels of another State Party in order to ensure compliance with conservation and management measures, even where the flag State is not a member of the RFMO.

- Article 23 provides that when a fishing vessel is voluntarily in a port, the port State may inspect documents, fishing gear, and any catch on board the vessel in order to ensure compliance with subregional, regional, and global conservation and management measures.

Thus enforcement against fishing vessels on the high seas is problematic unless both the suspect vessel and the enforcement vessel are flagged to a State that is a signatory to the Fish Stocks Agreement, or a CCAMLR Commission Member. The enforcement is problematic, but not impossible, because in practice the scenario that most frequently exists is that a suspicious vessel has allegedly fished without authorisation in the waters of a coastal State (such as Australia) and then fled to the high seas. Such scenarios allow for enforcement via Article 20(6) of the Fish Stocks Agreement that allows for a high seas inspection of the vessel and, in the event that the suspect vessel flees onto the high seas, Article 111 of the LOS Convention allows for hot pursuit (Stephens 2004: 12).

As Australia is already a signatory to the Fish Stocks Agreement, and a member of the CCAMLR Commission, what role exists for Australia regarding the enforcement of conservation measures on the high seas?

Australia is seen as a good world citizen in matters relating to the law of the sea. In both 2005 and 2006 Australia spearheaded considerable international diplomatic pressure to foster support in the International Whaling Commission for the continuation of the moratorium on commercial whaling (Campbell 2005c; see also Jabour *et al* this volume). Ultimately, their efforts were successful. Encouraging other States to ratify and implement the Fish Stocks Agreement is a subject deserving of the same levels of international diplomacy.

National Management of Sub-Antarctic Fishing

If CCAMLR has struggled with the issue of enforcement on the high seas, its member States with sub-Antarctic islands are often required to exercise national enforcement over the most productive of fishing grounds in the entire CCAMLR zone. In the case of the AFZ (Figure 6, *over page*), a 200 nm EEZ rich with Patagonian toothfish surrounds Australian sub-Antarctic and Antarctic territories.

Figure 6: Australian Fishing Zone and Australian Antarctic EEZ

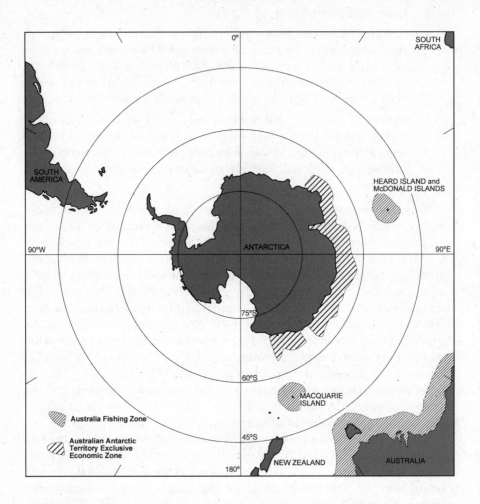

To date, Australian authorities have arrested nine IUU vessels allegedly fishing illegally for Patagonian toothfish in the sub-Antarctic EEZ. The value of the combined catches on the nine vessels is considerably in excess of AUD$10 million. The environmental cost of the illegal industry includes not only dangerous levels of overfishing of the target catch, but also the capture on longlines of endangered albatross species (see Hall this volume). A summary of the nine IUU fishing vessels is provided in Table 4:

Table 4: Details of Sub-Antarctic IUU Fishing Vessels Recently Seized by Australian Authorities

Vessel name	Flag State/ vessel owner	Date of arrest	Estimated value of catch AUD$	Bail and fines imposed AUD$	Fate of vessel, gear and catch AUD$
Salvora	Belize/Clayton Trading Co Uruguay	16.10.97	178,571	Captain and Fishing Master fined $50,000 each ($25,000 for each offence).	Vessel, catch and gear forfeited (value $1.07 million). Vessel released on bond. Vessel not returned – bond $1.47 million forfeited.
Aliza Glacial	Panama/Norway	17.10.97	250,000	Captain and Fishing Master failed to appear to answer charges.	Mortgagee action in Admiralty Law. Commonwealth legal costs paid from proceeds of sale. Vessel valued at $8 million.
Big Star	Seychelles/Big Star Int. Corp	21.02.98	1.5 million	Master fined $100,000. This was reduced on appeal to $24,000.	Vessel, catch and gear forfeited. Vessel released on bond and not returned – bond $1.5 million forfeited.
South Tomi	Togo/ Not disclosed	12.04.01	1.5-1.6 million	Master fined $136,000.	Catch and gear forfeited. Bond not set as owner's identity not divulged by lawyers. Vessel forfeited, to be disposed of at direction of Minister.
Lena	Russia / Alitas	06.02.02	900,000	Captain fined $50,000. First Officer and Officer fined a total $25,000 each.	Vessel, catch and gear forfeited. Bond not set as owner's identity not divulged by lawyers. Vessel forfeited, to be disposed of at direction of Minister.
Volga	Russia/Alitas	07.02.02	1.6 million	Charges against Ship's Master withdrawn following death. Fishing Master, Fishing pilot and Chief Mate charged.	International determination such that bond may be set as equal to the value of the vessel.
Viarsa 1	Uruguay	27.08.03	1 million	Captain and 4 crew charged. In Dec 04 the jury trying five crew members was dismissed after failing to reach a verdict. Status Conference in Jan 05 listed trial for 5 Sep 2005. On 4 Nov 2005 a Perth District Court Jury found all 5 accused persons not guilty of fishing charges.	Civil case in the Federal Court to recover the impounded $5million trawler, the value of the catch and income lost, is pending.
Maya 5	Uruguay	23.01.04	3 million	Captain and Fishing Master fined $30,000 each. Crew fined $1000 each.	Vessel catch and gear forfeited. Vessel currently used as a training vessel for Customs.
Taruman	Cambodia/Rulfend Co Operator: Rivadulla	06.09.05	1.5 million	Captain and Fishing Master fined $65,000 and $53,000 respectively. Remaining crew deported.	Vessel and gear (valued at $2.45 million) remain forfeit to Australia. Civil case unheard.

The Commonwealth legislation that deals with IUU fishing in the HIMI and Macquarie Island EEZ is the *Fisheries Management Act* 1991 (Cth). However, as the emergence and growth of IUU fishing has post-dated this legislation, significant amendments to the legal regime (mostly reactionary) have been introduced since 1999 (Rachel Baird 2004: 63 s 82).

In summary, these amendments have taken the s 100 strict liability offence of using a foreign boat without a licence for commercial fishing in the AFZ, and:

- provided for intentional offences (s 100A);

- provided for intentional offences where the foreign boat may not have been fishing but was equipped with nets, traps or other equipment for fishing (s 101A);

- provided for the liability of any support boat *outside the AFZ*, which is supporting a foreign fishing boat *within the AFZ* (s 101B);

- significantly increased financial penalties for foreign fishing boat offences (Sch 1);

- imposed forfeiture orders upon seized boats or support boats, their fishing equipment and fish; (ss 106A-106F);

- provided for the full recovery of any costs incurred in the hot pursuit chase of a foreign fishing boat (the Compliance and Deterrence Act);[4] and

- implemented the obligations arising from the coming into effect of the Agreement to Promote Compliance with International Conservation and Management Measures by Fishing Vessels on the High Seas,[5] (the United Nations Food and Agriculture Organization (UN FAO) Compliance Agreement implemented by the *Fisheries Legislation Amendment (High Seas Fishing Activities and Other Matters) Act* 2004.

The FAO Compliance Agreement requires that each State Party shall take measures to ensure that fishing vessels entitled to fly its flag do not engage in any activity which undermines the effectiveness of international conservation and management measures. Furthermore, no State Party should allow any of its vessels to be used for high seas fishing unless the vessel has been authorised to do so by an appropriate authority of the Party. High seas fishing authorisation will not be granted unless the said Party is able to exercise effectively its responsibilities with respect to that fishing vessel. Paragraph (5) of Article III seeks to limit the freedom of vessels with a bad compliance record in high seas fisheries from shopping around for a new flag.

---

4   *Fisheries Legislation Amendment (Compliance and Deterrence Measures and Other Matters) Act* 2004.

5   33 ILM 968.

The Australian legal amendments show a determination by the Government to close loopholes and stay in front of IUU fishers who attempt to harvest in the HIMI or Macquarie Island EEZs. The amendments are comprehensive, but Australia should pursue one further amendment to the Fisheries Management Act. This amendment would require courts, when sentencing, to consider the deleterious impact of IUU fishing on the ecosystem – including seabirds.

In 2006 the Australian Law Reform Commission completed a review of Part 1B of the *Crimes Act 1914: Same Crime, Same Time – Sentencing of Federal Offenders* (Australian Law Reform Commission 2006). Chapter Six of this report examines factors that must be taken into consideration as relevant to sentencing. Category V deals with factors relating to the impact of the offence and these are clearly stated to include the impact of the offence on the environment.

Despite clear scientific evidence on the environmental dangers of overfishing and the need to apply sustainable management practices to the toothfish fishery, environmental considerations have not been consistently taken into account by the courts when sentencing IUU offenders. In statutory interpretation law, the object or purpose for which an act was passed is an important consideration in how the law is to be interpreted (*Acts Interpretation Act* 1901, s 15AA (Cth)). The amendments to the Fisheries Management Act may have been passed for several reasons, (external affair treaty obligations, border protection and sovereignty) but the primary reason is the threat posed by IUU fishers to the sustainability of Patagonian toothfish stocks under Australian jurisdiction. Accordingly, these environmental considerations should be included in the Fisheries Management Act, the court proceedings, and the sentencing remarks. To not do so is to undermine or trivialise the importance of the environment.

In approaching the subject of how Australian courts can better include environmental considerations, some help can be obtained from the United Kingdom where a Sentencing Advisory Panel has produced *Environmental Offences: The Panel's Advice to the Court of Appeal* (United Kingdom 2000). This report offers interesting approaches to measuring the culpability of defendants accused of environmental offences. In paragraph 6, the report notes that certain factors must be taken to enhance or aggravate culpability. Of particular application to IUU fishing such factors must include:

- the offence is shown to have been a deliberate or reckless breach of the law, rather than the result of carelessness;
- the defendant acts from a financial motive, whether of profit or cost-saving; or
- the defendant's attitude towards the relevant environmental authorities (Australian Fisheries Management Authority or CCAMLR) is dismissive or obstructive.

Regarding sentencing, the Panel supports a fine as the most appropriate sanction. This is based on the fact that environmental offences are "non-violent and carry no immediate physical threat to the person". Of particular relevance to the Sch 1 fines listed in the Fisheries Management Act, the Panel recommends that the level of fine should be fixed in accordance with the seriousness of the offence and the financial circumstances of the individual defendant (including the defendant's economic gain as a result of the offence).

It is submitted that the UK sentencing report provides an excellent template for the way IUU fishing offences should be treated by the Australian courts. IUU offenders are deliberate with where they fish (or at least reckless with regard to sovereignty). They act from a financial motive of profit. They are dismissive or obstructive of management quotas set by the relevant fishery management authorities. Accordingly, these factors should enhance their levels of culpability.

The Big Picture of Australia's Fight Against IUU Fishing

The Fisheries Management Act legislative amendments must be viewed as part of the big picture that is Australia's total response to IUU fishing and border protection. In recent years, other parts of the big picture have included:

- provision of a full-time contracted vessel, *Oceanic Viking*, to conduct armed Customs/Fisheries year-round patrols of the Southern Ocean for improved at-sea surveillance and enforcement;

- completion of an Australian National Plan of Action on IUU Fishing (which addresses domestic responsibilities under the FAO International Plan of Action on IUU Fishing);

- promoting vessel monitoring systems in Australian and regional waters; and

- participating in the Organisation for Economic Co-operation and Development (OECD) Taskforce and FAO fishery consultations which have aimed to internationalise action against IUU fishing. (High Seas Task Force 2006)

This list of achievements is significant and shows a genuine attempt to deal with the problem of IUU fishing. However, when addressing the subject of fisheries law reform, it must be understood that any domestic Australian action will be severely restricted by the limitations of an outdated international legal regime for managing the world's oceans. The final part of this chapter examines the role that international law reform should play in Australia's Antarctic fishing agenda.

Reforming International Law

The 1982 Law of the Sea Convention (LOS Convention) is the product of 2000 years of customary law evolution, combined with two previous United Nations Conferences on the Law of the Sea (UNCLOS I in 1958 and UNCLOS II in 1960). Furthermore, it took another 10 years of intense negotiations to compile the 1982 Convention. Despite its impressive pedigree and widespread support (153 Parties), by the time the Convention entered into force in 1994, it was already overtaken by a number of significant developments such as increasing technology and an increase in distant water fishing fleets.

Article 312 of the LOS Convention notes that "after the expiry of a period of ten years from the date of entry into force of this Convention, State Parties may ... propose specific amendments to the Convention". The 10-year wait expired on 16 November 2004 but no amendments were proposed. Australia should support those international diplomatic efforts that aim to reform the LOS Convention. It is a Herculean agenda that would need to be negotiated in a world that is currently divided along many lines, but momentum has to come from somewhere.

The LOS Convention is based on numerous outdated principles, but three provisions in particular have a special relevance to Southern Ocean IUU fishing: Articles 87(1)(e), 73 and 111.

Reform of Article 87(1)(e)

Part VII, Section 1 of the LOS Convention deals with the General Provisions of the High Seas, and Article 87 lists the freedoms of the high seas, including (1)(e) freedom of fishing, subject to the Section 2 provisions on conservation and management of the living resources of the high seas. Article 87(1)(e) is derived from the 400 year old *Mare Liberum* customary law theories of Hugo Grotius, and although the theories have aged into the 21st century, they have not aged well. Freedom of fishing in contemporary fisheries law is an anachronism.

A central argument for reform lies in the global proliferation of RFMOs. Every law of the sea instrument in soft and hard law that has been brought into existence since the LOS Convention has recognised the need for States to cooperate in regional, subregional or global institutions (Lugten 1999: 4-14). Accordingly, RFMOs already cover a large portion of the high seas and ideally will eventually cover all oceans. If RFMOs are to be viewed as representing the future of global fisheries management, then clearly their authority will be undermined if the historic doctrine that the high seas are free for fishing is simultaneously continued.

Reform of Article 73

Article 73 stands in that part of the LOS Convention that deals with rights and duties of the coastal State within the 200 nm EEZ. Thus, (from all provisions) the coastal State has a *right* to explore, exploit, conserve and manage the living resources of the EEZ. It has a concurrent *duty* to promptly release (upon the posting of a reasonable bond) foreign vessels and crew that violate the fishery laws of the coastal State. It is submitted that Article 73 uses outdated concepts and terminology, does not consider any deleterious impact on the environment, and offers no deterrence measures. Accordingly, reform of Article 73 must begin by including the concepts of ecosystem and sustainability. Thus, "exploitation, conservation and management" in Article 73 must take an ecosystem approach, and must prioritise sustainability.

A final criticism of Article 73 relates to the words "arrested vessels and their crews". This provision essentially means that the hidden beneficial owners of IUU fishing operations break no international laws. IUU fishing vessels are traditionally owned by front companies registered in international tax havens. These front companies constitute the public face of a highly complex, transnational corporate structure that deliberately disguises the identity of the corporation's beneficial owners and controllers. Hidden behind their corporate veils, there is currently no legal obligation to acknowledge the existence of beneficial owners, and punishment or deterrence is impossible (Griggs and Lugten 2007).

Only by removing profits from the beneficial owners, and increasing their potentiality for being caught (and punished), will a true reduction in this conduct occur. Possible avenues for reform of both domestic and international laws include lifting the corporate veil to identify people behind incorporation, and using taxation accrual regimes as a tool to undermine the illegal fishing corporate use of tax havens (Bender and Lugten 2007).

Reform of Article 111

Where a vessel has violated the laws and regulations of a coastal State (such as Australia and the Fisheries Management Act), the coastal State is permitted (with restrictions) to pursue that vessel even onto and across the free high seas. The law of hot pursuit was invoked in the chase and capture of both the *South Tomi* and the *Viarsa 1* (see Table 4). The concept of the law is reasonable, but many of its restrictions are anachronistic, and in need of reform.

In particular, the restrictions in Article 111 can be interpreted as usurping many of the current measures that are actively promoted by the UN and OECD for addressing IUU fishing. Thus the UN promotes regional cooperation in combating IUU, but Article 111 provides that if the pursued ship reaches its own territorial sea, or the territorial sea of a third State, then the right of hot pursuit must end. Similarly, the OECD promotes (for certainty) the use of vessel monitoring systems as a vital tool in the struggle against IUU fishing. However, Article 111 refers to the pursuing vessel "satisfying itself" that a foreign vessel is within the relevant maritime zone. Such words defeat certainty so that courts are unclear as to the evidentiary standard required by the pursuing vessel. Technological developments are again excluded in the provisions that require a visual or auditory signal to stop. This ignores modern methods of communication, and the fact that both the pursued and pursuing vessels are likely to have radio, fax, satellite phone and electronic mail facilities on board (UN FAO 2007). It is clear that the doctrine of hot pursuit, as it is worded in Article 111, is eminently suitable to sailing ships and long-glasses, but out of place in the modern world.

Conclusion

This chapter has provided an overview of Australia's Antarctic agenda for Southern Ocean fishing. The overview has included an examination of the domestic fisheries regime under the *Fisheries Management Act* 1991, the regional fisheries regime under CCAMLR, and reform of the international legal regime for marine capture fisheries. It has been shown that Australia's Antarctic agenda for fishing is dynamic, innovative and flexible, but more needs to be done.

The chapter has described four recommendations that should be implemented for Australia to adequately address its future Antarctic fisheries agenda. First, the history of overexploitation of Antarctic marine living resources demonstrates that sustainability of the current primary target species – the Patagonian toothfish, must be the foremost priority. If IUU fishing for the toothfish is ignored then, as with previous target species (such as seals, whales, fin fish), the stocks will eventually become self-regulating and fishing will no longer be commercially viable. History suggests that the illegal industry will then move on to the next target species, which may be krill. This commercial approach to the harvesting of living marine resources contravenes numerous conventions in public international law including the LOS Convention.

Second, IUU fishing plagues both the high seas and zones of national jurisdiction. On the high seas south of the Antarctic Convergence, CCAMLR attempts to combat IUU fishing through its conservation measures, and enforcement of these measures is left to the CCAMLR Members. Australia should:

- make an ongoing commitment to at-sea patrol, and enhanced technological MCS (including satellites) of both the Australian EEZ, and the CCAMLR high seas;
- implement more bilateral or multilateral surveillance mechanisms with neighbouring States and Eastern Antarctic Coastal States; and
- promote globally the implementation of the United Nations Fish Stocks Agreement.

Third, enforcement of the Fisheries Management Act in remote zones such as the HIMI and Macquarie Island EEZs has required continuous legislative amendments and a series of such amendments (mostly reactionary) have been introduced since 1999. This chapter has recommended a further legislative amendment requiring courts, when sentencing IUU offenders, to take into consideration any deleterious impact on the environment.

Finally, the achievements of Australia's Antarctic fishing agenda have been accomplished in spite of the international legal regime, not with the assistance of it. Although many critics suggest that reform of the LOS Convention is an impossibility, the momentum to tackle this Herculean task must begin somewhere. In particular, Articles 87(1) (e), 73 and 111 of the LOS Convention inadequately address IUU fishing.

There is a clear need for both the domestic and international legal regimes to work together in order to address the worsening problem of undetected and unpunished hidden beneficial owners of illegal fishing vessels. Possible avenues of reform include lifting the corporate veil to reveal the identification of these beneficial owners, and the use of taxation accrual regimes in domestic law as a tool to undermine the profit motive in illegal fishing. Australia's excellent reputation as a good world citizen in all matters pertaining to the law of the sea, suggests that we are a State most suitable to promoting international and domestic law reform for the sustainability of Southern Ocean marine capture fisheries.

9

Saving Seabirds

Rob Hall

Over the past two decades, seabird conservation has become a significant item on the international marine policy agenda. During this period, albatrosses and some of the larger species of petrels of the Southern Hemisphere have come to be regarded as amongst the most threatened birds in the world. According to the World Conservation Union (IUCN) Red List of Threatened Species, most species of albatrosses are threatened with global extinction having a Vulnerable, Endangered or Critically Endangered conservation status, while the remaining albatross species are listed as Near Threatened (IUCN 2007).

Threats to the survival of albatrosses and petrels occur at sea and on land, with the primary threat generally recognised as stemming from longline fishing operations – each year, tens of thousands of these seabirds become what is known as bycatch, when they are incidentally drowned after ingesting baited hooks during the setting and hauling of longlines.

Since the recognition of the severity of the threats to these species of seabirds in the late 1980s, a number of mitigating measures and strategies have been developed. These have been incorporated in international and national initiatives to address the problem. This chapter examines these initiatives and the involvement of Australia within them. It is divided into three major parts. In the first, the nature of the threats that confront albatrosses and petrels is outlined. Second, international mitigation efforts through the establishment of an international seabird conservation regime to address these threats are discussed. In the third and final part, Australia's role in contributing to understanding the nature of this seabird conservation problem, as well as the development and implementation of these international initiatives, is assessed.

Major Threats to Albatrosses and Petrels

Albatrosses and petrels belong to the order *Procellariiformes*. There are 22 species of albatrosses and they are the largest of the petrels with wingspans measuring between 2-3 metres and weighing between 2-10 kilograms. Eighteen species of albatrosses breed in the higher latitudes of southern temperate areas, one species breeds primarily on equatorial Isla Española of the Galápagos Islands, and three species breed in the Northern Pacific.

Five species of albatrosses breed in Australian territory – the endemic shy albatross (*Thalassarche cauta*), which breeds on several islands off the Tasmanian coast, and the wandering (*Diomedea exulans*), black-browed (*Thalassarche melanophrys*), grey-headed (*Thalassarche chrysostoma*), and light-mantled (*Phoebetria palpebrata*) albatrosses that are known to breed on sub-Antarctic Macquarie Island. Fourteen other species of albatrosses are known to forage within Australian waters, but do not breed there (Baker *et al* 2002). All in all, and notwithstanding the coarse nature of population estimates and that the population status of many petrels is unknown, 43 Procellariiform species breed in Australian territory and 39 species forage within Australian waters but do not breed there (Baker *et al* 2002).

Albatrosses spend much of their lives at sea on foraging flights that cover vast distances and they typically come ashore on oceanic islands only to breed (Robertson and Gales 1998; Baker *et al* 2002). All Procellarii-formes are long-lived birds that come ashore to breed at about 7-12 years of age – some each year, others every two years. They have single-egg clutches with incubation and chick rearing shared by the parents. Egg incubation ranges from 6-12 weeks and chicks fledge from the nest between 3-9 months after hatching (Baker *et al* 2002).

While albatrosses and petrels tend to have low rates of natural mortality, they are vulnerable to threats brought about directly or indirectly by human activity. Since the late 1970s and 1980s when declining populations of albatrosses were first noticed, it became clear that the major threat increasing the mortality rate of these seabirds has been a consequence of longline fishing operations. Indeed, species of albatross and petrel form the major non-fish bycatch from longlining in the southern oceans – the Southern Ocean as well as the South Atlantic, and the southern parts of the Indian and Pacific Oceans.

Longline fishing began in the Southern Hemisphere during the 1950s. It is now conducted globally, targeting pelagic and demersal fin-fish and sharks. One of the most dangerous forms to seabirds is mid-water pelagic longlining for tuna that is undertaken by large fleets from Japan and other Asian countries (such as Taiwan, Indonesia and the Republic of Korea) in many parts of the world to meet the needs of the Japanese raw tuna markets. Domestic fleets of various countries, including Australia, also conduct tuna longlining operations (Robertson 1998).

Pelagic longlining for species such as tuna, involves the deployment of long main lines from which smaller branch lines or snoods are attached. Baited hooks are attached to these snoods. The pelagic longlines can be over 100 kilometres long with as many as 40,000 hooks. Demersal longlines (involving the deployment of short branch lines on a weighted mainline) target species such as Patagonian toothfish and Antarctic toothfish. Lucrative fishing grounds of these species are frequently situated over continental shelf breaks (often within or just outside State Exclusive Economic Zones or EEZs) and along high sea ocean fronts (beyond State jurisdiction) where water masses mix and upwell (Robertson 1998).

Albatrosses and petrels forage for food at the same locations, often attracted by fish waste discharged by longlining vessels. The seabirds get hooked and drowned during line setting and hauling – thus the bycatch problem. It is estimated that in the southern oceans, tens of thousands of albatrosses and petrels are killed annually with estimates ranging from 40,000 to 100,000 per year over the last decade or so (CCAMLR 2002). Because albatrosses are long-lived, immensely wide-ranging seabirds with low fecundity, such decimation bodes ill for the survival of many populations.

Many of those engaged in the longline fishing industry are reluctant to acknowledge that their operations are causing extensive decline in the populations of albatross and petrel species. As Robertson (1998) points out, the evidence that longline fishers are responsible for population decreases is circumstantial – albeit overwhelmingly so. Furthermore, fishers are reluctant to change fishing practices that have worked well in the past, especially if such changes involve the use of mitigation methods suspected of compromising fishing efficiency and, ultimately, income (Robertson 1998).

Many fishers also believe that the extent of seabird bycatch is exaggerated. Again, Robertson (1998) notes it is unlikely that fishers make the mathematical connection between the strike rate of seabirds per fishing vessel (which may be quite low) and the vast number of hooks deployed annually by all of the longlining vessels in the southern oceans (Robertson 2001).

While longline fishing is the primary threat to albatrosses and petrels, it is also important to recognise that other significant threats at sea include trawl fishery interactions (when, for example, seabirds become entangled in nets while scavenging for food); chemical contamination from organochlorines, heavy metals and oil spills; and ingestion or entanglement with marine debris (Baker et al 2002; Baker et al 2007).

On land, a major threat to albatrosses and petrels occurs at breeding colonies when increased mortality or decreased breeding success is caused by the predation of introduced mammals (such as cats and rats) and the degradation of nesting habitat by introduced herbivores (such as rabbits, cattle, sheep and goats). For seabirds breeding in Australian territory, with Macquarie Island being a case in point, rats and rabbits pose serious threats (Baker et al 2002).

With increasing concern about the conservation status of albatrosses and petrels and the identification of threatening processes that are sketched above, efforts to mitigate and/or eliminate them have been made in recent years at both the international and national levels. In regard to the former, these have centred on the formation of an international regime.

A Seabird Conservation Regime

An international regime is a cluster of rights and rules governing or regulating the actions and relations among members of international society that pertain to well-defined activities, resources or geographical areas (Young 1989). The primary function of international regimes is to facilitate cooperative action as a means for achieving desirable goals or values that cannot be obtained by its members acting individually. Albatross and petrel conservation is one such goal.

The cluster of rights and rules that constitute an international regime is often articulated or expressed in formal international agreements. This is the case with the seabird conservation regime that has been formed over the past decade largely through negotiation processes between interested States in various forums. It is centred, at present, upon a set of three major "hard law" (that is, binding) and "soft law" (that is, hortatory, non-binding) international instruments and measures that span different and overlapping zones of application – Conservation Measures promulgated by the Commission established under the Convention on the Conservation of Antarctic Marine Living Resources (CCAMLR), the Food and Agriculture Organization's International Plan of Action for Reducing Incidental Catch of Seabirds in Longline Fisheries (IPOA-Seabirds) and the Agreement on the Conservation of Albatrosses and Petrels (ACAP).

CCAMLR Conservation Measures

The first "hard law" initiative specifying measures to mitigate the incidental catch of albatross and petrel species was Conservation Measure 29/X (entitled "Minimisation of the Incidental Mortality of Seabirds in the Course of Longline Fishing or Longline Fishing Research in the Convention Area") that was adopted in 1991 by the CCAMLR Commission for its (then) 23 Members.

A majority of Southern Hemisphere albatross and petrel species range through the area covered by the Convention – south of the Antarctic Convergence. The issue of incidental mortality associated with fishing operations was first raised at the Third Meeting of the CCAMLR Commission held in 1984 (CCAMLR 1984). The need to collect data on incidental catch was discussed at both the Fourth and Fifth Meetings held in 1985 and 1986 respectively. It was not until 1989, however, that the issue of incidental catch re-emerged on the agenda of Commission meetings – the result of early data gathering and concern about the introduction of longline fishing during the 1988-89 fishing season in the Convention area and the potential threat this activity posed to seabirds (CCAMLR 1989b).

During the Ninth Meeting of the CCAMLR Commission in 1990, the issue of incidental catches of albatrosses received considerable attention. Australia presented a paper to the Scientific Committee of the Commission that described albatross mortality associated with longline tuna fisheries outside the Convention area – a conservative estimate of 44,000 albatrosses killed annually. Australian delegates also presented information on Australian-Japanese efforts to reduce albatross bycatch through the use of tori-poles with streamers erected at the stern of the fishing vessels to scare seabirds attracted to the food used as bait on the hooks attached to the longlines. Evidence indicating the significant decline in bird bycatch rate of 88 per cent using these devices was presented to the Committee along with the economic benefits of such devices (CCAMLR 1990a; CCAMLR 1990b).

The Commission also agreed that, before the evaluation of data, modifications of longline fishing techniques within the Convention area needed to be implemented. These modifications reflected the experiences of Australia, New Zealand and Japan in tackling the problem within the Southern bluefin tuna fishery and the development of the tori-pole concept and bait-caster technology by Nigel Brothers, a Tasmanian biologist working on the albatross bycatch problem. In short, the modifications included the deployment of tori-poles and streamers; the requirement that fishing operations be conducted in such a way that baits sink immediately they are in the water; the setting of longlines only at night; and the prohibition of dumping trash or offal while longline operations are in progress. These recommendations were prepared as a draft Conservation Measure and, although this proposed measure was not approved at this particular meeting of the Commission, it was agreed that it would be discussed again at the next one (CCAMLR 1990b).

It was at the Tenth Meeting of the CCAMLR Commission in 1991 that the conservation measure was formally adopted. France, however, reserved application of the measure in the EEZs of Kerguelen and Crozet Islands and as a result of these reservations, Conservation Measure 29/X came into force on 3 May 1992, except for waters around the French territories (CCAMLR 1991). The measure was subsequently modified as Conservation Measure 29/XIII in 1994 (with the addition of the requirement that every effort be made to release live birds from lines) (CCAMLR 1994). Also in 1994, the Commission established the Ad hoc Working Group on Incidental Mortality Arising from Longline Fishing (WG-IMALF) to review data on seabird bycatch, assess the performance of its seabird-related conservation measures and submit advice to the Scientific Committee (CCAMLR 2004a). This Group's name was amended in 2001 to the Ad hoc Working Group on Incidental Mortality Associated with Fishing (WG-IMAF) in the light of new seabird bycatch concerns associated with trawl fishing.

In 2002, after a new numerical system was introduced, this Conservation Measure was renumbered 25-02 and it now sits along side other

Conservation Measures that have subsequently been developed, *inter alia*, to minimise the incidental mortality of seabirds and marine mammals in the course of trawl fishing in the CCAMLR area (CCAMLR 2006/07). In addition, the CCAMLR Commission has also established seabird bycatch limits in exploratory fisheries and delayed the opening of fishing seasons until the end of the breeding season of most albatrosses and petrels (CCAMLR 2004a).

The CCAMLR Commission has also established an observer program that requires the presence of an independent observer (of different nationality from the vessel's flag State) on all members' vessels fishing for toothfish, icefish and crab and on all vessels engaged in exploratory fisheries in CCAMLR managed waters (Small 2005: 33). From this program, the Commission collects observational data on target and non-target species (including seabird bycatch) that facilitates the development of a greater understanding of the nature and extent of the seabird bycatch problem and the efficacy of mitigation measures deployed, as well as the enhancement of compliance to them.

Since their adoption and implementation, CCAMLR Conservation Measures have proved very successful in the CCAMLR managed area, with seabird mortality in regulated longline fisheries reducing from 6589 birds killed in 1997 to 15 birds killed in 2003. This represents a reduction of over 99 per cent. Within the French EEZ around Kerguelen and Crozet Islands, seabird mortality totalled 13,784 seabirds (93 per cent of which were white-chinned petrels) in 2003 (CCAMLR 2003), however in 2003-04 the number of seabirds killed reduced to 4008 following efforts by France in cooperation with the CCAMLR Commission (CCAMLR 2004b; Small 2005: 35). Moreover, later CCAMLR reports indicate further reductions of seabird mortality in most parts of the Convention area and in 2006, for the first time, no albatrosses were reported taken in regulated longline fisheries (CCAMLR 2006).

Notwithstanding such success, a substantial problem remains – illegal, unreported and unregulated (IUU) fishing in the CCAMLR area. The CCAMLR Commission was one of the first regional fisheries management organisations (RFMOs) to address this problem as it sought to manage its toothfish fisheries during the late 1990s (Small 2005: 33-4; see also Lugten this volume).

IUU fishing in the CCAMLR area is a complex problem involving vessels registered under a flag of convenience taking advantage of inadequate vessel monitoring by the flag States involved. Moreover, there is evidence to suggest that some vessels engaged in IUU fishing in the CCAMLR area are owned by so-called front companies that, in turn, are owned by nationals of Member States. In addition, there is evidence of transgressions by Member vessels from Uruguay, Russia, and Korea (CCAMLR 2001; CCAMLR 2003).

Apart from the serious depletion of fish stocks, such IUU fishing operations have had a major detrimental affect on seabird populations. In 2002, the CCAMLR Commission estimated that IUU fishing vessels not required to deploy the bycatch mitigation measures were responsible for between 39-52,000 and 70-93,000 seabirds being killed per year. This was judged to be a level of mortality "entirely unsustainable for populations of albatrosses, great petrels and white-chinned petrels in the Convention area, many of which are declining at rates where extinction is possible" (CCAMLR 2002).

The level of IUU fishing within the Convention area in 2003-04 was estimated to have been significantly smaller than in 2002-03 (an decrease of 75 per cent) (CCAMLR 2004b). The Commission indicated that it was not clear whether this decrease represented a real decline in IUU fishing, depletion of fish stocks or a relocation of IUU fishing to outside the Convention area. Moreover, it was not clear whether there had been a net decrease in seabird bycatch attributable to IUU fishing (Small 2005). In 2006, the total potential seabird bycatch in the unregulated longline fishery was estimated (for 2005-06) to be 4583 seabirds. This value is similar to the value estimated for the previous season and both estimates are the lowest reported values since estimates started in 1996. This was presumed to be a consequence of a reduction of unregulated toothfish catch and/or changes in the areas from where IUU fishing takes place. Nonetheless, the Scientific Committee of the CCAMLR Commission reiterated its conclusion that even these levels of IUU seabird bycatch were of substantial concern and likely to be unsustainable for some of the seabird populations concerned (CCAMLR 2005).

International Plan of Action-Seabirds

The soft law component of the seabird conservation regime is the IPOA-Seabirds. This was formulated in 1998 and adopted by the Food and Agriculture Organization of the United Nations (FAO) in 1999 within the framework of its 1995 Code of Conduct for Responsible Fisheries.

Essentially, the IPOA-Seabirds exhorts States with longline fishers to conduct an assessment of these fisheries to determine if a seabird bycatch problem exists. If this is the case, States should adopt a National Plan of Action (NPOA-Seabirds) for reducing such bycatch, which, in turn, should be implemented, monitored and regularly assessed at least every four years. States should also strive to cooperate through regional and sub-regional fisheries organisations or arrangements to reduce seabird bycatch in longline fisheries (FAO 1999; FAO 2007). The Plan also includes technical guidelines for developing a NPOA-Seabirds, together with prescriptions of appropriate mitigation methods, research and development plans, education, training and publicity, and data collection programs.

Supplementing and complementing the IPOA-Seabirds is the International Plan of Action to Prevent, Deter and Eliminate Illegal, Unreported and Unregulated Fishing (IPOA-IUU) adopted by FAO in 2001. This plan provides support for the seabird conservation regime, as it is unlikely that vessels avoiding compliance with fisheries management arrangements are also less likely to be concerned with the implementation of bycatch miti-gation measures.

IPOA-Seabirds originally exhorted States to start implementation of their NPOA-Seabirds no later than the FAO Committee of Fisheries (COFI) Session in 2001. By early 2007, eight States had produced one – the United States, Japan, the United Kingdom (on behalf of the Falkland Islands), New Zealand, Uruguay, Canada, Chile and Brazil. Australia is in the process of developing a NPOA-Seabirds to add to its Threat Abatement Plan that was implemented in 1998 and which contains a mixture of voluntary and mandatory measures. South Africa has a draft plan close to finalisation and it is understood that Namibia, Taiwan and the European Union are each in the process of developing one (Cooper and Riviera 2004; CCAMLR 2006).

While this soft law component of the seabird conservation regime is non-binding, it does not necessarily mean that it lacks significance. Although soft laws do not have the same legal standing as the text of a treaty, they are regarded as rules with which parties should comply and, accordingly, they possess a considerable practical significance (Lyster 1985). Soft law may also engender the participation of States that prefer to avoid binding international agreements, either because of competing national interests, or because of the lack of technical or fiscal means to participate in a binding agreement (Joyner 2000: 176, 182). Moreover, soft law may rapidly become part of customary law or even become hardened in treaties (Birnie and Boyle 1992). The FAO IPOA-Seabirds initiative illus-trates this point – provisions concerning the plan are incorporated in the hard law ACAP.

The Agreement on the Conservation of Albatrosses and Petrels

The second hard law component of the seabird conservation regime is the 2001 ACAP. This Agreement was negotiated in response to a resolution in 1999 by the Conference of Parties to the Convention on the Conservation of Migratory Species of Wild Animals of 1979 (CMS).

The CMS provides a framework for further action by its Parties to protect migratory species of wild animals during their trans-boundary migrations and to preserve their habitats. Attached to it are two Appen-dices. Appendix I of CMS lists migratory species which are endangered. Range State Parties to this Convention are required to prohibit the taking of these animals, with few exceptions, so as to give them full protection (Article III). Appendix II lists migratory species which have an unfavou-rable conservation status and which require international agreements for their conservation and management as well as those that would signifi-cantly benefit from the international cooperation that could be achieved by an international agreement (Article IV(1)).

The issue of threats posed to albatrosses and petrels had been raised by Australia at the Third and Fourth Meetings of the Conference of Parties (hereafter CMS-CoP3 and CMS-CoP4) in 1991 and 1994 (Cooper *et al* 2006). (Australia had become a Party to CMS after ratifying the Treaty in September, 1991.)

In 1997 at CMS-CoP5, Australia noted "the need for concerted and co-operative action by all range States" and called for "an active role by range States in the development of an Agreement" (CMS 1997: 41). This proposal by Australia was supported by Chile, Ecuador, France, New Zealand, Norway and Uruguay – all range States of Southern Hemisphere albatrosses (CMS 1997: 23, 143). Furthermore, Australia nominated the Amsterdam albatross (*Diomedea amsterdamensis*, a Southern Hemisphere species) to be listed on Appendix I to join the short-tailed albatross (*Phoebastria albatrus*, a Northern Pacific species) that had been listed earlier in 1979. Australia also nominated 10 other Southern Hemisphere species of albatrosses and the Netherlands nominated the other two Northern Pacific species to be listed on Appendix II. Both sets of nomination were successful (CMS 1997).

Two years later at CMS-CoP6 in 1999, South Africa nominated seven species of petrels to Appendix II and, following approval, this meant that two species of albatrosses were listed in Appendix I and 12 species of albatrosses, as well as seven species of petrels known to be impact upon by fisheries interaction, were listed on Appendix II (CMS 1999a). Also at CMS-CoP6, a Resolution on Southern Hemisphere Albatross Conservation was passed accepting Australia's offer to initiate further discussion in early 2000 with all Parties that are range States to develop an international agreement (under the framework provided by Article IV(1) of CMS) directed at the conservation of these species (CMS 1999a: 39-42).

At the same time that these developments were taking place at CMS-CoPs during the 1990s, there were two international conferences which sought to attract and disseminate the most current information on albatross and petrel biology and conservation: the Inaugural Albatross Conference held in Hobart, Tasmania in September 1995 (Robertson and Gales 1998) and the Second International Conference on the Biology of Albatrosses and Petrels held in Honolulu, Hawaii, in May 2000. In addition, the Group of Temperate Southern Hemisphere Countries on the Environment (also known as the Valdivia Group – comprising Australia, Brazil, Chile, France, New Zealand, Peru and the United Kingdom) also addressed the issue of albatross and petrel conservation at several meetings in 1998 and 1999.

At the Fourth Meeting of the Coordinating Committee of the Valdivia Group held in Wellington, New Zealand in 1998, support for the development of an agreement under the auspices of CMS for Southern Hemisphere albatrosses was gained, based on recommendations set out in a paper presented by Australia. An ad hoc working group was established to examine options for regional cooperation to address the range of threats to Southern

Hemisphere albatross populations and, at its first meeting in June 1999, developed a document which outlined potential elements of a cooperative instrument to restore and maintain albatross populations (Cooper *et al* 2006; CMS 1999b). The meeting asked Uruguay (the Coordinator of the Valdivia Group) to present the final statement and attachments as a report on progress to CMS-CoP6 that was to be held later that year in Cape Town, South Africa.

The outcome of all these developments was that ACAP was negotiated in two sessions in 2000 and in early 2001. Australia convened a meeting in Hobart from 10-14 July 2000, to which all Southern Hemisphere albatross and petrel range States were invited. Twelve range States and several non-government organisations (most notably, BirdLife International) attended the meeting that supported fundamental principles to develop the Agreement. At the meeting, following a proposal by the United Kingdom, it was decided that the Agreement would not be restricted geographically (Cooper *et al* 2006). The meeting also recognised that a further meeting was needed to conclude the Agreement and this was held in Cape Town from 29 January to 2 February 2001, when ACAP was adopted by consensus. Several months later, on 19 June 2001, the Agreement was opened for signature, by any range State or regional integration organisation, at a formal ceremony in Canberra, Australia.

Seven range States signed ACAP at this ceremony – Australia, Brazil, Chile, France, New Zealand, Peru and the United Kingdom. It is important to note that in the Agreement, the term range State is defined as "any State that exercises jurisdiction over any part of the range of albatrosses or petrels, or a State, flagged vessels of which are engaged outside its national jurisdictional limits in taking, or which have the potential to take, albatrosses and petrels" (Article I(h)).

ACAP entered into force on 1 February 2004 (the first five ratifying States were Australia, New Zealand, Ecuador, Spain and South Africa). Subsequently, by the early 2007, the number of members had risen to eleven after the UK (2004 – whose ratification was extended to its Territories in the South Atlantic), Peru (2005), France (2005), Chile (2005), Argentina (2006) and Norway (2007) had deposited their instruments of ratification, acceptance or approval with the Depositary, Australia.

ACAP consists on nineteen articles and two annexes. In terms of rules, Parties are required, *inter alia*, to: take measures to achieve and maintain a favourable conservation status for albatrosses and petrels and in implementing such measures widely apply the precautionary approach (Article II); take general conservation measures which includes supporting the implementation of actions elaborated in the IPOA-Seabirds (Article III); give priority to capacity building, through funding, training, information and institutional support, for the implementation of the Agreement (Article IV); and cooperate with other Parties in regard to provisions of an Action Plan (articulated in Annex 2) for the achievement and maintenance of a favourable conservation status for albatrosses and petrels (Articles V and VI). The Parties have rights to participate in the Meeting of the Parties (Article VIII); amend, make specific reservations and denounce the Agreement (Articles XII, XVII, XVIII); and maintain or adopt stricter conservation measures (Article XIII).

As indicated above, ACAP has two annexes. Annex 1 lists the albatross and petrel species to which the Agreement applies and when it entered into force in 2004, 21 species of albatrosses and seven species of petrels were listed. (At this time, 24 species of albatrosses were generally recognised and the three species not listed in this annex were the Northern Pacific species – the short-tailed (*Phoebastria albatrus*), Laysan (*Phoebastria immutabilis*) and black-footed (*Phoebastria nigripes*) albatrosses.) Annex 2 is the Action Plan referred to in Articles V and VI and it deals with species conservation, habitat conservation and restoration, management of human activities, research and monitoring, collation of information by the Advisory Committee, education and public awareness and implementation of the plan.

By not restricting the geographic scope of the Agreement, there is no impediment to the Parties agreeing to add Northern Pacific albatrosses and petrels to Annex 1 in the future. Moreover, Parties need not be Parties to CMS to sign, ratify, accept, approve or accede to the Agreement.

The major organ of ACAP is the Meeting of the Parties, the first of which was held in Hobart in November 2004 (hereafter referred to as ACAP-MoP1). It was attended by five of the six members that had, by then, ratified the Agreement: Australia, New Zealand, South Africa, Spain and the United Kingdom. Also attending were three signatory range States (Argentina, Brazil and France), three non-member range States (Namibia, Norway and the United States) and representatives, as observers, of several RFMOs, intergovernmental organisations and non-governmental organisations (including BirdLife International) (ACAP 2004).

There were several major outcomes of ACAP-MoP1 including adherence to requirements set out in Article VIII of ACAP that at its first meeting the Parties: establish an Interim Secretariat (to perform secretarial functions until a permanent Secretariat is established); establish an Advisory Committee; and adopt interim criteria defining emergency situations for albatrosses and petrels and the assignation of responsibility for action to be taken and their referral to the Advisory Committee for further consideration (ACAP 2004).

In regard to the Interim Secretariat, in-kind and financial support in Hobart was provided by Australia as host country pending the adoption and entry into force of a headquarters agreement for the permanent Secretariat (also to be located in Hobart). Also established at ACAP-MoP1 were two working groups to assist with the implementation of the Action Plan – the Taxonomy Working Group and the Status and Trends Working Group (ACAP 2004).

The Advisory Committee, established at ACAP-MoP1, met in Hobart in 2005 (ACAP-AC1) and in Brasilia in 2006 (ACAP-AC2) and two other working groups were set up at these meetings – the Breeding Sites Working Group (at the former) and the Seabird Bycatch Working Group (at the latter).

The Second Meeting of the Parties (ACAP-MoP2) was held in Christchurch, New Zealand, in November 2006. It was attended by nine of the ten members that had, by then, ratified the Agreement: Argentina, Australia, Chile, Ecuador, France, New Zealand, Peru, South Africa and the United Kingdom (that had, in 2006, also extended its ratification to its Territory of Tristan da Cunha). Also attending were one signatory range State (Brazil), two non-member range States (the United States and Uruguay) and representatives, as observers, of two RFMOs (CCAMLR and the South East Atlantic Fisheries Organisation – SEAFO), the United Nations Environment Program/CMS, and two non-governmental organisations (BirdLife International and Humane Society International). At this meeting, too, the Interim Secretariat of ACAP reported that it had been advised by Norway, Namibia and Brazil that they expected to ratify the Agreement within a short period of time (ACAP 2006).

At ACAP-MoP2, major outcomes included: adoption of an Agreement Budget 2007–09 with an average annual budget of AUD$464,517; adoption of the headquarters agreement between the Secretariat to ACAP and the government of Australia; and endorsement of the Advisory Committee's ongoing proposed Work Programme 2007-2009 setting out, *inter alia*, topics and tasks that are the responsibility of the working groups to undertake (ACAP 2006).

Furthermore, demonstrating that albatross taxonomy is a work-in-progress exercise, it was agreed at this meeting that the number of albatross species listed in Annex 1 of ACAP signifying the species to which the Agreement applies, be reduced from 21 to 19. The decision was based on scientific evidence that does not currently support the recognition of several closely related albatrosses as separate species: (i) the Antipodean albatross (*Diomedea antipodensis*) and Gibson's albatross (*Diomedea gibsoni*) is now considered synonymous at the species level and, following rules of taxonomic precedence, is now listed in Annex 1 as *Diomedea antipodensis* and, similarly, (ii) Buller's albatross (*Thalassarche bulleri*) and the Pacific albatross (*Thalassarche nov sp (platei)*) is now considered synonymous at the species level and is listed in Annex 1 as *Thalassarche bulleri*.

There were also several priorities expressed at ACAP-MoP2 to help ACAP achieve its objective of a favourable conservation status for albatrosses and petrels. One major priority was for Parties, range States and working groups to start the process of engagement with RFMOs that manage fisheries in areas that overlap with albatross distribution with the view to get them to implement effective seabird bycatch mitigation measures and observation programs in the way that the CCAMLR Commission has done (ACAP 2006).

Leaving aside the CCAMLR Commission, there are 12 other RFMOs whose areas of application coincide with known distributions of albatrosses and petrels (BirdLife 2004; Small 2005). Of the four longer established RMFOs, by 2005 only the Commission for the Conservation of Southern Bluefin Tuna (CCSBT) had adopted (in 1995) a requirement that all longline vessels in the Southern bluefin tuna fishery deploy streamers lines when operating south of 30 degrees South latitude. In the decade following the adoption of this requirement, the CCSBT has not, however, adopted any other mitigation measures despite proposals from Australia and New Zealand (both member States of CCSBT, along with Japan, the Republic of Korea and Taiwan and the cooperating non-member, the Philippines) for their deployment (CCSBT 2001; Small 2005: 39). Nor has CCSBT established any monitoring program to assess the effectiveness of, and compliance with, this particular measure (Small 2005: 39, 77).

It must be noted, however, that several of the more recently established RFMOs have begun to address the seabird bycatch problem. For example, in October 2006, SEAFO adopted Conservation Measure 05/06 on reducing incidental bycatch of seabirds in the SEAFO Convention area. It included the provision that each Party shall seek to achieve reductions in levels of seabird bycatch across fishing areas, seasons, and fisheries through the use of effective mitigation measures such as bird-scaring streamer poles, night-setting requirements, the prohibition of offal dumping while gear is being shot or set, and the release of live captured birds (SEAFO 2007). The Western and Central Pacific Fisheries Commission (WCPFC) also adopted, in December 2006, a mandatory Conservation and Management Measure (2006-02) obliging its Commission members, Cooperating Non Members and participating Territories to require their longline fishing vessels to use at least two seabird bycatch mitigation measures in areas south of 30 degrees South and north of 23 degrees North (WCPFC 2006).

Concern was also expressed at ACAP-MoP2 about the lack of information on the level of seabird bycatch as a consequence of IUU fishing and it was agreed that there was an urgent need for RFMOs to provide estimates of IUU fishing in their management areas. Another priority expressed was the need for Parties to undertake capacity building activities in range States that require training, information and institutional support to implement the Agreement (ACAP 2006).

Considering that ACAP has been in force for only a short period of time, it is not possible to make any meaningful assessment of its effectiveness towards achieving its primary objective. What can be said, however, is that much has been achieved in what Young (1994) refers to as constitutive effectiveness – that is, in terms of structures and processes established. In addition, by the end of 2006, ACAP had ten members; two other range States, Brazil and the United States, had been active participants at ACAP meetings (indeed, Brazil hosted ACAP-AC2) and both had submitted reports of their activities in regard to the implementation of ACAP 2004-06.

Notwithstanding these considerations, it must be recognised that ACAP does not have among its member Parties some crucial States – most notably those with major high seas fishing fleets (especially Japan, the Republic of Korea and Taiwan). This is clearly a major impediment to the attainment of the objective of the Agreement for those species of albatrosses and petrels listed in Annex 1, and perhaps, Northern Pacific species that may benefit from listing in the future.

What can be gleaned from the foregoing discussion is that several States (and individuals from them) have played leadership roles in contributing to the understanding of the nature of the seabird conservation problem, the development of mitigation methods as well as to the development and implementation of the seabird conservation regime – most notably, the United Kingdom, New Zealand, South Africa and Australia. The non-government conservation organisation, BirdLife International, has also played a prominent role, especially through its Global Seabird Programme and its participation at ACAP meetings.

Australia's Involvement in Seabird Conservation

In regard to Australia's contributions, Australian seabird scientists and delegates to CCAMLR Commission meetings in the late 1980s and early 1990s played significant roles by providing evidence linking longline fishing operations outside the Convention area to the incidental mortality of tens of thousands of albatrosses annually. They also provided information on mitigation efforts used initially by Australian, Japanese and New Zealand fishers operating in the Southern bluefin tuna fishery to reduce albatross bycatch through the use of streamer poles. This prompted further intensive research on mitigation measures that have proved effective in reducing the level of seabird bycatch.

While these developments were taking place in 1992, the Australian Nature Conservation Agency funded the preparation of a global review of albatross populations and threats. As Baker *et al* (2002) note, this 1993 review by Tasmanian seabird scientist Rosemary Gales highlighted the scarcity of information on the status of albatross populations and set out an assessment of all threats known at the time to be affecting albatross populations. Importantly, this review provided impetus and focus that shaped ongoing seabird conservation policy development in Australia and internationally.

Further impetus was generated at the National Seabird Workshop held in Canberra in 1993. Organised by the Biodiversity Group of Environment Australia, the Workshop provided an opportunity for State and Commonwealth government policymakers and seabird and fisheries scientists, community groups and the fishing industry to further develop solutions to address threatening processes (Ross *et al* 1996). Furthermore, in 1995, the Australian Antarctic Division and the Tasmanian Parks and Wildlife Service supported the staging of the Inaugural Albatross Conference held in Hobart.

Australia also played a pivotal role in discussions on albatross and petrel conservation within CMS-CoPs and the Valdivia Group's meetings during the 1990s. Australia raised the issue of the severe threats faced by albatross and petrel populations, largely stemming from longline fishing operations, and proposed the creation of an agreement for their conservation and management at CMS-CoP3, CMS-CoP4 and CMS-CoP5. Furthermore, Australia nominated 11 species of albatrosses for listing on CMS Appendices at CoP5 and convened the first (in Hobart in 2000) of the two meetings during which ACAP was negotiated. Australia was among the first signatories and ratifiers of ACAP; Australia hosted ACAP-MoP1 and ACAP-AC1, both held in Hobart.

With the creation of ACAP, Australia has served as Depositary for the Agreement and has also hosted and given substantial in-kind and financial support to the Interim Secretariat of ACAP until the permanent Secretariat has been established. Its offer to host the permanent Secretariat in Hobart was accepted at ACAP-MOP1. Three of the four Working Groups established to assist with implementation of the Agreement's Action Plan are convened by Australian representatives – the Status and Trends Working Group, the Taxonomy Working Group and the Seabird Bycatch Working Group.

Clearly, all these contributions demonstrate Australia's significant commitment to the conservation of albatrosses and petrels sustained over two decades of involvement in the issue. What can be concluded, too, from this overview of the major threats to albatrosses and petrels and the seabird conservation regime that has been developed to address them, is that much has been achieved in a relatively short period of time through the international efforts of a relatively small group of dedicated people (representing interested States, government agencies, scientific bodies, intergovernmental organisations and non-governmental organisations).

It is clear, though, too, that there is much work still to be done if the major threats to the survival of albatross and petrel species (particularly those threats associated with longline fishing operations) are to be diminished or overcome. The challenges are many. Although mitigation measures have proved effective in reducing seabird bycatch in the CCAMLR area, the need for their further uptake by RFMOs whose areas of management also coincide with albatross and petrel populations is crucial. There is also the need for high seas fishing States that have yet to sign and ratify ACAP to do so. These States would then need to implement and comply with its requirements. Capacity building and maintenance in range States is needed, too. Tackling IUU fishing is also critical, as is the need for more States to develop, implement and comply with a NPOA-Seabirds. Threats on land at breeding sites need also to be addressed through appropriate programs, especially those concerning the eradication of feral species. Listing of the three species of Northern Pacific albatrosses in Annex 1 of ACAP and the concurrent accession to the Agreement by the States through which these species range (Japan, Canada and the United States – all of which have established a NPOA-Seabirds) may also contribute to the further development of international momentum around ACAP.

All these needs are paralleled by the necessity for the continuation of scientific work concerning such matters as population status and tends, demographic parameters, taxonomy, breeding locations, foraging distribution and threats. This is required to assist with the ongoing implementation of the Agreement's Action Plan as new knowledge gained from such work provides an essential base upon which future decisions by ACAP-MoPs (as well as those by the CCAMLR Commission and other RFMOs) will be taken.

There seems plenty of scope for Australia to continue its commitment to seabird conservation. And there are sound reasons why Australia would choose to do so. Apart from the instrumental value of this commitment to seabird conservation as a means to address the threats to albatrosses and petrels, there is a symbolic dimension that reinforces the way Australia wishes to be seen by several audiences. To the international community, it shows that Australia is very active in working towards fulfilling its obligations not only in regard to ACAP and CCAMLR, but also under such broader instruments as CMS, the Convention on Biological Diversity, and the Fish Stocks Agreement. Furthermore, many of the Parties to ACAP are also Parties to the Antarctic Treaty and its associated instruments such as CCAMLR. Australian involvement in seabird conservation through ACAP and CCAMLR and the leadership roles it has played in these international initiatives addressing threats to albatrosses and petrels serves to enhance Australia's standing as an influential actor in Antarctic and southern ocean affairs – a key objective of Australia's Antarctic policy.

Acknowledgements

The author expresses his appreciation to Warren Papworth (Executive Secretary, Interim Secretariat, ACAP), Barry Baker (Institute of Antarctic and Southern Ocean Studies, University of Tasmania) and Michael Double (Australian Antarctic Division) for the advice and information they provided during the preparation of this chapter. They are, of course, absolved from responsibility for any error of fact or interpretation in the chapter.

10

The Great Whale Debate:
Australia's Agenda on Whaling

Julia Jabour, Mike Iliff and Erik Jaap Molenaar

Introduction

The great whale debate has been ongoing since whaling acquired a strong public perception of being cruel, unsustainable and unnecessary during the middle of the 20th century. A *volte face* by whaling States including Australia, Canada, the Netherlands, New Zealand, Peru, South Africa, the United Kingdom and the United States of America culminated in the adoption of a moratorium on commercial whaling from 1985-86 to conserve whale stocks, some of which were thought to be close to extinction. The moratorium is still in place today.

In November 1978, Australia's last coastal whaling company, Cheyne's Beach at Albany, Western Australia, closed down, effecting shortly thereafter a complete policy reversal for the Australian Government on what has since become an intensely emotive and highly politicised international issue. The closure was purported to be for economic reasons, putting over 100 people out of work. However, two years later whaling activities carried out by Australian citizens were criminalised. Thereafter a whole of government approach existed that was fundamentally and intractably anti-whaling. Today, all that remains of the Cheyne's Beach operation is a slipped whaling vessel and a few chattels for tourists to photograph.

Relics like the Cheyne's Beach complex – known in tourist brochures as Whale World – serve as a reminder of what official government rhetoric today calls "the bad old days" (Campbell 2005a). Whaling, Australians are told, is no longer in the country's national interest. The government has taken on the role of a "moral entrepreneur" (Nadelman 1990: 482), proselytising its view to both its domestic constituents and its international contemporaries.

This chapter will illustrate that, in relation to whaling, Australia's national interests are, indeed, representative of the "cosmopolitan moral

view" (Nadelman 1990: 484) that lethal activities like whaling are anachronistic and therefore have no place in modern civilised society, prompting
the evolution of customary practice in this regard. There is evidence, however, that this is not a view universally shared.

The aim of this chapter is to illustrate how Australia pursues its global
anti-whaling agenda. It investigates the nature of Australia's whaling
policy and how this is implemented in domestic legislation. It also examines the international legal situation with respect to whales and whaling,
to ascertain whether Australia has other options available to it in the
pursuit of its policy goals. In so doing, this chapter also locates the sources
of rights of pro-whaling States within the international legal regime, and
examines the robustness of Australia's policy in that context. It concludes
by speculating about possible future directions. The fact that the locus of
much of the contentious whaling activity is the Southern Ocean makes this
an Antarctic issue, despite profound reluctance by the Antarctic Treaty
Parties to address the matter as part of usual Antarctic business.

Current Australian Policy

The Frost Report and its Legacy

Australian policy has been zealously anti-whaling since the publication
of the Frost Report in 1978 (Frost 1978). A number of key policies, both
domestic and international, were derived from it and the later findings of
the government-commissioned National Task Force on Whaling in 1997.
These included:

- to maintain a permanent ban on commercial whaling in the
  maritime zones of Australia, to apply to both Australians and non-
  nationals; and

- to pursue a permanent international ban on commercial whaling
  (in the short term) by amending the convention on whaling (in the
  long term). (Environment Australia 1997: xi-xii)

The report also recommended that the government work within the
International Whaling Commission (IWC) and ensure that delegates to
meetings "should be selected not only for their expertise but also because
they are personally committed to supporting Australia's anti-whaling
policy" (Environment Australia 1997: 15).

The first of the two key policies is now entrenched in Australian
domestic law and until recently was thought to be relatively unproble-
matic for the government. However, the ongoing action by Humane
Society International (HSI) in the Federal Court (see also Rothwell and
Scott, Stephens and Boer this volume) has challenged the utility of an Australian Whale Sanctuary in Antarctica, given that HSI's action insists on the
legal application of Australian law to non-nationals. The second policy,

while partially achieved through the International Convention for the Regulation of Whaling's (ICRW)[1] moratorium on commercial whaling, is also problematic, particularly in terms of its permanency.

The Task Force report was used to formulate and strengthen government policy and today it underpins the aggressive pursuit of a permanent international ban on commercial whaling, including whales taken by lethal scientific research. Australia is a fervent participant in the annual meetings of the IWC as the States with an interest in whaling routinely duel with those that have an interest in banning whaling completely. Scattered around both sides are a retinue of middle-minded States that, for various reasons, align themselves with one bloc or the other, or choose to remain non-aligned. Australia has achieved some success in its strategic policy: It was a proponent of the establishment of the Southern Ocean Whale Sanctuary, and the moratorium has remained in place for over 20 years. But it has not achieved its ultimate goal of a permanent global ban on commercial whaling entrenched in an amended Convention.

Domestic responsibility for whales is currently with the Commonwealth Department of the Environment and Water Resources. Since the late 1970s responsibility for whales has rested within the environment portfolio and traditionally ministers have been extremely active in supporting and promoting government policy. This is particularly so in those few months around the annual IWC meeting and the activities of the research fleet in the Southern Ocean when the issue is artificially inflated in importance by constant media attention, providing numerous opportunities for a minister to collect no-cost electoral points. Despite the ICRW being a multilateral treaty, the Department of Foreign Affairs and Trade keeps a low profile in whaling matters compared, for example, to their role as head of delegation to Antarctic Treaty Consultative Meetings. This solitary approach to whaling responsibility is at odds with the way in which Australia has handled other international issues, for example its opposition to Antarctic mining in the 1980s (see Hemmings *et al* this volume). Then, a whole of government solidarity helped to secure a successful outcome, that is by overturning the minerals convention. Of course this may have been driven by the implications for Australian sovereignty and the allocation of unowned resources. On the other hand, Australia's opposition to whaling in the IWC is argued from a basis of sustainability, for which there is little empirical evidence.

The government has funded a new $AU2.5 million marine mammal research centre, hosted by the Australian Antarctic Division of the Department of the Environment and Water Resources. The aim of the Australian Centre for Applied Marine Mammal Science is to conduct research that fills gaps in existing knowledge about marine mammals (including cetaceans), including within the broad framework of Australia's Antarctic Science

---

1   161 UNTS 74.

Program Science Strategy 2004/05 to 2008/09 (AAD 2007a). This official strategic science document includes the following statement: "[A] significant research capability in cetacean biology will be developed to provide scientific data to support Australia's policy position in the International Whaling Committee [sic]" (AAD 2007a: 5). This approach was reinforced on the Centre's website (AAD 2007b).

Domestic and International Perceptions of Our Policy

In formulating its anti-whaling policy, Australia canvassed public opinion through the public enquiries of 1978 and 1997. There is no empirical evidence, however, that the majority of Australians currently support the government's policy (as may well be the case for public opinion on any government policy). The government has also relied heavily on the support and advice of representatives of environmental non-government organisations (NGOs), in particular The World Conservation Union (IUCN), the International Fund for Animal Welfare (IFAW) and Humane Society International (HSI). NGO representatives are sometimes included in the annual Australian IWC delegation.

Australia is aware of its international position and the effect its policies have on its neighbours and trading partners. Japan, in particular, is in Australia's sights over its lethal research in the Southern Ocean, despite being Australia's major trading partner for 40 years (Truss 2006). In this respect it must be said that the public disagreement between the two States in the IWC context does not appear, publicly at least, to have upset relations between them in other areas. For example, they are proceeding with negotiations on a bilateral Free Trade Agreement worth more than an estimated $AU50 billion in two-way trade (Truss 2006) while having just signed a bilateral security declaration (ABC 2007a).

The Australian Government has been reluctant to acknowledge that a position on whaling other than its own is legitimate and that it can be in accordance with international law. However, it has publicly recognised the need for subsistence catches of whales by some indigenous cultures to meet genuine traditional, cultural and dietary needs. Notwithstanding, at the announcement of Iceland's resumption of commercial whaling in November 2006, Australia was one of 26 States to sign a *démarche* condemning the Icelandic decision. The group clearly did not perceive Iceland's actions as synonymous with an indigenous culture meeting a genuine traditional need by whaling. The *démarche* came about because even though Iceland re-joined the IWC in 2002, it did so with a reservation to the moratorium. A number of States, including Australia, objected to the reservation at the time but the IWC ruled that it did not have competence to decide on the legal status of reservations and the matter is unresolved.

How robust are Australia's strategic policy goals? Whaling and the conservation of whales are regulated by a specific convention, the ICRW. Other aspects of the activity, such as international trade in whale products, are subject to separate regimes. Australia's domestic legal framework will be examined first. However, the manner in which Australia pursues its strategic policies within the IWC is not just a matter of aligning with its national interest and domestic obligations. It also depends on rights and obligations States have under the international law relevant to whaling and the conservation of whales.

Australia's Domestic Legal Framework

The recommendations made by the Frost Inquiry in 1978 led to the repeal of the *Whaling Act* 1960 (Cth) in 1979 and its replacement by the *Whale Protection Act* 1980 (Cth). The latter Act was eventually repealed by the *Environment Protection and Biodiversity Conservation Act* 1999 (Cth) (EPBC Act).

Section 225 of the EPBC Act establishes the Australian Whale Sanctuary, which comprises the Exclusive Economic Zone (EEZ) of continental Australia and its External Territories, including the Australian Antarctic Territory (AAT). Sections 229-232 contain various offences in relation to whales in the Australian Whale Sanctuary, which are also applicable to non-nationals. As Section 225 does not exclude application to Australia's Antarctic EEZ, the Australian Whale Sanctuary applies to non-nationals anywhere in the EEZ.

Under Australia's domestic legislation therefore, Japanese scientific research by lethal means (also known colloquially as "scientific whaling") in the EEZ off the AAT is illegal under this Act. However, in view of the delicate balance of sovereignty maintained through Article IV of the 1959 Antarctic Treaty,[2] Australia has never enforced its legislation against foreign vessels. The HSI case discussed below (and elsewhere in this volume) challenges that situation.

Humane Society International and Kyodo Senpaku Kaisha Ltd

In November 2004 HSI took action in the Australian Federal Court against a Japanese company, Kyodo Senpaku Kaisha Ltd, for killing whales in the Antarctic section of Australia's Whale Sanctuary in breach of the EPBC Act (see also Rothwell and Scott, Stephens and Boer this volume). HSI essentially sought a declaration from the Court that the Japanese activities were illegal.

It is useful to note that:

- HSI had standing to bring the action to restrain the offences in the absence of government action;
- a breach of the EPBC Act did occur;

---

2   402 UNTS 71.

- Japan is conducting its scientific research by lethal means in the EEZ off the AAT;

- Japan does not recognise Australia's sovereignty over the AAT (Government of Japan 2005) and thus does not acknowledge the existence of an EEZ; and

- Japan is conducting its scientific research as permitted by the ICRW.

The Australian Government was invited to submit its views to the Court. The Attorney-General's submission agreed there was no dispute as to the application of the EPBC Act to non-nationals and non-Australian flagged vessels in the AAT's EEZ. However, in acknowledgement of Japan's non-recognition of Australia's Antarctic claim (*ergo* the EEZ also), the Attorney-General submitted that the AAT claim is not one of sovereignty in the full sense but rather is one of limited entitlement. Justice Allsop concluded therefore, that the Japanese government would regard any attempt by Australia to enforce Australian law against Japanese vessels and nationals in the Antarctic EEZ to be a breach of international law on Australia's part and would give rise to an international disagreement with Japan. Furthermore, any attempt at enforcement could be "reasonably expected to prompt a significant adverse reaction from other Antarctic Treaty Parties" and any such action would also "be contrary to Australia's long term national interests" ([2005] FCA 664 at [13]-[14]).

In his decision that leave to serve be denied, Justice Allsop confirmed his agreement with the government's opinion that it was more appropriate to pursue diplomatic solutions to activities of this kind ([2005] FCA 664 at [16]). That this view was of doubtful validity was supported by HSI's successful appeal. It could be argued, for example, that the court should not have dealt with Australian-Japanese relations with regard to Antarctic claims or Australia's long-term national interest, as these are not juridical matters. Whether or not the application of the EPBC Act in this case would jeopardise the delicate Antarctic diplomatic balance should have been irrelevant.

Accordingly, when HSI lodged an appeal to the Full Bench of the Federal Court on 17 June 2005 they did so on the basis of the Court's:

- failure to exercise *prima facie* right to exercise of jurisdiction;
- failure to consider legislative intention to apply to non-nationals;
- erroneous consideration of political and diplomatic issues;
- consideration of irrelevant issues; and
- erroneous finding that proceedings are futile.[3]

HSI won the appeal (*Humane Society International Inc v Kyodo Senpaku Kaisga Ltd* [2006] FCAFC 116) and the documents have been served on

---

3   Notice of Appeal # NSD995/2005, dated 17.06.05.

Kyodo Senpaku Kaisha in Japan. While it will have little or no effect on the international regulation of whaling, the determination that weight was erroneously attached to the political rather than the legal aspects of the case will endure.

International Law Relevant to the Conservation of Whales and Whaling

International Convention for the Regulation of Whaling

Australia was among the original States that signed the ICRW on 2 December 1946 and became a Party upon its entry into force in 1948. There are 73 Parties to the Convention, which are also members of the IWC established under Article III. An integral part of the ICRW is its attached Schedule, which contains the agreed definitions and technical conservation and management measures. For example, paragraph 10(e) of the Schedule contains the moratorium on commercial whaling on all whale stocks, which has been in effect since 1985-86.

The ICRW applies to "factory ships, land stations, and whale catchers under the jurisdiction of the Contracting governments and to all waters in which whaling is prosecuted by such factory ships, land stations, and whale catchers" (Article I.2).

Article VIII(1) entitles Parties to grant its nationals permits to engage in scientific research. This right is not subject to the approval of the IWC. At the time of writing, only Japan was exercising this right. As there is no accepted definition of scientific research, and no exclusion for the taking of whales by lethal means, this activity is not in breach of the Convention *per se*. Furthermore, Article VIII(2) requires that whales taken under special scientific permit shall be processed (if practicable) and the proceeds dealt with according to directions from the permitting government. That the whale meat from Japanese scientific research ends up in the market place is therefore not inconsistent with the right granted in this provision, despite protests to the contrary.

In 1994 the IWC adopted the Revised Management Procedure (RMP) which seeks to ensure that once the moratorium is lifted, sufficient account is taken of the high risks of over-exploitation and thereby loss of marine biodiversity. The Revised Management Scheme (RMS), which complements the RMP on matters of supervision, control and data gathering to ensure that catch limits are not exceeded, has not yet been adopted. While the lifting of the moratorium is not formally linked to the adoption of the RMS, within the IWC there is broad support for a RMS package between three elements: the moratorium, scientific research by lethal means and compliance (IWC Chairman 2005: 3).

The process of decision-making under the Convention is of crucial importance to the stalemate on this package.

Decision-making Under the ICRW

The making of decisions is governed by specific procedures: a three-quarters majority is required for decisions on the core regulations contained within the Schedule; a simple majority for all other decisions (Article III.2). When proposals require a three-quarters majority, members can avoid becoming legally bound through the objection or "opting-out" procedure (Article V.3). By invoking this procedure, Norway and the Russian Federation have not become bound to the moratorium on commercial whaling and Japan has not become bound to the Southern Ocean Sanctuary to the extent that it relates to Antarctic minke whales (Schedule paragraphs 7(b) and 10(e) footnotes).

As simple majority is the general rule rather than the exception, this also applies when the IWC has to determine whether or not it has competence (compétence de la compétence). This, for instance, occurred during the 53rd and 54th IWC Meetings (2001 and 2002) and the 5th Special IWC Meeting (2002) in relation to Iceland's instrument of adherence to the ICRW, by which it made a reservation to the moratorium. At the 5th Special Meeting, the IWC eventually ruled it had no competence to determine the legal status of reservations made by States when acceding to the ICRW (Molenaar 2003: 44). Australia and various other IWC members objected to the Icelandic reservation and Australia accepts Iceland as a member of the IWC but not its reservation (Embassy of Australia 2003).

One of the most significant problems with decision-making and general behaviour on the part of IWC Members is the fact that the Convention does not have its own dispute settlement procedure. However, compulsory dispute settlement under the United Nations Convention on the Law of the Sea (LOS Convention;[4] see below) in cases of a breach of good faith, for example, cannot be ruled out (Triggs 2005). As proposals relating to whales within the IWC are extremely politically charged, there is often pressured block-voting and efforts by the pro- and anti-whaling camps to encourage like-minded States to obtain membership in order to influence decision-making. As a consequence of the qualified majority used within the IWC and the present sizes of the opposing blocks, it has become very difficult to alter the core status quo in relation to whales. But there may be recourse through other international legal avenues.

In the absence of specific provisions in the ICRW, contracting Parties can only amend the Convention with the unanimous agreement of all (Birnie 1985: 193; Brownlie 1990: 625). It is unclear whether any IWC Member has ever proposed an amendment to Article VIII to define "scientific research" in a way that excludes lethal techniques, thereby putting an end to activities by Japan under this Article. Despite a resolution being passed by the Scientific Committee in 1957 to limit the extent of the scientific "catch" (Tønnessen and Johnsen 1982: 579-80), the most common action the

---

4   1833 UNTS 396.

Members take in this regard is the annual ritual of passing a resolution under Article VI (which is non-legally binding) condemning lethal scientific research. This indicates a complete lack of faith in any chance of success at amending the Convention.

United Nations Convention on the Law of the Sea

Australia ratified the United Nations LOS Convention and became a party upon the Convention's entry into force on 16 November 1994. At the time of writing, participation in the Convention was so wide (153 Parties) that it essentially represents universal international law. The LOS Convention's overarching objective is to establish a universally accepted, just and equitable legal order for the oceans involving a fundamental redistribution of rights over marine resources, both living and non-living. On account of their sovereignty within their internal waters, territorial sea and archipelagic waters as well as their sovereign rights in the adjacent EEZ and outer continental shelf (Articles 2, 49, 56 and 77 respectively), coastal States have very extensive authority over marine living resources therein.

The fact that the ICRW predates the LOS Convention by several decades explains why the coverage of the ICRW is not influenced by the LOS Convention's division of the oceans into maritime zones and the rights of coastal States and flag States therein or why it does not in one way or another defer to the LOS Convention. The circumstance that the ICRW is older, however, does not affect the sovereign rights of coastal States over marine mammals in their EEZs under Article 65 of the LOS Convention. This means that whether or not a coastal State such as Australia is a Party to the ICRW, it has a right under Article 65 to regulate the exploitation of marine mammals more strictly than the ICRW (such as Australia declaring its EEZ a whale sanctuary). The reverse is not possible. That is, a Party to the ICRW cannot authorise whaling in its own EEZ by invoking Article 65 of the LOS Convention if it is also legally bound to a moratorium on whaling under the ICRW.

The sovereign rights of a coastal State (less comprehensive than sovereignty) in its EEZ are granted for "the purpose of exploring and exploiting, conserving and managing the natural resources" (Article 56(1)(a)). Articles 61-73 impose further limitations on these sovereign rights. Most importantly, Article 61 requires coastal States to ensure that the harvesting of living resources in their EEZs is aimed at producing the maximum sustainable yield and does not lead to over-exploitation. Article 62(1), on the other hand, requires coastal States to "inter alia ... promote the objective of optimum utilisation of the living resources in the exclusive economic zone without prejudice to article 61". The superiority of conservation above utilisation is common sense: without measures to avoid over-exploitation, there cannot be long-term utilisation.

Furthermore, Articles 63-67 of the LOS Convention lay down regimes for international cooperation for different categories of species whose ranges of distribution are not confined to a single coastal State's EEZ. Whales fall within two of these categories: highly migratory species (Article 64 and Annex I(17)) and marine mammals (Article 65).

Section 2 of Part VII of the LOS Convention implicitly recognises that all States have a right to engage in whaling on the high seas, subject among other things to their Treaty obligations as well as general obligations on the conservation (but not optimum utilisation) of the living resources of the high seas. Article 120 on Marine mammals stipulates that "Article 65 also applies to the conservation and management of marine mammals in the high seas".

A key feature of the LOS Convention's Part XV on Settlement of Disputes is compulsory third Party dispute settlement procedures entailing binding decisions, which can be brought unilaterally by a contracting Party against another contracting Party. However, one of the automatic limitations under Section 3 of Part XV covers disputes on the coastal State's regulation of whales within the EEZ (Article 297.3). The ICRW does not have a dispute settlement procedure of its own and Japan has used this absence to support its view that access to the compulsory dispute settlement procedure under the LOS Convention cannot be presumed.[5]

Convention on the Conservation of Migratory Species of Wild Animals

Australia is one of the current 91 Parties to the Convention on the Conservation of Migratory Species of Wild Animals (CMS)[6] (CMS 2007). The CMS aims to conserve migratory terrestrial, avian and marine species throughout their range of distribution. Various forms of regulatory action are possible, for instance prohibitions of intentional taking, habitat protection and the development of agreements that do not merely deal with conservation but also with management, thus encompassing utilisation (Articles I(1)(a), (f), (h) and (i); Articles III, IV and V). Various species of whales are included among the species threatened with extinction that are listed in Appendix I, as well as in Appendix II, which lists species that need or would significantly benefit from international cooperation by means of global or regional agreements.

Australia is one of the signatories to the non-legally binding Memorandum of Understanding (MOU) for the Conservation of Cetaceans and their Habitats in the Pacific Islands Region (CMS 2007), within the framework of Article IV(4) of the CMS. The MOU does not have a utilisation component (MOU paragraph 1). Among the reasons for Australia and New Zealand participating in, and probably even driving the negotiations

---

5   *Australia and New Zealand v Japan*, Arbitral Tribunal constituted under Annex VII of the United Nations Convention on the Law of the Sea, Award on Jurisdiction and Admissibility of 4 August 2000 at 38(i).

6   1651 UNTS 355.

of this MOU, is that its comprehensive approach to the conservation of whales in the Pacific is in part an alternative to the designation of a South Pacific Sanctuary under the Schedule to the ICRW (which would solely concern directed take). A proposal for such a Sanctuary failed to get the required three-quarters majority at the 56th Annual IWC Meeting (2004) and was not submitted again in 2005 or in 2006. As participation in the CMS by States in the Pacific is currently minimal, the MOU may eventually help to broaden participation in the CMS. While this could also affect voting patterns within the Conference of the Parties to the CMS, there is no indication that this is a major driver for the MOU initiative.

Convention on International Trade of Endangered Species of Wild Fauna and Flora

Australia is one of the current 168 Parties to the Convention on International Trade of Endangered Species of Wild Fauna and Flora (CITES),[7] the main objective of which is the protection of endangered species against over-exploitation through the regulation of international trade. Whales caught on the high seas are regarded as "trade" under CITES Articles 1(c) and (e). International trade in endangered species is regulated by means of listing species on three different Appendices, each requiring different regulation. All species of whales are listed on Appendix I or II. Norway, Japan and Iceland are all Parties to CITES. However, as each has exercised its right to use the objection procedure (Article XXIII), in relation to *Balaenopteridae* species (for example, minke, humpback, fin), they are exempt from trade restrictions on these whales. These reservations essentially keep the market for whale meat open among States that wish to trade.

Customary International Law

Can Australia rely on the development of customary international law to support its policy positions? While custom is nowadays a relatively minor source of international law, it has certainly not become obsolete. It can therefore not be ruled out that gradually more and more States take the view that they are under an international obligation not to engage in commercial whaling, or even any type of whaling. At a certain time State practice could become sufficiently uniform and widespread to transform this into a rule of customary international law, binding all States that have not persistently objected to it during the rule's formation. As the IWC still has several prominent pro-whaling members as well as a group of States that pursue a more pragmatic middle course, and in view of the fact that several non-Parties to the ICRW are currently engaged in whaling activities, this process is not likely to be completed in the near future, if ever.

---

7   993 UNTS 243.

In this respect, the principle of good faith, which is not laid down in the ICRW, is arguably a rule of customary international law. While IWC Resolution 2001-1 on Transparency within the International Whaling Commission focuses in particular on transparency, it does so in tandem with the principle of good faith (IWC 2001). While this resolution was adopted as a consequence of alleged vote-buying by pro-whaling States, it is intended to have a more general application. Accordingly, the IWC:

> STRESSES in particular the importance of adherence to the requirements of good faith and transparency in all activities undertaken by the IWC and in all activities by Contracting Governments in respect of their involvement with the IWC. (IWC 2001)

The resolution also makes reference to the *pacta sunt servanda* rule in Article 26 of the 1969 Vienna Convention on the Law of Treaties,[8] which is in fact directly linked to performance in good faith (Preamble). Perhaps even more important is the reference to Article 300 of the LOS Convention on 'Good faith and abuse of rights', which has significant implications for compulsory dispute settlement under the LOS Convention.

Current Considerations

The IWC in 2006

In 2006 the IWC was at a crossroads. The moratorium had been in place for 20 years, and membership recruitments meant that voting on the various issues, which had effectively become proxies for a vote on the moratorium itself, moved closer to a balance between the pro- and anti-whaling groupings. In 2006, for the first time in 24 years, the pro-whaling group gained a simple majority (by one vote) in the Meeting, resulting in the adoption of the St Kitts and Nevis Declaration which effectively confirmed the original (1946) IWC role as that of conservation rather than preservation of whale stocks (IWC 2006a). While the Declaration has no immediate consequences for the role or function of the Convention or the IWC, it can legitimately be claimed to be a contemporary statement of the intent of the majority of IWC Members. It is also an important indicator that Australia, the anti-whaling group and the moratorium on which they pin their hopes may be under significantly greater pressure in the future.

The longer term outcome from the so-called Tiger Room Meeting of predominantly pro-whaling delegates, which was held in St Kitts and Nevis following the passing of the Declaration, is more difficult to predict. The Japanese delegation has repeatedly used the term "normalise" to describe its agenda for the IWC (IWC 2006b), and its published Mission Statement for the follow-up meeting in February 2007 sets the aim of the conference as to discuss and put forward specific measures to resume the

---

8   1155 UNTS 332.

function of the IWC as a resource management organisation (Fisheries Agency of Japan 2007). It also notes "discussions at the Conference will be based on the [ICRW] which established the IWC together with the principles of sustainable use, science-based conservation and management, and respect for cultural diversity" (Fisheries Agency of Japan 2007: 1).

In spite of the fact that the tone of the Mission Statement is extremely conciliatory, stressing that the Conference aims to "build confidence and trust among participants" and the outcomes "may include a list of short-term and long-term recommendations to the IWC" (Fisheries Agency of Japan 2007), Australia, together with most of the anti-whaling States, chose to boycott it. Their view was that to attend would suggest tacit support for the normalisation agenda, which clearly includes sustainable harvesting of whales, and this is a step they were not prepared to take. The position of the USA is interesting. After initially announcing they would boycott the conference, Commissioner Hogarth subsequently indicated that the USA would attend, a move which provoked the ire of the NGOs, with one claiming:

> To its allies in the IWC the US decision may be taken as a betrayal ... To the media and the public ... the decision to attend may be interpreted as providing this unnecessary and misguided conference with a stamp of legitimacy. (Animal Welfare Institute, 2006)

In the event, the USA did not attend the Normalization Conference and the conference recommendations to be presented to the 2007 IWC meeting were extremely bland. The focus of the recommendations was on the achievement of consensus, however unashamedly in the context of sustainable harvesting of whales. It is difficult to see any effect on the IWC as a result of the Normalization meeting.

Australia's Role Within the IWC

If Australia is not prepared to entertain multilateral brokering of a position of normalisation, what will its role be within the IWC? Withdrawal is hardly an option as both Frost and the Task Force recognised the IWC as the most appropriate forum from which to pursue its strategic goals.

In the light of the St Kitts and Nevis Declaration and possible consequential normalising of the IWC, Australia must face the very real prospect that simply attending the annual IWC meeting and lobbying new and existing members to vote for whale preservation may not be enough to hold the anti-whaling position. However, the pro-whaling camp only barely have a simple majority now and is a long way from the three-quarters majority required to lift the moratorium. Therefore, this may not be the direction in which Japan chooses to lead the Tiger Room group. Particularly in view of the boycott by the anti-whaling States, it takes little imagination to see this group declare itself the only legitimate adherents to the ICRW.

Joji Morishita, the public face of the Japanese IWC delegation, has suggested that if the pro and anti-whaling groups within the IWC cannot "agree to disagree" on the cultural values aspects of the whaling issue, and abide by the strict wording of the ICRW, then those who cannot should withdraw from the organisation. He suggests splitting the IWC into two organisations; one to manage sustainable whaling, the other to totally protect whales (Morishita 2006). This seems to be a totally nonsensical idea as the notions are oxymoronic.

The recommendations of the meeting of the Tiger Room Group, and the subsequent debate in the 2007 IWC meeting will determine the next move.

Less-known Threats to Whale Populations

Most Australians would be surprised to hear that the major global threats to whale populations are likely to come from the effects of global warming. While such changes may be capable of eliminating all the great whales through destruction of their feeding habitat, there is little contemporary scientific certainty about the magnitude and temporal aspects of global warming (Branch and Butterworth 2001; Burns 2003). The next most serious threat comes from pollution of the oceans by organochlorines and heavy metals (Busbee et al 1999; Barsh 2001; Coghlan 2002). Together, these factors could kill many times the number of whales annually than all whaling operations combined. Ship strikes, accidental netting entanglement and anthropogenic underwater noise probably account for similar numbers of whale deaths as do whaling operations (IWC Bycatch sub-Committee 2004; NOAA 2004; Best et al 2005; WDCS 2005). The Conservation Committee of the IWC has identified these issues, but its reports to the main body of the IWC are being lost in the noise of claims and counter claims on Japanese scientific whaling (IWC 2006c, 2006d). The IWC has no mandate to regulate these issues and anti-whaling States such as Australia would achieve more success if they concentrated their efforts in other international fora.

The Role of NGOs

In 1997 the Task Force acknowledged the utility of the networks and expertise of conservation NGOs and recommended that the government promote dialogue and work with them to help achieve their mutually held objectives (Environment Australia 1997: xiii). In fact, since the early 1970s, conservation NGOs have been leading the anti-whaling movement as a flagship for their conservation agenda and have been responsible for shaping government and public opinion in Australia and worldwide. It is also true that whales provide outstanding publicity for fundraising by NGOs and have been exploited in this respect for a considerable period. The activities of the Sea Shepherd Society and Greenpeace vessels in conflict with the Japanese research fleet in the Southern Ocean, from which the government naturally distances itself (Turnbull 2007), have been well documented by the popular press. While their actions may raise concerns among the more conservative environmental NGOs, they have certainly also raised awareness of the cruelty issues and hardened public sentiment against the Japanese.

Conclusions

With the increase in numbers of whales sighted in Australian waters, and in particular near the coast, there has been rising public awareness of whales and whaling issues. As long as both conservation NGOs and governments focus public attention on the cruelty of whaling and away from the sustainability issue, public opinion will remain strongly anti-whaling, leading to the conclusion that there are a number of possible scenarios available to the factions.

It is possible that the status quo in the IWC will remain, with Japan continuing its scientific whaling, Iceland and Norway continuing commercial whaling under their reservation to the moratorium and some aboriginal subsistence whaling alongside.

Commercial whaling could recommence through a range of scenarios, from a withdrawal from the IWC by pro-whalers to harvest (almost certainly in accordance with the RMP), through to a move within the IWC in which a majority vote of pro-whaling States declares them the only *true* IWC members by remaining faithful to the principles of the ICRW. The former scenario is the one that is least desirable as it could eventuate in unregulated harvesting thereby complicating any chance of the anti-whaling States like Australia achieving their goals. The latter would require a three-quarters majority of Parties succeeding in setting aside the moratorium. The suggested possible removal of minkes and humpbacks from the IUCN Red List of Endangered Species could have an effect on this situation in the medium to long term (IUCN 2007). It is difficult to forecast how the demand for whale meat would be affected by an increase in availability, but it appears unlikely that short-term demand would rise to anywhere near the catch limit under the RMP of some 6000 animals based on current population estimates. In any case, whaling within the limits set by the RMP ensures that population sustainability is assured. Sustainability, however, depends on other factors in addition to harvesting effort.

Some scientific and popular science reports (for example, Burns 2003; Atkinson *et al* 2004; The Royal Society 2005; Kolbert 2006; Ruttimann 2006; Ainley *et al* 2007) indicate that the current rate of climate change, particularly aspects such as ocean acidification and global warming, will alter the marine environment in which cetaceans live. Although there is still a long way to go to achieve the level of certainty desired by policy-makers, early indications are that impacts may be profound in the long term, although with negative niches possibly being filled by opportunistically positive ones (for example, Ainley *et al* 2007). The Australian Government is being proactive in this regard by sponsoring marine mammal and climate change science to support its policy positions.

Australia has substantial domestic law in the form of the EPBC Act to help preserve whale stocks in its jurisdiction, yet it has not enforced the Act against the Japanese in the Antarctic EEZ, preferring instead a diplomatic approach. That approach does not stretch to attending the Japanese-sponsored Normalization Conference, however. Nor does it mean Australia will commence an international dispute settlement procedure against Japan or raise Japanese research (or even whales generally) in Antarctic fora such as Antarctic Treaty Consultative Meetings or the Commission for the Conservation of Antarctic Marine Living Resources (CCAMLR) meetings, despite the keystone species status of whales in Southern Ocean ecosystems (ASOC 2005b). Even though Australia is an outspoken Antarctic claimant, it would not wish to upset the status quo by broaching the subject of whales in Antarctic Treaty System forums. Here, whales have been legally and diplomatically eschewed through the recognition of high seas rights (Antarctic Treaty Article VI) and by direct reference to the primacy of the ICRW (CCAMLR Article VI). Despite all the main protagonists from the IWC being present at either ATCMs or CCAMLR Commission meetings, the topic is not mentioned as part of usual Antarctic business.

It is unlikely Australia will ever be in a position to change the ICRW to prevent lethal research, given that it requires consensus. The only scenario in which this could occur would involve all pro-whalers withdrawing from the Convention. This means that it is highly unlikely Australia will ever achieve its goal of a permanent international ban on commercial whaling. The Australian government has intractable beliefs, bolstered by perceived public approval and verified by the media and conservation NGOs. While successive Australian governments continue their role as moral entrepreneurs in the great whale debate, they will attract no-cost votes from their constituents – an attractive proposition indeed – while the futility of their efforts is likely to remain both heroic and irrelevant. Finally, its stated position is to take a strong diplomatic approach to issues raised inside the IWC, particularly Japanese scientific research, but it is clear that this in no way impinges on business as usual in other areas such as trade and security.

11

Emerging Issues of Australia's Sub-Antarctic Islands: Macquarie Island and Heard Island and McDonald Islands

Lorne K Kriwoken and Nick Holmes

Introduction

Macquarie Island (Macquarie) and Heard Island and McDonald Islands (HIMI) are spectacular, remote Australian sub-Antarctic islands located in the Southern Ocean (Figures 7 and 8). Macquarie and HIMI are home to an abundant and diverse array of unique sub-Antarctic wildlife. The vastness of the Southern Ocean and the isolation of these islands mean they provide crucial habitat for fauna, flora and microbial life. On Macquarie and HIMI 3.5 and 1.3 million seabirds annually breed and moult, largely represented by five penguin species (PWS 2006; AAD 2005c). Research indicates that 850,000 pairs of endemic Royal penguins are found on Macquarie and 1 million pair of Macaroni penguins on Heard Island. Endemic cormorant species are found on both islands. Of particular importance is the breeding habitat for threatened migratory species, such as the wandering albatross, with less than 20 breeding pairs known for Macquarie and only one for Heard Island (see Hall this volume). Seals represent the other major vertebrate and include Antarctic and sub-Antarctic fur seals, Southern elephant seals on HIMI, and New Zealand fur seals on Macquarie. One seventh of the world's population of elephant seals (80,000) are found on Macquarie (PWS 2006).

In addition to wildlife, HIMI and Macquarie provide remote outposts for a specialised suite of vegetation, notably on Heard Island, which has been affected by a dramatic glacial retreat of 70 to 80 per cent over the past 50 years. The cold, windy environment means slow growth and low profiles, with no trees. The tallest species are slow growing mega-herbs, and three endemic vascular species on Macquarie. Plant communities include cushion beds, herbfields and tussock grasslands.

Macquarie is 1500 kilometres (km) from Hobart, half way between Tasmania and Antarctica. Steep rocky beaches rise sharply to an undulating glacier-free plateau roughly 100-300 metres (m) above sea level, with Mt Hamilton the highest point at 433 m. Macquarie is 34 km long, up to 5 km wide with an area of 12,785 hectares (ha).

Heard Island (36,800 ha) and McDonald Islands (360 ha) are 4100 km from Perth and about 1700 km north of Antarctica. The French sub-Antarctic Kerguelen Islands are 380 km to the north west. The most prominent feature on Heard Island is Australia's tallest mountain and only active volcano, Big Ben, rising to 2750 m. Recent volcanic activity has in fact doubled the size of the McDonald Islands.

The aim of this chapter is to compare and contrast Macquarie and HIMI and provide an analysis of the most important and emerging issues over the next decade. Climate change is not considered here. The chapter begins with a brief outline of early discovery, industry and science. This is followed by an overview of legislative, institutional and management arrangements, with particular attention given to World Heritage status. Emerging issues are then presented. The management, scale and impact of human activities are introduced, focusing on both science activities and commercial tourism. This is followed by an assessment of quarantine, disease, alien introduction issues, commercial fishing pressures and enforcement problems. The chapter concludes with a comparative analysis of emergent issues for both sub-Antarctic groups.

Discovery, Industry and Science

Macquarie Island

Hasselburgh's 1810 expedition in the sealing brig *Perseverance* is credited with discovery of Macquarie and commencement of the sealing industry. Oil was derived from elephant seals, king and royal penguins until 1919. Historical sites and artefacts from seal and penguin harvesting work gangs are scattered around much of the island. Macquarie was visited by polar explorers such as Borchgrevink, Scott, Shackleton and Mawson on their way to Antarctica. These early activities inevitably introduced a wide range of alien species that have had, in some cases, disastrous consequences for the flora and fauna of the island.

In 1820 Bellingshausen collected the first known specimens of flora and fauna, followed by Scott in 1881 and Hamilton in 1885. The 1911-14 Australasian Antarctic Expedition (AAE) under Mawson established the first scientific research station and the first radio link between Australia and Antarctica. Mawson returned in 1930 with the British, Australia, New Zealand Antarctic Research Expedition (BANZARE) in 1930 to make collections and scientific observations. It was largely Mawson's influence that forced the cessation of oil gathering and the proclamation of Macquarie as a wildlife sanctuary in 1933.

In 1948 the Australian Government established and staffed a permanent scientific base for Australian National Antarctic Research Expeditions

(ANARE) personnel (now know as the Australian Antarctic Program (AAP)). The Australian Antarctic Division (AAD), a division of the Commonwealth Department of the Environment and Water Resources, operates the station today. AAD undertakes a range of science activities including upper atmospheric science, biology, climatology, geology and zoology. Parks and Wildlife Service (PWS) began operating research and management programs in 1972. The research station occupies a low flat isthmus at the north of the island. There is no airstrip, with access only by sea, usually by inflatable boats. There are no landing facilities for ships. Helicopters are used to resupply the station from ships anchored off the northern eastern coast.

Heard Island and McDonald Islands

Kemp, a British explorer, first sighted HIMI in 1833 and 20 years later an American, Captain Heard, rediscovered the islands. The sealing era began in 1855 largely with American gangs. *HMS Challenger* paid a brief visit in 1874. In 1929 BANZARE visited and the scientific era commenced in earnest in 1947, when Australia made a proclamation over the islands (Bush 1982). There were no protests made by the United States at the time and today they recognise Australia's sovereignty over HIMI. ANARE occupied HIMI between 1947 and 1955 and then there was a 10-year hiatus until the South Indian Ocean Expedition in 1965 made the first ascent of Big Ben. The adjoining McDonald Islands were only first landed in 1971. Scientific surveys by ANARE commenced in 1980. Extensive marine surveys (benthic trawls) were carried out in the early 1990s targeting benthic fish (Meyer *et al* 2000: 19). The first commercial Antarctic tourist cruise ship, *Lindblad Explorer*, first visited in 1981 (Keage 1981: 21-3). ANARE visits have been largely infrequent and from the 1950s to the 1980s the *MV Kista Dan*, *MV Thalla Dan* and the *MS Nella Dan* were used as expedition ships. Most recently the *RV Aurora Australis* has supported AAD activities, including a summer party in 2003-04.

Legislative, Institutional and Management Arrangements

Macquarie Island

The island was declared a Tasmanian Wildlife Sanctuary in 1933, a Tasmanian State Reserve in 1972, and an international Biosphere Reserve in 1977 under the United Nations Educational, Scientific and Cultural Organisation's (UNESCO) Man and the Biosphere Program. It was declared a restricted area in 1979 thereby requiring all visitors to acquire permits from the managing authority. The World Heritage Committee inscribed Macquarie and waters out to 12 nautical miles (nm) on the World Heritage List for its outstanding geo-conservation significance in 1997. Macquarie satisfied two of four natural criteria as a location that is "an outstanding

Figure 7 Macquarie Island

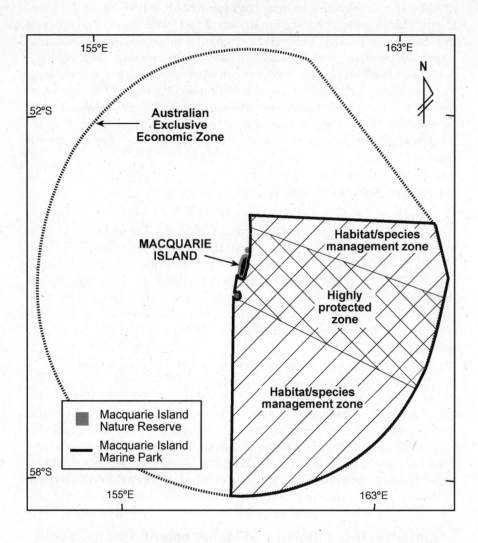

example representing major stages of the Earth's evolutionary history, including the record of life, significant on-going geological processes in the development of landforms, or significant geomorphic or physiographic features" and a site "containing superlative natural phenomena or areas of exceptional outstanding natural beauty and aesthetic importance" (PWS 2006: 4-5). Macquarie is unique in the world in that it is composed entirely of oceanic crust and rocks from the earth's mantle where rocks from the mantle are being actively exposed above sea level (PWS 2006: 4-5). The inscription on the World Heritage List did not include its rich fauna and flora values. There is a curious situation whereby the seemingly secure geological structure of the island is in a sense protected as a key natural criteria for its World Heritage listing. In contrast the biological values, which are far more at risk, were not included in the listing.

In October 1999, the Macquarie Island Marine Park, representing over 16.2 million ha, was declared to protect the unique and vulnerable marine ecosystems of the south-eastern portion of the Macquarie Island Region (Environment Australia 2001). The Marine Park was divided into three zones: a Highly Protected Zone (assigned International Union for Conservation of Nature (IUCN) category Ia) and two Habitat/Species Management Zones (IUCN category IV) either side of the Highly Protected Zone (Figure 7).

The State Government of Tasmania, through the Tasmanian Parks and Wildlife Service and the Nature Conservation Branch, a division of the Department of Tourism, Arts and the Environment (DTAE), are responsible for research and management of Macquarie and the surrounding waters to three nm. The Australian government has responsibility for the management of the area from three nm to the 200 nm Exclusive Economic Zone (EEZ) (Environment Australia 2001).

Conservation legislation for Macquarie is present at both the Federal and State levels and includes, *inter alia*, the *Environment Protection and Biodiversity Conservation Act* 1999 (Cth) (EPBC Act), the *Nature Conservation Act* 2002 (Tas) and the *National Parks and Reserves Management Act* 2002 (Tas). Macquarie is managed in accordance with the Macquarie Island Nature Reserve and World Heritage Area Management Plan 2006 (PWS 2006). A management objective of the Plan permits tourist visits under strictly controlled conditions and allows visitors to experience the island's natural values.

Heard Island and McDonald Islands

HIMI is an Australian External Territory subject to the *Heard Island and McDonald Islands Act* 1953 (Cth). The territory was placed on the Register of the National Estate in 1983. Management of the Territory is under the *Heard Island and McDonald Islands Environment Protection and Management Ordinance* 1987 (Cth). The HIMI territory is managed as an IUCN category Ia as a strict nature reserve since 1996, in accordance with the provisions of the Heard Island Wilderness Reserve Management Plan made under the Ordinance. In 2005 the Heard Island and McDonald Islands Marine Reserve Management Plan was finalised (AAD 2005). The Australian Fisheries Management Authority (AFMA) declared an additional one nm buffer zone to prohibit commercial fishing. Fishing is prohibited in the 12 nm zone surrounding the Wilderness Reserve and although fishing vessels are allowed to enter the one nm buffer zone, they cannot conduct fishing activities. Fishing is therefore prohibited in the 6488 square km area that makes up the Wilderness Reserve and the surrounding buffer zone. The Australian Fishing Zone (AFZ) and the Australian EEZ extend from 12 to 200 nm. The boundary to the northwest of HIMI is subject to the

Australia France Maritime Delimitation Agreement. Commonwealth of Australia laws that extend to external territories also apply. HIMI also falls under the jurisdiction of the Convention on the Conservation of Antarctic Marine Living Resources (CCAMLR) and is located in CCAMLR Statistical Division 58.5.2.

HIMI was inscribed on the World Heritage List in 1997 because of its outstanding natural universal values. The World Heritage nomination states:

> HIMI is a unique wilderness, a place of spectacular beauty which contains outstanding examples of biological and physical processes continuing in an essentially undisturbed environment. Significant biological processes include colonisation and speciation, while the island groups' physical processes provide valuable indicators of the role of crustal plates in the formation of ocean basins and continents and of atmospheric and oceanic warming. (AAD 2005c: 4)

The HIMI nomination met two natural criteria: "an outstanding example representing major stages of the Earth's evolutionary history, including the record of life, significant on-going geological processes in the development of landforms, or significant geomorphic or physiographic features" and "an outstanding example representing significant ongoing ecological and biological processes in the evolution and development of terrestrial, freshwater, coastal and marine ecosystems and communities of plants and animals". The Strategic Assessment of Nationally Important Wetlands Managed by the Commonwealth found that HIMI satisfied six of the Ramsar criteria for wetlands of international importance (Watkins and Jaensch 2003).

The HIMI Marine Reserve was declared by proclamation under s 344 of the EPBC Act on 16 October 2002 for the purpose of protecting the conservation values of HIMI and the adjacent unique and vulnerable marine ecosystems. A total of 85 per cent of the Reserve was declared as a highly protected marine reserve and 15 per cent a conservation zone, covering 6.5 million ha. The Marine Reserve includes the World Heritage listed island, the territorial sea, a marine protected area and extends in parts to the boundary of the 200 nm EEZ (Figure 8). AAD is the responsible Commonwealth agency.

The HIMI Management Plan incorporates the Parks Australia Strategic Planning and Performance Assessment Framework. Outcomes are developed in Key Result Areas including: natural heritage management; cultural heritage management; joint management (not applicable to HIMI); visitor management and park use; stakeholders and partnerships; business management; and biodiversity knowledge management (AAD 2005c: 9). The Plan includes an aim or list of aims that describe the desired results of Reserve management activity and a series of prescriptions that control activities and strategies for managing the Reserve to meet the aim(s).

Figure 8 Heard Island and McDonald Islands

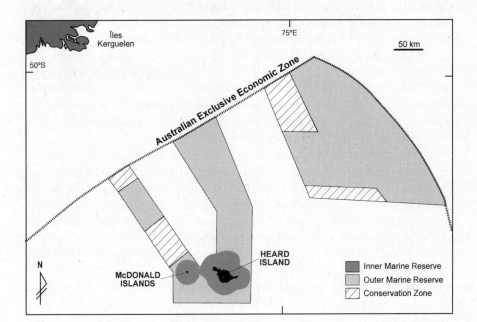

Emerging Issues

Human Use: Science and Management

Science has long been supported by AAD on Macquarie, most notably since 1948 with the construction of a base at the northern end on the isthmus. The station consists of several buildings for science and support, including laboratories, living quarters, trade workshops and the Australian Bureau of Meteorology weather station. Several vehicles are used on station including four wheel drive "quad" bikes, tractors, a forklift and a bulldozer. The vast majority of science programs are undertaken in the summer, with up to 40 people living and working on the island, dropping to around 20 over winter. The island is resupplied once a year. From the station, access to the remainder of the island is by foot via a series of tracks, supported by irregular small boat operations, using five field huts with limited facilities.

All human activity on Macquarie (science, management programs and tourism) is required to be consistent with the primary objectives of environmental conservation outlined for the island (PWS 2006). Thus, proposed human activities require permits, may require environmental impact assessment, and are subject to zoning and activity restrictions. Researchers are required to obtain permission and approval from Federal and State government bodies, (including the Antarctic Animal Ethics Committee if vertebrate animals are involved), PWS, plus approvals from relevant academic bodies where appropriate. Within DTAE, approvals are assessed by the Macquarie Island Research Activities Group (MIRAG), which consists of members from the Nature Conservation Branch and PWS. Approvals can take up to 18 months, and include public scrutiny of proposed projects. The approval may require an environmental evaluation outlining how the proposed activities would impact the values of the reserve, including World Heritage values, how they would be alleviated, and justification for the activities (PWS 2006).

Management zoning has also been adopted on Macquarie to protect the island from human impact. Zone A – Services Zone, covers a portion of the isthmus and allows buildings, facilities and scientific equipment. The objective is to concentrate human impact and activity in and around the station limits. Zone B – Limited Access Zone, includes the terrestrial area of the main island and seastacks and allows limited facilities such as walking tracks and field huts for management, scientific or educational tourism use. Zone C – Marine Zone (State waters), extends from the low water mark to 3 nm and the Commonwealth waters to 12 nm. The management plan only applies to those waters to 3 nm in the State reserve. Special Management Areas are designated in the Reserve to further pro-tect natural or historical values. Tourism Management Areas (TMAs) are located at the isthmus, Sandy Bay and Lusitania Bay and are discussed in the next section. Limited access is provided for educational tourism associated with summer only commercial tourism activities.

The presence of ANARE on HIMI has been more sporadic than Macquarie. Except from 1947 to 1954 when there was a permanent human presence, research expeditions have been summer based and few in num-bers. This pattern is likely to continue as there is no call for a permanent station. In addition, the remote geographical location of HIMI means that even a summer expedition has very high costs. The last summer expedition was in 2003-04 when 28 scientists and support staff visited. Expeditions are planned to occur every three years.

Expedition planning now has to consider the requirements of the HIMI Management Plan, which divides the Reserve into seven zones (main use, visitor access, heritage, wilderness, restricted, inner marine and outer marine). Each zone is designated a specific IUCN category to ensure the protection of areas susceptible to the impacts of human activities. The main use zone is at Atlas Cove and Spit Bay and supports access and support for long-term facilities. The visitor access zone areas are at Atlas Cove, Spit Bay and Long Beach. These three areas support short-term, land-based visitor activities such as commercial tourism. Low-impact activities include walking, photography and wildlife observation. Atlas Cove and the ANARE Station have been recognised as having heritage significance in the Plan. The Atlas Cove, Heard Island Cultural Heritage

Management Plan was prepared in 2005 (Vincent 2005) by AAD to identify the heritage significance of the site and to guide future management. This Plan is especially important given that past indiscretions may have compromised its heritage significance (Kriwoken *et al* 1989). Human activities in the wilderness and restricted zones are tightly controlled.

Human Use: Tourism

HIMI and Macquarie present opportunities for tourists to experience unique wildlife and plant communities, spectacular scenery and rare historic artefacts (Kriwoken *et al* 2006; see also Johnson and Kriwoken this volume). Commercial tourism is guided by management plans requiring minimisation of impacts from visitation over the short austral summer. Tourism to these regions is deemed a legitimate use, with management of this activity balanced against the primary objectives of environmental conservation (AAD 1995c, 2005; PWS 2006). Visiting these areas requires a significant logistical undertaking and, to date, visits have been limited to private yachts and commercial expedition-style operations carrying fewer than 100 passengers, with a high level of interpretation by lecturers and guides. Tourism to Macquarie and HIMI is inextricably linked to the growth in Antarctic tourism. However, while visitor numbers exceeded 49,000 in the Antarctic in 2005-06 (IAATO 2007), visitation to HIMI and Macquarie is likely to remain low because of the high cost, notoriously bad weather and the long sea passages on these trips (Cessford and Dingwall 1994; Kriwoken and Rootes 2000; Kriwoken *et al* 2006).

Tourism began on Macquarie in 1990. Since that time over 5000 tourists have visited, averaging 350 per season. Macquarie is usually part of longer expeditions to the Ross Sea in Antarctica or to New Zealand's sub-Antarctic islands (Sanson 1994; Cessford and Dingwall 1994). Similar to science and management programs, tourism on Macquarie is subject to permitting, zoning and activity restriction. Tourists are offered experiences within three TMAs, where wildlife and landscape are considered more resilient to visitation. Landings are permitted at two TMAs. The Sandy Bay TMA includes penguin colonies and fields of megaherb. The ANARE station TMA allows tourists to interact with scientists and support personnel living at the station, and visit cultural sites, such as digesters used to render down seal blubber. The Lusitania Bay TMA allows zodiac cruising adjacent to a spectacular king penguin colony.

Strict guidelines exist for Macquarie tourism in order to minimise environmental impact. A quota of 750 visitors per summer is in force. Tourist operators must obtain a permit outlining specific performance criteria associated with safety and environmental controls. Spatial restrictions are guided by the TMAs and restrictions apply to the maximum numbers ashore (60 at Sandy Bay, 100 at the isthmus) with shore parties required to be no larger than 15 people (including at least one guide) (PWS 2004). Only a small number of activities are offered, such as short guided walks, photography and wildlife observation. Other adventure activities conducted in Antarctica, such as ocean kayaking and diving, are not allowed. Within each TMA, impact is further managed through a code of conduct stipulating minimum approach distances when viewing wildlife (PWS 2004), zodiac operation guidelines that include speed limitations near wildlife concentrations, boardwalks over sensitive sites, and guidance and interpretation offered by PWS staff.

To date, tourism has had a negligible impact on Macquarie when compared to the research and management activities undertaken by PWS and AAD (PWS 2006). Nevertheless, research into human activities, including tourism, is ongoing (Holmes *et al* 2003, 2005), and long-term monitoring of tourism is considered a research priority (PWS 2006).

Similar to Macquarie, HIMI offers visitors unique wildlife viewing opportunities, cultural insights into the sealing era and a chance to view a remote and foreboding landscape. However, unlike Macquarie, which is included as a part of expeditions to the Ross Sea or New Zealand's sub-Antarctic islands, HIMI is not usually included in these itineraries and consequently tourist visits are few. Landing on Heard Island has only occurred 245 times (includes tourism, scientific and sealing expeditions) and McDonald Islands only twice (AAD 2005c). Those few tourist visits primarily include private expeditions in ocean-going yachts, amateur ham radio operators and mountaineering parties undertaking an ascent of Big Ben. HIMI has also been irregularly visited by commercial tourist operators as a part of a semi-circumnavigation of Antarctica. Similar to Macquarie, HIMI has strict guidelines for human activities. Commercial tourism visits are restricted to the visitor access zone areas.

Quarantine, Disease and Alien Introduction

Introduction of alien, or non-native, species or disease by human activities represent one of the largest potential conservation threats to Antarctic and sub-Antarctic environments (Frenot *et al* 2005; Jones *et al* 2003). The consequences of introductions can significantly alter the ecology of these environments, with native plants and animals at risk from increased competition or predation. HIMI and Macquarie both share strict precautionary measures to prevent introduction to alien species, however they contrast in the previous introductions of alien species, and subsequent impact on the islands.

On Macquarie, a host of alien species were introduced for domestic purposes. There are three plant, 28 invertebrate (amongst the highest recorded on any sub-Antarctic Island), plus three terrestrial vertebrate (ship rat, house mouse and European rabbit) alien species (Frenot *et al* 2005; PWS 2006). There are three other alien bird species (redpoll, European starling and mallard), however they are likely self-introduced. It is unknown how many marine invertebrate alien species have been introduced (Lewis *et al* 2003). By far the species with the greatest negative impact was the cat. The avifauna on Macquarie evolved without such a predator. Cats were estimated to take 60,000 seabirds per year (PWS 2006) and have since been removed following an intense five-year eradication effort. Rabbits also present a significant impact, with increased grazing reducing habitat for seabirds, increasing erosion and altering the land-scape. Since 1978, the myxoma virus was used as a control measure to reduce rabbit numbers from 150,000 to 16,000 in 2002 (Copson and Whinam 2001). In 2005, eradication of rats, rabbits and mice began, model-led in part on the successful aerial baiting program to remove Norwegian rats from New Zealand's sub-Antarctic Campbell Island (Towns and Broome 2003).

By comparison, Heard Island has suffered considerably less than Mac-quarie in terms of alien species, and hence has a very high conservation value. A number of species were introduced to Heard Island during the sealing days (AAD 2005c), although only two alien plants and two alien invertebrates are known to exist. No known alien species are thought to exist on McDonald Islands, thus supporting its extremely high conser-vation value (AAD 2005c).

Given the high potential threat of introducing alien species, quarantine practices to Macquarie and HIMI are strict. Science program support has been recognised as a significant vector for alien species transmission, such as seed dispersal on the clothing of AAP expeditioners (Whinam *et al* 2005). As a consequence, AAD expeditioner clothing excludes the use of Velcro (Clifton 2004). Tourism is also recognised as a significant vector for alien species or disease transmission, particularly given other sub-Antarctic locations may also be visited on a single voyage, potentially translocating new species (Lewis *et al* 2003; Frenot *et al* 2005). Consequently, standard procedures for the International Association of Antarctica Tourism Opera-tors (IAATO) include disinfecting boots and the vacuuming of pockets for seed propagules (IAATO 2005c).

Similarly, transmission of disease to native populations is recognised as a significant threat to Antarctic flora and fauna (COMNAP 2003). Avian influenza or Newcastle disease could have dramatic consequences for native bird populations on HIMI and Macquarie. Strict guidelines exist for AAD operations in regards to animal products that can be brought to the islands that could inadvertently operate as vectors for disease trans-mission. For instance, no avian products (that is, eggs or other poultry products) are to be taken to Heard Island (Clifton 2004). In addition, response plans exist in case of unusual animal mortality that may be a consequence of potential disease outbreaks (AAD 2004c). Similar guide-lines exist in regards to plant products. Because of native Brassica on HIMI and Macquarie, other members of this family, such as cauliflower and broccoli, must not be taken ashore on HIMI (AAD 2005c) or beyond station limits on Macquarie (PWS 2006).

Commercial Fishing

Australia's Oceans Policy provides a framework of integrated and ecosystem-based planning and management for Australia's marine jurisdictions (Australia 1998: 2). As part of the Policy, Australia has developed Regional Marine Plans based on large marine ecosystems. The first plan produced was the South-east Regional Marine Plan, which included over 2 million square kilometres off southern New South Wales, eastern South Australia, Victoria, Tasmania and Macquarie Island. An assessment report on the resources of Macquarie was produced in 2002 (NOO 2002). From November 1994 to April 1996 an Australian fishing company conducted exploratory mid-water pelagic trawling targeting Patagonian toothfish (NOO 2002: 10-12). Longline fishing is banned from the Macquarie AFZ to protect species such as the endangered wandering albatross (see Hall this volume). In order to gain a better understanding of fish stocks, AFMA set up a fishery assessment group, followed by a Macquarie Island Fishery Interim Management Policy. A total allowable catch of 510 tonnes of Patagonian toothfish was set in 2000 with conditions including: trained observers, collecting fishery and environmental data, and information on bycatch and gear used (NOO 2002: 13). In addition, a Sub-Antarctic Fisheries Bycatch Action Plan was developed (AFMA 2001) to account for direct and indirect impacts on the marine environment. The Plan extends to HIMI as well. The long-term potential yield for the Macquarie fishery is unknown at present. The potential for commercial fisheries is said to be very low given the size of the shelf, rough seas and the distance from ports (Scott 2000: 33).

Commercial fishing surrounding the Îles Kerguelen region, which includes HIMI, began in the early 1970s with limited exploratory fishing starting in 1975 (Meyers *et al* 2000: 41). In the 1997-98 season, 2417 tonnes of Patagonian toothfish and 67 tonnes of icefish were legally caught in the Australian EEZ surrounding HIMI. Commercial fishing by Australian companies commenced in 1997, regulated under the *Fisheries Management Act* 1991 and administered by AFMA. In 2001 a draft "Strategic Assessment Report – Heard Island and McDonald Islands Fishery" and the draft "Heard Island and McDonald Islands Fishery Management Plan" were released for public comment. In April 2002 the Assessment of the Heard Island and McDonald Islands Fishery was released (Environment Australia 2002). The assessment recognised that the management was sufficiently precautionary and capable of controlling, monitoring and enforcing the fishery. A significant concern was raised regarding the illegal, unreported and unregulated (IUU) fishing for Patagonian toothfish (Fallon and Kriwoken 2004; see also Stephens and Boer, and Lugten this volume). Illegal longline fishing for Patagonian toothfish has occurred in the northern and central areas of the Kerguelen Plateau and the north-eastern region of the HIMI AFZ (Meyers *et al* 2000: 41).

Petuna Seafoods Ltd from Devonport, Tasmania was granted a licence in 2003 to operate a longline vessel fishing for Patagonian toothfish off HIMI. The operational conditions were considered some of the most stringent for any vessel operating in CCAMLR waters and included: fishing in the winter, retention of fish offal and waste, use of streamers, setting of longlines at night and specific requirements on the sinking speed of the longlines (Robertson 2005: 18). Over the 2003 and 2004 winter seasons nearly 3 million hooks were set and not one seabird was caught through incidental bycatch (see Hall this volume). Robertson (2005: 19) has argued that an adaptive management approach has worked effectively in this fishery to ensure that conservation measures have been met and fisheries operations are allowed to continue.

Under the EPBC Act, s 147 requires that Strategic Environmental Assessments (SEA) for all fisheries managed by the Commonwealth of Australia be completed by mid-2005. The HIMI Fishery Management Plan has been subject to SEA, however the new draft HIMI Marine Reserve Management Plan has not been subject to a similar assessment. Marsden (2005) has argued that whilst the two Management Plans are regulated under different legislative provisions (s 147 for fisheries plans, s 146 is discretionary for the marine reserve plan), they should both be subject to the SEA process.

Concluding Remarks

Australia's Macquarie and HIMI are spectacular, isolated sub-Antarctic environments. As World Heritage areas they both represent outstanding natural universal values. As such, Australia has both international and national obligations to protect, conserve and interpret those natural values to present and future generations. Although remote islands in the Southern Ocean, they both face growing pressure from a number of sources over the next decade. Both islands share some of these pressures, some are unique.

The presence of AAD will directly impact how science, planning and management will be supported at both islands. AAD has considered reducing or removing its science activities and logistic support on Macquarie. Logistic support for AAD researchers on Macquarie includes a voyage at the beginning and end of the summer program to drop off and pick up scientists and support staff, including a voyage dedicated to resupply. However, since 2003 this has been reduced to one voyage (PWS 2006). This requires scientists to either arrange alternative transport with a commercial tourist ship or spend a full year on the island. This is occurring at the same time as an air link to Antarctica is being established to reduce the time taken by expeditioners to reach the continent. Future changes in AAD priority or funding for research on Macquarie, including removing all support, could significantly alter the type of research undertaken on

Macquarie. If AAD ceases to support work there, an alternative could be the increased use of logistical support from the private sector. In contrast, AAD will continue to support summer only expeditions to HIMI as funding allows. This is likely to occur every three years at this stage.

Commercial tourism to both groups is quite different. Macquarie is an integral stop off for Antarctic tourism expeditions heading south to the Ross Sea or the New Zealand sub-Antarctic islands. Tourism on Macquarie is generally considered well managed and offers a representative experience of the island without significant effects. Presently, tourism is highly regulated and the numbers do not seem to adversely affect the flora or fauna. Management guidelines ensure that visitor numbers are limited and their onshore activities tightly controlled. Onshore visits are for short periods only, yet the sense of isolation and remoteness of the location, and the rewarding views of large numbers of wildlife, appear to have a profound effect on visitors. Tourism to HIMI is quite different because it is not part of a regular itinerary to Antarctica and it is more geographically remote than Macquarie. It is likely that tourism will continue on a very small scale with occasional visits from operators offering a circumnavigation of Antarctica. Private yachts and mountaineering parties are likely to remain few in number and low in impact.

The issue of quarantine, disease and alien introduction is a high priority issue for both Macquarie and HIMI. Strict measures are in place to prevent alien introductions and impact on the islands. Macquarie has obviously been subject to a host of alien species and eradication is a top priority for managers. The cat eradication program is an excellent example of a long-term, strategic undertaking by the Tasmanian PWS but the result has been an unforeseen explosion in rabbit populations, which are now having a devastating effect on the terrestrial ecosystem. Heard Island is quite different for a number of reasons. First, it is an External Territory under Federal jurisdiction and does not suffer from Federal-State tensions in the same way that Macquarie does. This tension is presently manifest in the inability of the two jurisdictions to agree on responsibility for funding eradication programs. In order to resolve this tension, it might be timely to consider if the Tasmanian Government should relinquish jurisdiction over Macquarie and transfer responsibility to the Australian Government. This might ensure that adequate funding would be made available to secure the long-term sustainability of the island. Secondly, HIMI has limited numbers of alien species and therefore has a high conservation value. McDonald Islands has only recorded two landings by humans and represents, with Prince Edward Island, the only sub-Antarctic islands with no known alien species.

Commercial fishing for Patagonian toothfish is a recent resource extraction activity off the islands. In both locations, trawling appears preferable to longlining because of incidental mortality of seabirds that occurs from longlining. However, trawling can also impact the composition of benthic communities. Greater research needs to be undertaken on marine ecology and toothfish biology before expanding the quotas for the Patagonian toothfish fishery. Current estimates of toothfish biomass are uncertain and are likely to remain so until further research is completed. AFMA and others need to investigate the extent that HIMI and islands in the Kerguelen region share a single or straddling Patagonian toothfish stock. Once this is undertaken, then the stock assessment must take into account fishing pressure from nearby areas. At similar latitudes there are active squid, crab and myctophid (lanternfish) fisheries and these may be exploited in the future. The concern over IUU fishing is most apparent in the HIMI fishery, given the remote location of the EEZ and the problem of surveillance and enforcement (see Lugten, and Stephens and Boer, this volume). Most recently there has been a heightened awareness of the need for increased surveillance and enforcement in Australia's Southern Ocean EEZ. In the 2005 Federal budget AFMA received an additional AUD$10.1 million from 2006 to 2009 to increase its efforts in protecting Australia's EEZ in the Southern Ocean. The Australian Customs Service (ACS) also received an additional AUD$120.9 million. AFMA and ACS will jointly support armed patrols in the HIMI EEZ to deter IUU fishing and protect Australia's commercial fishing industry.

The final point relates to regional marine planning and possible boundary expansion. Australia's Oceans Policy includes Macquarie in the South-east Regional Marine Plan. This process has been a very useful exercise in data gathering and interpretation for large marine ecosystems. However, there are a few anomalies with respect to World Heritage area boundaries and recent designations of marine reserves. The Macquarie Island World Heritage area and the Australian Register of the National Estate only include waters out to 12 nm, yet the Macquarie Island Marine Park includes some 16.2 million ha surrounding the island. Similarly, the HIMI World Heritage area and the Register only include the waters out to 12 nm, yet the HIMI Marine Reserve covers 6.5 million ha. The examination of the possible extension of the World Heritage area boundaries to include the marine area from 12 to 200 nm is warranted. At HIMI two significant plans have been recently released: the HIMI Fishery Plan and the HIMI Marine Reserve Management Plan. Only the Fishery Plan has been subject to a SEA. It might be prudent to instigate a regional marine planning process for HIMI to integrate these two plans and possibly subject the Marine Reserve Management Plan to a SEA process. A regional marine plan could integrate sectoral commercial fisheries interests and conservation requirements and would be binding on all Commonwealth agencies.

Acknowledgements

The authors thank the School of Geography and Environmental Studies, the Antarctic Climate and Ecosystems Cooperative Research Centre, University of Tasmania and Sustainable Tourism Cooperative Research Centre for their support. A special word of thanks to the editors for their comments and suggestions. All errors and omissions remain the responsibility of the authors.

12

A Caution on the Benefits of Research:
Australia, Antarctica and Climate Change

Aynsley Kellow

This chapter considers the place of climate change in Australia's Antarctic agenda, arguing that since the prohibition on minerals exploitation introduced with the Protocol on Environmental Protection to the Antarctic Treaty (Madrid Protocol), this issue provides an important justification for Australian engagement with the continent, and especially a justification for maintaining the expense of a substantial presence. It presents arguments to support this conclusion, but also argues that the significance lies more in terms of the impact of Antarctica on Australia's climate than in terms of Australia's impact on Antarctica through the emission of greenhouse gases (GHGs). It presents a brief case study of climate change in the south-west of Western Australia to highlight the kind of impacts which might be better understood through Antarctic research. The chapter also sounds a note of caution that the benefits from such research are problematic and unlikely to result in a clear justification that expenditure on scientific research in Antarctica will necessarily be seen as representing an acceptable investment. In other words, some commitment to the ideals of pure scientific research is still likely to be necessary to maintain the commitment of successive Australian governments.

Some might be surprised at the statement that Australia's climate change connection to Antarctica is primarily not to do with the impact of Australia's activities on the continent such as might constitute a breach of its Antarctic Treaty obligations, but that concern can be quickly allayed, even if it is admitted that global anthropogenic change might impact upon it in some way. There is currently evidence of both ice loss from the Western Antarctic shelf, and gain on the Eastern Antarctic shelf, and it is not clear whether either of these changes represents damage. First, in a physical sense, Australia's contribution to the problem is so small as to be indistinguishable from background variability, but it is also the case that there is little legal or moral basis for arguing that Australia bears responsibility for any resulting changes.

It is difficult to see that Australia could be held to be in breach of its obligation under the Antarctic Treaty relating to "the preservation and conservation of living resources in Antarctica" (Article IX. 1(f)), especially because the rather weak and vague obligation under Article X is related only to activity "in Antarctica" that is contrary to the principles or purposes of the Treaty. Australia's emission of greenhouse gases could hardly be construed as being an activity "in Antarctica", and merely declining to accede to a protocol to an international convention in itself could hardly be construed to constitute such an action.

Moreover, any purely moral claim on Australia would also appear to be rather weak, since it is one of the few States close to meeting its allocated target under the Kyoto Protocol to the United Nations Framework Convention on Climate Change (UNFCCC 2007), with some being substantially over target. Not only do Australia's annual emissions barely rate in the global scheme of things, but the Kyoto approach also masks the fact that elevated carbon dioxide levels in the atmosphere is not a matter of annual emissions (of flows) but one of contributions to accumulation (of stocks) which occurs because carbon dioxide is thought to have a residence time in the atmosphere of 100 years. The responsibility for any damage caused to Antarctica is thus a function of historical contributions to accumulated carbon dioxide, to which the United Kingdom and Germany have made the greatest contribution, rather than the United States (the highest contemporary emitter).

Australia's interest in Antarctica is therefore more about what climate change refracted through physical changes in Antarctica might mean for it, rather than what its contribution to climate change might mean for Antarctica. Or, perhaps more accurately, Australia's climate variability – whatever its cause – has much to do with what happens in Antarctica and the Southern Ocean.

I shall return to this point in looking at climate variability in Western Australia, but first I shall set out the case that climate science now represents a significant part of the justification for the science investment in Antarctica, and thus for the Australian Antarctic Program.

Justifying the Australian Antarctic Project

Much of the early history of human activity in Antarctica is of feats almost archetypical of the "golden age" of exploration, of men exploring the unknown white continent, seemingly in pursuit of knowledge. Elsewhere, empire usually followed exploration, but the riches of Antarctica were much less obvious than those of Gambia, and the justification for the commitment of substantial resources to the exploration of the Antarctic continent by successive Australian governments remains problematic (Doyle and Kellow 1995).

As one would expect, the rationale for an Australian presence in Antarctica has evolved over time. For example, during the 1960s, Hanessian summed up Australia's "traditional" position towards Antarctica in the following terms: "Australia's active Antarctic policy is based on considerations of security, prestige, science and possible economic gain. It has strong bipartisan support in Parliament and in the press" (Hanessian 1965: 14). It is fair to say that the security driver for Australian policy has diminished greatly in the intervening period, thanks in part to the prohibition on military activities in the Antarctic Treaty, but also because of a general decline in naval power (save perhaps that of the United States) in the unipolar world that emerged with the end of the Cold War. There is now a greatly diminished threat to Australia's shipping trade from the prospect of Antarctic-based sea power, and Australia's relatively greater economic integration with Asia also makes it less concerned with the small residual risk, as the shipping routes important to its international trade on balance lie elsewhere. Thus, Wace argued that in the early 1980s any strategic benefit that could be derived from the Australian sovereignty claim had been lost. Moreover, the Australian Navy had no ice-strengthened vessels and there was little or no expertise in ship handling or other naval activities in ice-strewn seas (Wace 1983: 8).

Prestige is arguably still a factor, but the economic driver is now also much diminished. The two major economic reasons for an economic interest in Antarctica can be summed up as fish and minerals. The Southern Ocean is enormously rich biologically and one of the most productive marine environments on earth with massive amounts of krill and other species attesting to the rich nutrients the marine environment provides. Second, the possibilities of exploiting newly discovered non-renewable resources, such as oil, gas and other minerals, were an early attraction. This Australian interest dates back to at least 1921, when the then Prime Minister, WM Hughes, stated in a cablegram to a representative in London:

> Prime value Antarctic from economic stand-point as evident today apparently lies in animal life, principally fish, seals, whales and penguins, but extensive coal bearing area known to exist and encouraging prospects for copper, molybdenite, lead and other metallic minerals also obtained while from geological formation every reasonable possibility discovery gold. (Doyle 1985: 13)

Hughes added "and in view of the potential economic value of these regions desire you strongly urge that Australia should share in control with New Zealand" (Doyle 1985: 13).

The resource-based justification for the expense of Australia's Antarctic Program effectively ended in 1989, when the Australian Government announced it would not sign the Convention on the Regulation of Antarctic Minerals Resource Activities, which had been negotiated for the previous six years, and instead advocated the establishment of a kind of wilderness park, an idea that eventually in October 1991 became the Madrid Protocol. As Bergin noted (1991: 216), this constituted a dramatic shift in Australia's position on Antarctica. While the potential for discovery of some minerals such as gold and oil is rather speculative, there are known to be substantial deposits of both coal and iron ore in the Prince Charles Mountains in the Australian Antarctic Territory, and so Australia's foreswearing of the minerals of Antarctica could be seen a substantial sacrifice. This was, however, a time when Australian politics was witnessing the emergence of environmentalism as a political force, and the decision created no immediate disadvantage while permitting the government to appeal to green voters.

This left science as a reason for an Antarctic presence, and it is fair to say it has been difficult to determine whether science was the reason for maintaining Australia's sovereignty claim or vice versa. Phillip Law, a former senior administrator in Australian Antarctic affairs, considered that for the 50 years before the International Geophysical Year (IGY) in 1957, the main motive for Australia's Antarctic policy was territorial conquest, but, he argued, the inspiring precedent set in the IGY, resulted in an appreciation of the potential value of Antarctica as an "untapped reservoir of knowledge, and a unique uncontaminated laboratory" (Law 1962: 21). Law wrote that "scientific research remains as the paramount activity in future Antarctic work" (Law 1962: 21). Barry Jones, as Minister for the Department of Science and Technology, endorsed Law's ideas in 1984 and cited the various scientific breakthroughs that had occurred in Antarctica, stating that "it's the scientific discoveries that will really matter. That's why we have to be there" (Jones 1984: 39). But Antarctic science is an expensive undertaking, and continued political support cannot be taken for granted.

Successive Australian governments have constantly reinforced the point that Australia's supreme objective in maintaining sovereignty over Antarctica was the acquisition of scientific knowledge. The Antarctic Project has been promoted to the Australian public as being about noble scientists in the pursuit of knowledge. As one source put it:

> This quest for knowledge is in itself more commendable than the old fashioned quest for land. What raises it to an even higher plane is the fact that the whole vast spectrum of knowledge now brought back from the Antarctic is made available, as a matter of course, to all mankind. This Utopian state of affairs is due partly to the International Geophysical Year and partly to the Antarctic Treaty. (Cameron 1974: 238)

But the usefulness of the noble endeavour of science is nevertheless significant in maintaining Australia's sovereignty claims. For example, the initial report of the Antarctic Research Policy Advisory Committee in 1979 argued that since Australia's presence in the Antarctic was demonstrated by scientific research and, because most international involvement in the area focused on scientific research, the quality achieved in scientific programs was important if the government wished to maintain its claim of sovereignty over the Australian Antarctic Territory. A paper prepared for the Department of Foreign Affairs in the mid-1980s reinforced this point:

> It is axiomatic that Australia's Antarctic research program should aim to serve Australia's national interests and policy objectives in the Antarctic. This requires us to maintain a credible, high quality and preferably high impact Antarctic scientific program on a year-round basis. (ASAC 1986: 13)

Antarctica and Climate Science

To a large extent, modern climate science grew out of the scientific enterprise in Antarctica. Joseph Fourier had first raised the possibility that emissions of carbon dioxide might produce an enhanced greenhouse effect in 1827. Then, in 1896, Svente Arrhenius predicted an increase in air temperature of between 4 and 6 degrees celcius as the result of elevated carbon dioxide levels, and in 1938 Guy Callendar also concluded that the planet was getting warmer because of carbon dioxide emissions. Callendar was responsible for the first modern reconstruction of historical atmospheric carbon dioxide levels. One problem for early climate modellers was the limited availability of data, with nothing approaching global data available until the 1950s (Christianson 1999). The 1957-58 IGY supported concerted international efforts to generate data, including the commencement of the measurement of carbon dioxide at Moana Loa in Hawaii, which now forms the basis of our understanding of the accumulation of carbon dioxide. From these beginnings came the Global Atmospheric Research Program that formed the basis of the contemporary scientific effort to understand global climate change.

In 1956, Plass had aroused new interest in carbon dioxide as a factor in climate change. Revelle and Suess (1957) predicted that fossil fuels might soon induce rapid changes in world climate and warned that humanity was conducting, unawares, a great geophysical experiment on the Earth's climate. To track the experiment's progress, Revelle proposed a monitoring station for atmospheric carbon dioxide at Mauna Loa, Hawaii, as part of the IGY. The Mauna Loa station has since then documented a rise in the atmospheric concentration of carbon dioxide, due primarily to human activities.

But Antarctica has also played a role in our knowledge of carbon dioxide in the more distant past. Analysis of air trapped in bubbles in ice cores, such as that from Law Dome (Etheridge *et al* 1996), provide a record of carbon dioxide levels extending before the period of direct atmospheric measurements. Continuous direct measurements date from 1958 and confirm the ice core data, however the longest ice core records extend this record back 650,000 years (Siegenthaler *et al* 2005).

Antarctic research has made other significant contributions to our understanding of the global atmospheric environment. For example, the discovery of the Antarctic ozone "hole" (Farman *et al* 1985) helped elevate the general issue of anthropogenic atmospheric change in the public consciousness and thus helped build the political support, which led to the successful negotiation of the 1991 Montreal Protocol on Substances that Deplete the Ozone Layer, the first global response to the problem of ozone-depleting chemicals. Science had earlier suggested that chlorofluoro-carbons (CFCs) could destroy stratospheric ozone, but the discovery of pronounced ozone thinning over Antarctica provided powerful obser-vational evidence that such changes were indeed occurring in the atmos-phere. But the main significance for Australia of Antarctic research related to climate change has less to do with questions of whether it is anthropo-genic in nature and more to do with understanding the processes of climate variability which impact Australia regardless of causation. Indeed, it is possible that variable factors in the Antarctic climate system might have significance for the global climate system.

The significance for Australia comes because much of Australia's climate system depends on what happens to its south. Not only do many of the weather systems that affect it originate there as part of the transport of energy from the tropical regions towards the poles, but ocean currents are also important. Any changes in ocean circulation can have sizable consequences, because the oceans store so much energy that they act like a flywheel on the coupled ocean-atmosphere system. The oceans contain many times more energy than the atmosphere, and thus moderate the climate system by storing energy. But they are also capable of releasing this energy back to the atmosphere so that warming of the oceans can continue to have an effect long after any atmospheric warming has abated. Ocean currents therefore transport large amounts of energy from one part of the globe to another, and so play an important part in climate variability. Currents are driven, *inter alia*, by winds, the earth's rotation and fresh melt water, with differences in density between seawater driving what is known as thermohaline circulation.

Cold winds sweeping down from the Antarctic plateau and out to sea freeze the surface of the water, but the ice formed is constantly scoured by the wind, with new ice forming behind it. The water is kept ice-free by this mechanism, but as the ice forms differentially from fresh water, the water left behind becomes highly saline and very dense, sinking to the bottom and gradually flowing northwards, taking nutrients and oxygen to produce highly productive upwellings which are important for fisheries and forming an important part of ocean currents that contribute to the pole-wards transportation of energy from the tropics.

Over the past 25 years, the role of the El Niño-Southern Oscillation (ENSO) in driving Australia's drought cycles (and weather patterns else-where) has become well established. El Niño brings drought to Southern

Australia, while La Niña brings torrential rain. Science is some way from understanding fully the ENSO phenomenon, with forecasting skill stretching only to months rather than years, but such cyclical variations also appear to be underlain by less regular discontinuities that are even less well understood. While El Niño tends to receive more attention because of its impact upon agricultural productivity, there is evidence that the hazards brought by La Niña might be more significant (Kuhnel and Coates 2000). Ocean currents can play a longer-term, even more dramatic role in climate variability, however, with periodic changes to patterns capable of producing profound consequences. It is clear that one such event, known as the Pacific Climate Shift, occurred around 1976, with changes in patterns of warm and cold water currents affecting climate in locations as far apart as Western Australia and Alaska.

In addition to an enhanced greenhouse effect due to elevated levels of greenhouse gases in the atmosphere, therefore, there is both short-term and long-term variability in ocean currents that can have a significant impact upon climate variability, and science that improves our under-standing of these processes promises to be a significant benefit flowing from Australia's Antarctic research program.

It is also possible that research in the Southern Ocean could assist with measures to mitigate elevated levels of carbon dioxide. Phytoplankton in the oceans plays a significant role in removing carbon dioxide from the atmosphere. Indeed, the oceans take up more carbon dioxide than land-based sinks, and their ability to do so is often limited by the availability of minerals such as iron. Iron fertilisation is considered to be a possible way of addressing the risks of anthropogenic climate change, and there is much to be learned about both the impacts and efficacy of iron fertilisation through the conducting of large-scale experiments.

This is not to say that monitoring the mass of ice on the Antarctic continent is not an important part of climate research, as any significant loss of ice would cause a substantial sea level rise. The Antarctic ice sheet averages a thickness of 2500 metres and contains around three-quarters of the earth's freshwater. The largest contribution of global warming to sea level rise is nevertheless likely to come from the thermal expansion of the oceans and the retreat of mountain glaciers, with most climate models suggesting that temperatures in Antarctica will remain below freezing point, with increased snowfall likely to contribute to the addition of ice to the continent. The observational science appears not yet to be settled on such questions. A paper published in *Science* in 2006 found evidence (using satellite measurements of gravity) of a decline in ice in Antarctica (Velicogna and Wahr 2006), but it was based on only 34 months of data and had as its starting point a time of exceptionally thick ice as recorded by other means in the period 1982-2003 (Davis *et al* 2005). By selecting only 34 months of data, the paper ignored the evidence that ice mass had been growing for 20 years. The West Antarctic ice sheet has been declining, but the much larger East Antarctic ice sheet appears to have been gaining mass (Zwally *et al* 2005). There has been some warming around the Antarctic Peninsula, and ocean currents have contributed to the collapse of the Larsen B Ice Shelf in February 2003, but as it was floating on the surface, this will not contribute to sea level changes. Nevertheless, concerns persist that this might trigger an acceleration in glacial discharge, thus contributing to a loss of ice mass and substantial sea level rise, although such a prospect is largely speculative – though a convincing justification for research programs monitoring the Antarctic ice mass.

As this example suggests, much remains to be understood about the complex interaction between Antarctica and the global climate, and Australia's climate science is thus making a substantial contribution to an understanding of climate variability and ways of addressing the risks of climate change. It is thus making a significant contribution to the value equation over Australia's Antarctic Program. It is not that science for its own sake could not be justified to the Australian public to some extent, but science which promises benefits that can be measured in terms of decreasing the costs of climate impacts provides an enhanced ability to win popular support, especially given the importance of climate variability (especially drought) in the Australian economy (and psyche).

Perhaps of greater concern than speculative concern over any changes in the Antarctic ice sheet, is the impact of climate change on sub-Antarctic regions. There is evidence that the region of the Antarctic Peninsula is warming, and clearly any changes in atmospheric temperatures or in the path of cold or warm ocean currents will have important consequences for sub-Antarctic islands such as Macquarie Island and Heard Island and McDonald Islands. These islands face other, more immediate threats. The most notable example is perhaps the damage being caused by introduced rabbits and rats on Macquarie Island as a result of the successful eradication of feral cats. There have been suggestions that pest populations have expanded as a result of global warming, but any such effect is surely secondary to the effect of removing the only predator for the pest species.

Nevertheless, there is greater diversity of botanical life on the sub-Antarctic islands than in Antarctica itself, thanks to their enjoying temperatures above zero, and any change in climate will certainly place their ecology at risk.

Understanding Climate Variability: Benefits and Challenges

Despite the relevance of research that promises to throw light on climate variability, the chaotic nature of the global climate system might limit the ability of science to deliver on that promise. Perhaps one of the most celebrated examples of climate change impacting upon Australia is that of the decline in water supply for Perth in the State of Western Australia, where the government decided in April 2005 to add a desalination plant to a recycling plant at Kwinana in response to a worsening demand-supply situation. The state opposition had even proposed a grandiose scheme of constructing a canal the vast distance from the Kimberley to supply Perth's burgeoning demand. Seemingly, the stakes are high in improving our understanding of climate variability.

But an examination of the facts of the case of Perth's water supply suggests both that the potential pay-offs are considerable, but also that the ability of climate science to provide useful, policy-relevant advice is limited. This is partly because the problem has been wrongly constructed as primarily one of climate variability, when there have been more factors at play. But it is also because the nature of the science itself is highly uncertain and inherently incapable of providing definitive answers – not just because the error terms in the science are large, but because it is seeking to describe coupled, non-linear chaotic systems.

To take the first point, it is true that yields to Perth's dams declined from an average of 338 gigalitres (GL) per annum during the period 1911-76 to 167 GL per annum during 1976-2001 – a decline of about 50 per cent, and clearly giving rise to a serious problem for a growing metropolis. But the reduction in rainfall in the region was not commensurate with the reduction in catchment yields, declining only by about 10 per cent from 880 mm to 790 mm per annum (Western Australia 2002). Indeed, rainfall outside the south-west corner of the state has increased during this period, so rain appears to have been relocated slightly further north-east by the Pacific Climate Shift. Nevertheless, there is now about 10 per cent less rain falling in the catchments for Perth's water supply, and that is large enough to be significant. It should be noted, however, that the reason that the yield from these catchments has declined by around 50 per cent has more to do with land management practices than with climate change with the thickening of vegetation in catchments exacerbating the effects of the slight decline in rainfall as a result of vegetation taking more of the available water by transpiration. One option that water policymakers have considered is to thin vegetation that has been allowed to thicken for environmental reasons, and substantial increases in yield would result from this option.

The Western Australian Government, as noted above, has responded to the water supply problems of Perth with an approach that uses multiple steps, including committing to a reverse osmosis desalination plant. Together with considerable groundwater resources and the Kwinana recycling plant, Perth is (ironically) probably better placed than other state capitals to cope with future rainfall uncertainty. During the drought affecting Australia at the time of writing, Perth has less stringent water restrictions than other mainland capitals as a result. But substantial investments such as the desalination plant and exploitation of new groundwater resources depend upon the reliability of estimates of future yields from water catchments, and thus on climatology. It is not clear, for example, that the sudden decline in rainfall from 1976 represents a return to the norm after a prolonged period of atypically high rainfall from the early part of the 20th century, a brief period of low rainfall, or a long period of low rainfall.

Any improvement of the science relating to weather systems in the Southern Ocean or in future ocean current patterns, such as might be contributed by Australia's Antarctic science program is thus of considerable significance. The Western Australian response has been to create a system of water infrastructure that is robust under various future scenarios, with the desalination plant (at highest marginal cost of supply) being able to be off-loaded in times of abundance. Improved knowledge of future rainfall is of enormous importance for Western Australia, since a wrong forecast might lead to over-investment or under-investment in water infrastructure (including investment of the wrong kind).

Antarctic climate-related science potentially can thus make an important contribution to the welfare, not just to Western Australia, but also to the nation as a whole (and, indeed, globally, since much of the information has the form of a global public good). But there is a need to enter a note of caution about the ability of science to deliver on this promise – my second point.

As the Pacific Climate Shift all too clearly demonstrates, coupled ocean-atmosphere climate systems are non-linear, chaotic systems. Climate does not change just by some slow, gradual process, but also by sudden shifts that might involve sudden cooling as well as sudden warming. Nobody knew why climate changed in 1976, even though observers knew only too well at the time that something strange was happening (Namias 1978). And nobody really has much of an idea now as to what caused the shift, and therefore whether another shift might be just around the corner. In other words, both ENSO and longer-term climate shifts have no readily apparent periodicity, and might not be amenable to yielding better understanding, even when substantial scientific effort is devoted to trying to unravel their mysteries.

This suggests that the nobility of the less applied scientific enterprise is likely to continue to be an important (if not the main) foundation for justifications for the expense of the Australian Antarctic science program. The best that can probably be hoped for is to understand more about what drives ENSO so as to extend by even a few months the forecasting ability for policymakers and users of such information (particularly farmers and water utility operators). This is not to diminish the value of such a contribution, but to sound a note of caution about the ability of science – given the nature of the phenomena involved – to deliver much more any time soon. Science will have to be accepted for its own sake, or for other purposes, if it is to provide a durable basis for justifying Australia's presence in Antarctica.

Conclusion

As the strategic importance of Antarctica has declined, and the Madrid Protocol has taken the mineral resources of the continent off the agenda, science has assumed greater relative importance as a justification for the Australian commitment to Antarctica, helping to legitimate the continuing claim of sovereignty Australia continues to hold. The emergence of climate change as an issue has enhanced the salience of the science justification for a substantial commitment of resources, adding an element of material interests to the reliance on the nobility of disinterested science, conducted for its own sake. While the possibility of a substantial loss of the Antarctic ice sheet cannot be ruled out conclusively, such a prospect lays a greater hold to the popular imagination than it does to the scientific community, so that Antarctica probably has greater importance for understanding climate variability than does climate change for Antarctica. There is arguably a greater risk from climate change for the sub-Antarctic islands, but in neither case is it likely that Australia has any international liability for such an impact. As the brief case study of climate variability and Western Australian water resources shows, the potential benefits from such research are considerable, though there is a need for caution about overselling the potential of research to yield policy-useful knowledge of coupled, non-linear, chaotic ocean-atmosphere climate systems. There is the promise of great benefits in developing better understandings of Australia's climate variability, but the nature of the science means that such insights might prove elusive, and other justifications for Australia's scientific program are likely to remain important.

13

Globalisation's Cold Genius
and the Ending of Antarctic Isolation

Alan D Hemmings

What power art thou, who from below
Hast made me rise unwillingly and slow
From beds of everlasting snow?[1]

Introduction

Human activity in Antarctica, here taken to include the entire area south of
the Antarctic Convergence or Polar Front (Figure 1 at beginning of book),
only began in the late 18th century, and until the mid-20th century was, bar
infrequent and usually short-lived exploring expeditions, essentially
confined to seasonal exploitation of living resources – principally seals and
whales. Post World War II, and particularly since the International Geophysical Year (IGY) of 1957-58 and the adoption in 1959 of the Antarctic
Treaty,[2] permanent scientific endeavour joined marine mammal harvesting
as a significant human activity in Antarctica, and year-round and summer-
only stations were established on the continent and adjacent islands south
of 60 degrees South latitude. These were overwhelmingly operated by
government agencies, and few states were active in Antarctica until the
1980s.[3] Low levels of tourism began in the late 1950s, but were discontinuous over the next several decades. From the 1960s both whaling
(Tønnessen and Johnsen 1982: 638) and sealing (Bonner 1985: 218-19)
declined, but from the 1970s, distant-water fishing fleets began to operate in

---

1   "Cold Genius" in Henry Purcell's 1691 semi-opera *King Arthur*, libretto by John
     Dryden.
2   402 UNTS 71.
3   At adoption of the Antarctic Treaty in 1959, 12 states were Consultative Parties; in
     1969 still 12; in 1979: 13; in 1989: 25; in 1999: 27; and in 2007: 28.

Antarctic waters south of the convergence and harvesting of krill and finfish (and later other taxa) began (Croxall and Nicol 2004: Figure 1).

So the picture in Antarctica until well into the 1980s was of limited human activity focused in three classes: marine mammal exploitation (declining); scientific research activity (stable) and fishing (increasing). Antarctica was subject to an expanding legal regime under the Antarctic Treaty System (ATS), including conventions addressing the regulation of sealing and marine living resource exploitation. Throughout the 1980s, negotiations proceeded on a minerals convention, and whaling was subject to its own regulatory convention outside the ATS. However, what still really governed human activity levels in Antarctica were its remoteness from the main areas of global human activity, the rigours of the environment, limited technological capacity (with access to the technologies essential for Antarctic operation still largely confined to governments), and the situation of the Antarctic dispensation within a broader Cold-War rubric. Further, surrounding the Antarctic, with its limited human activity, was a wide belt of ocean in which very little human activity, bar transit, was evident. Human activity in Antarctica was thus limited, narrowly focused, governmental, and insulated from global trends. Antarctica was, accordingly, a place apart; a place outside the increasingly interconnected-world elsewhere.

This has now changed. The basket of ideas and issues embraced in the popular imagination by the term "globalisation" is now relevant to discussions about Antarctica. Although still obviously a place different in detail from elsewhere, Antarctica's isolation from the wider world is over. Unless we choose otherwise, Antarctica now faces basically the same sort of future as any other part of the planet. This development, although we see now with hindsight that it was already underway, did not form a significant part of the public policy debate around Antarctica in the 1980s. The publication that the present volume takes as its parent, *Australia's Antarctic Policy Options* (Harris 1984a), does not even include the word "globalisation". For Australia, as much as the wider international community, these changes are profoundly significant. Australia is claimant to 42 per cent of the Antarctic continent, as what it calls the "Australian Antarctic Territory" (AAT), and seeks to give effect to both national and international legal obligations there (Stephens and Boer this volume). This, coupled with Australia's objective interests in the future of a relatively proximate continent which, *inter alia*, is a potential competitive source of minerals and living resources, give it reason for a close interest in possible Antarctic futures.

This chapter examines the end of Antarctic isolation, as a place once remote, forbidding and "uninteresting" is opened up by technology and subject to commercial pressures and commodification. It briefly explains the developments that have led to this and explores the implications for a region hitherto conceived of, and operated as, a place apart. Consideration is given to the challenges posed to the histórically fragile and contingent Antarctic regional governance structures now struggling with fast-moving globally organised activities, with their standing or hegemony contested by newer global institutions and norms. The increasing normalisation of Antarctica as a place of varied and not necessarily consistent values, aspirations and interests, and the issues posed in relation to the near-past norms of the ATS, is explored. What sort of Antarctic future might we be heading for, who are the winners and who the losers? Where is Australia in all this, and how will "globalisation" affect the Antarctic?

Globalisation – Concept and Terms

Indiscriminate use of the term "globalisation" tends to confound several different elements. To overcome this, three different terms have been proposed by Steger (2003, 2005a, 2005b):

- "Globality" – for the social *condition* characterised by the existence of global economic, political, cultural and environmental interconnections and flows that make many of the current existing borders and boundaries irrelevant; (Steger 2003: 7)

- "Globalisation" – for the set of social *processes* thought to transform our present social condition into one of "Globality"; (Steger 2003: 8) and

- "Globalism" – for the dominant global *ideology* driving the process. (Steger 2005a, 2005b: 4)

To ensure clarity in the use of the terms, hereafter whilst the quotation marks will be dropped, the first character of the term will always be upper case.

The discussion of this chapter will use the second and third terms more frequently than the first, since it is focused on the drivers and processes operating in a part of the world – Antarctica – rather than the global condition *per se*. Globalisation as a process is intuitively obvious. The ideology of Globalism is perhaps best explicated by what have been called its six core claims (Steger 2005b: 52-90):

1. globalisation is about the liberalisation and global integration of markets;
2. globalisation is inevitable and irreversible;
3. nobody is in charge of globalisation;
4. globalisation benefits everyone;
5. globalisation furthers the spread of democracy in the world; and
6. globalisation requires a war on terror.

On first glance, some of these claims may seem peripheral in relation to Antarctica. Some analysts see Globalism in positive terms, albeit an ideology in need of recasting or humanising (Stiglitz 2006). Others see it more negatively (Bello 2002), and some even assert that as an idea it has already collapsed (Saul 2005). This chapter attempts not to take a values stance, but it does assume some continuing reality to the ideology, and its salience to the end of Antarctic isolation.

The End of Isolation

The isolation of Antarctica was in one sense ended when the first explorers were able to find it, and survived to return home with the news. But through the 19th and really up to World War II in the 20th century, human presence in the region was spatially and temporally patchy and Antarctica still essentially isolated as far as the rest of the world was concerned. Thereafter, and particularly from IGY, there were permanent scientific stations and seasonal marine mammal harvesting, but it was not until the late 1970s that significant modern commercial interest in the region began. From this period onwards, Antarctica has been increasingly integrated into global systems, and it is this transformation that is seen here as marking the substantive end of Antarctic isolation. Bush (2001: 139) has characterised this as "the emergence on the Antarctic scene of highly capitalised actors of the globalised economy". So, although not entirely confined to this, it is largely the arrival of *global commercial interests and activities* in Antarctica which is seen here as the proximate causal factor. Underlying this, of course, are technological, political and attitudinal transformations in wider international society.

Commercial Interests

Six clusters of commercial interest in Antarctica can presently be discriminated as fishing, minerals, tourism, bioprospecting, Antarctic services and education. Whaling in its present quasi-scientific guise is not here considered (see Jabour *et al* this volume).

Fishing in Antarctic waters was triggered in part by the processes that led to the Third United Nations Convention on the Law of the Sea (LOS Convention)[4] through the displacement by consequential Exclusive Economic Zones (EEZ) of fishing fleets to remoter areas of High Seas. But it was also stimulated by the collapse of fish stocks elsewhere (Pauly *et al* 2000), the use of fishing fleets to project influence in the region by some centrally planned economies, and advances in communications, navigational and deepwater fishing technologies. The ATS responded by adopting the 1980 Convention on the Conservation of Antarctic Marine Living Resources

---

4   1833 UNTS 396.

(CCAMLR).[5] Authorised catches for the 2005-06 season were 13,704 tonnes for toothfish and circa 125,000 tonnes of krill, although an additional 3080 tonnes of toothfish was estimated for the Illegal, Unreported and Unregulated (IUU) fishery within the convention area (ASOC 2006c). Recently, fishing for Southern bluefin tuna, a species subject to its own international instrument, the 1993 Convention for the Conservation of Southern Bluefin Tuna (CCSBT)[6] has commenced in CCAMLR waters. The relative responsibilities of CCAMLR and CCSBT in the management of this fishery are still to be resolved (Hemmings 2006a).

Interest in mineral resources in Antarctica, particularly in relation to hydrocarbons, was primarily stimulated by perceived global vulnerabilities, and price rises, following the mid-1970s production limits imposed by the Organisation of Petroleum Exporting Countries (OPEC), and by western anxieties about future dependencies on strategic metal reserves dominated by the problematic or unstable regimes in the communist Soviet Union and apartheid South Africa. The Antarctic was simply one of a range of prospective new sources examined. But again, the belief that the undoubtedly difficult operating environment would at some point become technically feasible was underpinned by experience in polar environments evolving in the Arctic and growing experience of deep water operations in places such as the North Sea and Atlantic coast of Brazil. As it happens, the minerals genie was formally confined to its bottle in the Antarctic by the prohibition on any activity relating to mineral resources other than scientific research by Article 7 of the 1991 Protocol on Environmental Protection to the Antarctic Treaty (Madrid Protocol).[7] However, there have been indications of continuing minerals interest from a number of Antarctic Treaty Consultative Parties (ATCP), most obviously Russia (Russia 2001; ASOC 2001b: Agenda Item 15).

Tourism really only commenced its present growth phase in the late 1980s (Bastmeijer and Roura 2004: Figure 1) accelerating during the 1990s as former Soviet ice-class shipping became available for western charter, and accelerating again post 2000 with the entry into the market of large to very large general-purpose cruise liners. The first stimulus to growth in the Antarctic tourism industry may, ironically, have been the increased public profile of the region achieved during the 1980s and early 1990s as a product of the public policy debate about the acceptability of possible future Antarctic minerals activity. However, it is clear that a substantial facilitator of tourism growth in the 1990s was the ready availability of ice-class vessels and their skilled Russian crews. With the ending of the Cold War, attitudes within ATCP states towards the realisation of economic benefits from the region also changed (see below). In the 2005-06 austral summer

---

5   19 ILM 841.

6   1819 UNTS 359.

7   30 ILM 1455.

30,877 tourists entered the Antarctic Treaty area on ships and a further 1165 overflew the continent (Antarctic Treaty Secretariat 2006: 35). If crews are included, a substantially higher figure is reached. From a smaller tourism base than in 2005-06, passengers, staff and crew entering the area in 2003-04, using International Association of Antarctica Tourism Operators (IAATO) data, were estimated at 44,266 (Murray and Jabour 2004: 314). Over the 14 seasons 1992/93-2005/06, tourist ships have increased from 12 to 44, the number of voyages from 59 to 249, and the number of tourists landed from 6704 to 25,167 (IAATO 2006a: Table 1). In the 2006-07 season, a single vessel, the 109,000 tonne cruise liner *Golden Princess*, alone carried 3700 persons into the Antarctic Treaty area (Hemmings 2006c).

Bioprospecting is the search for, extraction and testing of chemical compounds and genetic material from living organisms (Hemmings and Rogan-Finnemore in press 2007). Extremophile organisms from Antarctic environments are of high interest, bioprospecting has been underway there for some years (Hemmings and Rogan-Finnemore 2005a) across terrestrial, freshwater and marine environments, and no specific regulatory structure is in place (Jabour-Green and Nicol 2003; Hemmings 2005). Bioprospecting is a spinoff from increasingly sophisticated Antarctic scientific research and its revelations about biodiversity in the region. Like tourism, it appears to have been a beneficiary of the reassessment of economic potential by states – in this case, within the Antarctic research and national program communities.

"Antarctic Services", as the term is employed here, means the raft of supply, operational sub-contracting, logistics and other support services for Antarctic operations, whether conducted by national programs, fishing, tourism, bioprospecting or other industries. Generally these are presently delivered at the small number of key departure points for the Antarctic, and thus *outside* the Antarctic as such. However, these services are both diversifying and deepening and need not be confined out of area. Some services, such as the support services provided to the United States (US) National Science Program in Antarctica, have long been provided by corporations, and in these instances, plainly involve being in the Antarctic alongside the client. Other services, such as salvage, necessarily require travel to Antarctica, albeit infrequently. The key departure points (often referred to as Gateways) are Ushuaia (Argentina), Punta Arenas (Chile), Cape Town (South Africa), Hobart (Australia) and Christchurch (New Zealand). For these cities, Antarctic Services are multi-million dollar income streams to the local economy, and for some this is viewed as critical, and support and marketing is provided by either local or central government. In the case of Hobart, an office of the State of Tasmania's Department of Economic Development, Antarctic Tasmania, has been established to co-ordinate Antarctic opportunities (Antarctic Tasmania 2006). One cannot be in any doubt when in Hobart that there is a live local political and commercial interest in Antarctica.

Globally, education has emerged from a stand-alone category of activity to be viewed as a commercial activity too. There are indications of this in relation to Antarctica, with specialist courses at, for example, the University of Tasmania and the University of Canterbury in New Zealand. An International Antarctic Institute, which is a virtual university ("virtual" here relating to the non-physical basis of organisation, rather than its existence *in* Antarctica), involving these and other international centres is under development. Antarctic studies are viewed as a growth area, albeit still a niche education market.

A speculative further commercial cluster is the virtual use of Antarctica. At present, one can see the limited virtual use (imagery of Antarctica used in advertising or branding) as a development within the "Antarctic Services" cluster above. However, is it inconceivable, given the peculiar juridical status of the Antarctic Treaty area, that we might see attempts by service or financial entities to domicile their activities in some sense in a virtual Antarctica to achieve benefits and/or avoid obligations elsewhere?

The Underlying Drivers of Transformation

Perhaps the most obvious driver of transformation in Antarctica is technological advance, and the increasing access to those advanced technologies by a broader community than has historically been the case. During the early years of the ATS, Antarctic operations posed considerable challenges essentially beyond the capacity of any but the 12 original signatories to the Treaty, and even within these states capacity was confined to a national operating agency and/or the military. This had significant policy implications, because it meant that the Antarctic regime had to regulate only a very limited community, and even within that community a fairly limited range of possible activities. Even amongst states, most had limited mobility within Antarctica, and most were operating in the severe environments there with less sophisticated technologies than were the norm at home. In a sense, everyone was still "camping".

In the past decade or so, there has been what one might call a revolution in Antarctic affairs as automation, remote sensing, new materials technologies, communications and modelling capabilities have been applied there. The requisite technologies are now accessible by a far larger group of states (albeit the access of many is still constrained by their high costs), and (critically) a diverse range of commercial and non-commercial non-government entities. From the 1980s, entities as diverse as private fishing companies, tourism operators and Greenpeace, were able to professionally operate in Antarctica because of their access to sophisticated ships, aircraft and (in the case of Greenpeace) a year-round Antarctic station, and other advanced technologies. This access to technology is plainly part of a wider global development, but its consequences in Antarctica have been particularly significant. Technology has largely disappeared as the rate-limiting step for Antarctic operations, amongst those with money in any case.

This has occurred in parallel with substantial political and attitudinal changes following the end of the Cold War. The substantial literature on the geopolitical consequences of the end of that phase of international relations lies outside the remit of this chapter. But from the dynamics and power-relationships within the Antarctic Treaty Consultative Meetings (ATCMs), through the pattern of membership of the various instruments, to the imperatives that inform ATCPs in relation to their Antarctic stances and activities, one sees a profound shift from the XV ATCM in Paris in 1989, to any recent ATCM.[8]

One may, without prejudice to its successes, see the ATS as a product of the Cold War. Little surprise then, that the end of that Cold War would have implications for its operation. In place of the bloc orientation of national positions that was evident until as recently as 1989, facilitated by the fact that the most substantial human activity ashore was science conducted by government agencies – science which allowed more ready cooperation across the blocs, and which was emphasised as an organising principle precisely because of this (what Herr and Hall in 1989 termed "science as the currency of influence") – we have seen the emergence of more complex inter-relationships. While cooperation is still one of the Antarctic verities, it is accompanied now by greater evidence of competition. This competition may be considered unremarkable elsewhere in the world, but it is a new departure in Antarctica, and may not be an easy fit with the historic practice of scientific and operational cooperation. It may be one thing for national programs to carry each other's scientists on their aircraft, or make their facilities freely available when the project is pure science, but will they (or their legislators) be quite so happy if the scientist being assisted is engaged in bioprospecting and potentially an economic competitor of their own citizens?

Post Cold War, many ATCPs seek to maximise the economic benefits of Antarctic research and resource access, consistent with their international obligations under the ATS. With Australia, for example, one can see a codification of this in the last of four government goals for the Australian Antarctic Program being to "undertake scientific work of practical, *economic* and national significance" (AAD 2000: 6 emphasis added). There is a "strong undercurrent of the promotion of Australian national interest" (Haward *et al* 2006: 442). There always has been, but what that national interest is has changed subtly since the end of the Cold War.

In the case of claimant states, there is an additional consideration. So long as human activity in the Antarctic was limited, and perhaps largely under the direct control of partner governments, practical challenges to sovereignty were minimal. The innovative containment of sovereignty positions through Article IV of the Antarctic Treaty (Rothwell and Scott this volume) will be enough. But once the prime purpose of the ATS is no

---

8   The author has attended ATS diplomatic meetings since 1989.

longer largely containing the east-west confrontation of the Cold War,[9] and technology and economic interests mean that people are looking to realise economic benefits from the region, the picture becomes more complicated. For a claimant state there is a particular urgency to it, rather than others, being the beneficiary of activities within its claimed area. In the first instance, it goes against the grain to assert a claim to something and yet allow others to appropriate it (and nationalism is nowhere more alert than in relation to rights to territory). It may also undermine your legal position in relation to that claim if another essentially determines and/or conducts the activities there. Without some countervailing imperative, this is likely to drive the claimant to try to exclude others (extremely difficult in the unresolved Antarctic juridical environment, unless through ATS mechanisms) or to get in ahead and dominate the activity. There is some evidence of both approaches being used by claimant states – some instances of states strongly promoting an activity where they clearly receive (or expect to receive) benefits, other instances of attempts to constrain an activity which the claimant believes it will not be the primary beneficiary of, and/or which may indeed erode its claimant position.

The corollary of this is the stance adopted by states which are not claimants, and may have strong positions of opposition to assertions of sovereignty. The clearest exemplars of this are the US and Russia. Because of its extraordinary political and economic position, the US is the single most significant actor in Antarctic affairs. It appears to favour, in Antarctica as elsewhere, open access arrangements subject only to minimal ATS constraints (Bush 2001: 135). Such arrangements, whatever their intellectual or moral grounding, have apparent benefits for the US. If (say) Antarctic tourism and/or bioprospecting are largely unregulated by the ATS, US entities (which will likely predominate) will have more open access, and at the same time will potentially undercut the effective sovereignty of any claimant state. After all, if the dominant activity in, for example, the AAT were *not* conducted by Australian entities, and those who operated there were constrained by neither Australian domestic legal obligations, nor significant ATS regulation, for all practical purposes Australian territorial sovereignty might be moot.

A further complication emerges. In an Antarctic where substantial commercial activity occurs, this activity is likely to have continuity with activity outside the Antarctic Treaty area. The Antarctic activity in question may in practice be a regional manifestation of a global industry. This would seem to be the case with fishing, tourism and bioprospecting, for none of which a meaningful boundary is provided by ATS boundaries. Historically, the ATS has been predicated upon Antarctic exceptionalism, and the peculiarly Antarctic orientation of the activities managed under the ATS. Antarctic arrangements (with the exception of the vexed whaling

---

9   It was also about other things, including containing Argentine, Chilean and British rivalry in the Antarctic Peninsula (Dodds 1997, 2002).

question) and the Antarctic regime in general, have been walled off from wider international arrangements. The *modus operandi* of the ATS has been to add narrowly targeted instruments, addressing specific Antarctic issues, as those issues appear. This approach has been aided by the fact that until recently, not only were there few real activities to be regulated by the ATS, but a sort of *cordon sanitaire* existed around the Antarctic region in which nothing, bar transit, actually occurred.

The reality now is that the Antarctic region is no longer hermetically sealed, and there are activities occurring right up to its boundaries, and increasingly across these. So, to canvass just a selection of potential issues, we see:

- a prohibition of mineral resource activities under the Madrid Protocol, but rights to such activities in the Antarctic marine environment inherent in Part XI of the LOS Convention;

- in CCAMLR a regime for regulating Antarctic fisheries and eco-system management, but activities (albeit presently limited) in its area over which CCSBT, rather than it, has control;

- a commitment not to assert new claims or enlargement of claims under Article IV of the Antarctic Treaty, but submissions by clai-mant Australia in relation to the extended continental shelf under Article 76 of the LOS Convention, including that appurtenant to the AAT;

- an absence of any specific regulatory structure for bioprospecting under the Antarctic Treaty or Madrid Protocol, but potential inter-est in this matter in the Convention on Biological Diversity (CBD) and the International Seabed Authority (ISA); and

- a similar absence of any specific regulatory structure for Antarctic tourism, in the face of a rapidly expanding and globally enormous industry.

The traditional argument that the ATS was able to address resource issues as they emerged, and substantially in advance of their conversion into major activities, was underpinned by a demonstrated capacity to adopt instruments, which appeared at decadal intervals. However, not-withstanding some institutional development, the last substantive ATS instrument to be adopted (the Madrid Protocol) was in 1991, and no other instrument is even under negotiation in 2007. Perhaps the ATS has seen no more than the relative decline in multilateralism evident globally since the end of the Cold War, but unfortunately this has in Antarctica coincided with the greatest expansion of human activity. And of course, the alter-native pursued elsewhere, unilateral action or bilateral agreement, is rather problematical in the unusual legal context of Antarctica.

There are political developments that seem altogether less complica-ted. The closing of the Cold War has seen a number of newly independent or formerly effectively satellite states, particularly in Europe, join the ATS. Their reasons for doing so are many and various, but at least one rationale (to judge by comments by their representatives at least) is that participating in the ATS is a demonstration of long sought-for global citizenship. If this is indeed the case, it is an encouraging sign of an enduring moral standing of the ATS.

These strategic level changes are accompanied by changes at a more mundane operational level. Antarctic operations are expensive, and that expenditure is continuously under review. Justifications for expenditure – whether for research funding, operations, institution-building – are sought, and the prospect of economic benefit is an attractive argument in most contexts. National Antarctic programs, and individual researchers, started flagging their Antarctic activities as potentially economically advantageous from the mid 1990s. This is not to say that such arguments were never deployed before, but across a range of ATCPs, the relative profile of such arguments appeared to increase from this time. This has been evident in the case of bioprospecting, and has potentially wide consequences (Hemmings and Rogan-Finnemore 2005b: 237-8).

Broader societal changes are impacting on Antarctica too. Globally, the affluent amongst us are increasingly situated in consumer societies, where entertainment, travel and personal fulfilment are the new rights. This has created a tremendous market for, *inter alia*, Antarctic goods. These may be travel to Antarctica as a tourist, they may be virtual uses of the place to signify standards or value in other goods, and they may be existential public goods – the sense that there is a place such as this, and that we have ethical duties in relation to it. And variously, these are the grounds upon which such different entities as the tourism industry, Hollywood, vodka distillers, David Attenborough or environmental organisations appeal to us. Howsoever they do so, the Antarctic is now a vastly more familiar idea than ever before. This has both positives (if you do not know, how can you care about it?) and negatives (is Antarctica becoming just another commodity, and in the process losing its claim to particular care?) but it is unlikely that Antarctica will ever return to the obscurity that it once had.

Challenges to Antarctic Governance

The ATS provides a restricted form of governance for the region, although the tools it has available to it are rather limited – four treaties, two annual two-week meetings, limited intersessional work through sub-groups and two Secretariats. This structure is fragmented, discontinuous, still involves only a fraction of the international community and moves slowly by consensus. At its heart it still has major unresolved issues such as sovereignty and associated difficulties of agreeing appropriate jurisdiction. For some eventualities it has procedures and standards in place, for others – including regulation of some very large commercial activities – it has next to nothing. It has been innovative, but not recently. It is not uncharitable to see this as a rather thin governance regime.

For so long as human activities in Antarctica were limited, this did not greatly matter. The regime was appropriate to its tasks. It is not clear that this continues to be the case as activity in the region increases in complexity, scale, diversity, and particularly speed, and is increasingly conducted by multinational corporations. For the present, the ATS probably has the capacity to keep abreast of developments. It can, following past practice, elaborate new conventions under the ATS to address existing or emerging activities, including the big commercial activities. But, its failure to substantially develop the ATS further over the past 16 years means it will be running to catch up. The increased number of ATCPs, with their often divergent interests, while deepening its international mandate also adds complexity to decision making, but this is not yet intractable. There may be difficulties with the pattern of ATS development historically followed, where new instruments are added without amendment of any previous instrument. This has resulted in a somewhat internally inconsistent and complicated ATS. There is nothing to prevent ATCPs from revising and even combining instruments. However, "since even sovereign nations find it difficult to control the large multinational corporations that globalisation has spawned" how might the ATS be expected "to regulate them in an effective manner?" (Herber 2007: 60).

If the capacity of the ATS to manage, *inter alia*, modern commercial activities remains an open question, a more substantive question is whether there is now the political will and commitment to preserving a distinctly Antarctic regime at all, or whether Globalism now makes the very idea of a separate continental regime look archaic.

Antarctic Futures

The Antarctic may be at the hinge point of two quite different organisational futures. On the one hand, we could see a revival of interest within the ATS in regionally focused responses to the various current and emerging activities in Antarctica, on the other a recognition that the period of Antarctic exceptionalism is over, and that such regulation as is required is generally best achieved through global instruments and norms.

If the political judgement is made that there are legitimate arguments for maintaining the region as a separate entity, whether to secure particular geopolitical, scientific or environmental public goods, or these in combination (the classic ATS trinity of peace, science and the environment), then the existing state powerbase within the ATS makes that maintenance feasible. The revitalised ATS will still face considerable challenges. It may be that in order to maintain something like the ATS, states need to accept significant constraints on economic activities in Antarctica. Without either resolution of territorial sovereignty positions or the sort of "Sponsoring

State"[10] arrangements explored for the now defunct 1988 Convention on the Regulation of Antarctic Mineral Resource Activities (CRAMRA) – arrangements that now appear very Cold War era – many commercial developments seem likely to be zero-sum-games in terms of ATS internal stability and external acceptability.

In the event that a specific Antarctic regime is no longer the prime means by which the region is to be addressed, we face a very much more complex situation. We do not at this point seem to be seeing any inclination to collapse the ATS. All of the ATCPs appear to have, as their declaratory position, its maintenance. The question is really about the degree to which it might be further developed. If it ceases to be the main game, what we are likely to see is a period of relative decline – some historic core issues remaining within its purview, other sorts of issues, and particularly emergent commercial issues, largely dealt with elsewhere – or not at all. Under this scenario, the ATS becomes a quaint rump, preoccupied with the not altogether respectable issue of Antarctic sovereignty, but largely irrelevant as far as the operative issues in the region are concerned – Antarctica's own Treaty of Tordesillas.[11]

The prospects for Antarctica under this sort of scenario would be interesting. Without the underpinning of state sovereignty or the quasi-condominium provided by the ATS, substantial development of global instruments and norms may be necessary to provide effective governance in Antarctica. In the absence of such development, when it came to commercial activities, Antarctica might become in practice a continent for commerce, and non-state decision makers the prime determinants of its future, with all the issues that this would raise. Globalism is often characterised as inimical to the Westphalian states-based system, even in those parts of the world where sovereign states are established. How much more of a challenge might it be in the setting of Antarctica?

If we take Steger's (2005b) six core claims and examine them against Antarctica, we can perhaps see some difficulties with the Globalisation project there. Globalisation may be about the liberalisation and global integration of markets, but hitherto there have been no markets in Antarctica *per se*. Whether Globalisation is inevitable and irreversible is no more obvious in Antarctica than anywhere else, and who the beneficiaries are of potential destabilisation of the ATS would be a useful debate. If Globalisation spreads democracy in the world, that is wonderful, but it is not immediately clear how this occurs within the Antarctic region. Steger may be indulging himself with the suggestion that Globalisation requires a war on terror, but one of the foundational purposes of the Antarctic Treaty and

---

10 CRAMRA Article I.12.

11 Of 1494 which set the demarcation line between the Spanish and Portuguese empires following Pope Alexander VI's 1493 edict *Inter caetera* (Grewe 2000: 233-4) – a dispensation soon largely ignored by most other states.

the system that it anchors was precisely the demilitarisation of the continent, at the height of the Cold War.

Conclusion

Antarctica has changed from a place where activities were limited and almost entirely within the control of governments to a place where a fast-evolving (and fast-paced) menu of activities, increasingly outside government control are pursued. With its natural defences breached by technology, and its regulatory regime's Cold War rationale overtaken by events, Antarctica is now increasingly exposed to global forces. Globalism, in its present form, seems to dispute the very idea of a distinct and regionally focused set of norms for Antarctica. The major instruments of Globalisation – multinational corporations and their governmental supporters, and their prime focus – commercial opportunity, seem increasingly reluctant to have special rules for this part of the planet.

Antarctica's thin international governance regime appears under pressure and commercial competition is beginning to displace scientific cooperation as the driver of policy in the region. The Antarctic system will not collapse tomorrow, but it does appear to be in relative decline, and power is shifting from states to non-state entities, and particularly to commercial interests. The international community, and states such as Australia which have clear interests in Antarctica, may wish to consider whether the benefits promised (benefits which in the case of Antarctica have not been clearly enunciated) balance the risks to the present collaborative effort to govern Antarctica through the ATS, flawed as some may believe it to be.

This transformation in the Antarctic political reality appears to be another manifestation of the broader international process of Globalisation. In contrast to the live public debate around the merits or problems of Globalisation elsewhere, the process is proceeding without comment, largely beyond public view in relation to Antarctica. This surely is not a desirable state of affairs. Whatever one's perspective or preference, decisions about the future of some 10 per cent of the planet should be in the public domain. Beyond that, it may perhaps be preferable, even if one does not share sympathy with the particular path chosen, for decisions to be deliberately arrived at, rather than achieved through drift or stealth. This chapter is a small contribution towards opening a debate.

Acknowledgments

The ideas developed in this chapter have their roots in a short visiting lectureship at the University of Tasmania's Institute of Antarctic and Southern Ocean Studies in 2001 and an Erskine Fellowship at the University of Canterbury's Gateway Antarctica Centre for Antarctic Studies and

Research, in 2003. To both institutions, and their respective Directors, Garth Partridge and Bryan Storey, I extend my appreciation. I also acknowledge the role of helpful discussions with fellow participants in the Looking South project, particularly Julia Jabour, Marcus Haward, Don Rothwell and Shirley Scott. My thanks are also extended to Kees Bastmeijer, Klaus Dodds, Bernard Herber, Michelle Rogan-Finnemore, and Ricardo Roura for stimulating discussions of these matters over many years, and to my colleagues in scenario building for UNEP's *Global Environment Outlook 4* project. The stances taken and opinions expressed remain of course the sole responsibility of the present author.

14

Looking Forward, Looking South: An Enduring Australian Antarctic Interest

Alan D Hemmings, Lorne K Kriwoken and Julia Jabour

Introduction

Lord Palmerston famously argued that States had no permanent friends, only permanent interests. Since 1933 and the assertion of the Australian territorial claim as a result of the British Order in Council and the Commonwealth's *Australian Antarctic Territory Acceptance Act* (see Rothwell and Scott this volume), Australia has had one paramount Antarctic interest – maintaining that claim. But, whilst a territorial claim is generally the first act in a sequence of events, wherein some real use or exploitation of the claimed area follows, and thus in time the legal basis to claim becomes in a sense a proxy for something more (people, a way of life, some obvious signs of possession and use), the peculiarities of the Antarctic situation have meant this is not what we have seen in the case of the Australian Antarctic Territory (AAT).

The AAT has (like other territorial claims) to a very considerable extent, continued to exist only as a legal construct. Aside from the *Australianisation* evident at and around its three continental stations, Australian activity in the area has been of a piece with any other Antarctic scientific enterprise for more than half a century, and conducted alongside the activities of other States (currently China, India, Romania and Russia have stations in the AAT) which in their turn have similarly acculturated their own immediate environs. The context in which the AAT has been governed and regulated, like all the rest of Antarctica south of 60 degrees South latitude, has been international rather than national, via the Antarctic Treaty System (ATS). Beyond the Byzantine architecture of the Antarctic sovereignty edifice, in practice the AAT is no more *Australian* than the moon.

But, the centrality of the claim to the AAT for Australia's Antarctic project appears undiminished, notwithstanding some ebb and flow in the level of attention paid to Antarctica.[1] Why might this be? How is it that a modern, internationalist state like Australia still rationalises its Antarctic engagement, in the first decade of the 21st century, through recourse to a territorial claim, long after such rationales have ceased to be respectable elsewhere? Is there some enduring validity to this stance in Antarctica?

This concluding chapter explores the deep structure of Australian engagement with Antarctica, the substantive basis for a continuing national commitment to the great continent to our south. What specifically are Australia's interests – as both a member of the global community and as a self-interested State? Are Australia's interests reconcilable, or is Antarctica now like many other issues, one where divergent and perhaps incommensurable interests must be recognised? Mechanistically, how might these interests be realised? Are Australian interests always best viewed through the prism of nationalism and from the stance of a territorial claimant? What continuities, and what breaks from the past, might we glimpse as we look forward? How does Australia best secure its objective, and perhaps vital, interests? And how are we placed to confront those Rumsfeldian "known unknowns" and "unknown unknowns" when they inevitably arise?

Australian Antarctic Interests

If one went back to first principles, what would Australia's Antarctic interests be? Probably, on objective grounds, something like:

- avoiding political instability to the south of Australia, whether on the continent, surrounding islands or across the Southern Ocean;

- understanding and being confident about gaining advance warning of climatic, oceanographic and other events that could have direct or indirect consequences for continental Australia (now including global climate change);

- preventing, or at least ensuring a significant role in controlling, any activities in Antarctica that could have significant negative consequences for Australia (these might be use of the area for hostile purposes,[2] economic activities that might threaten vital Australian economic interests[3] or activities morally repugnant to Australians[4]);

---

1   The immensely helpful recent Australian Institute of International Affairs project whereby the nine volumes of *Australia in World Affairs 1950-2000* have been made available on a searchable CD-ROM shows peaks of Antarctic interest in that series in the periods 1956-60, 1976-80, 1981-90 and 1991-95, seemingly clustering around periods of ATS regime development (AIIA 2006).

2   Indeed, fear of Antarctica's use for military purposes was a concern for Australia pre Antarctic Treaty.

3   One of the factors behind Australia's repudiation of the Convention on the Regulation of Antarctic Mineral Resource Activities (CRAMRA) was the zero-sum-game Antarctic minerals might pose for Australian minerals.

4   Such as current whaling activities.

- encouraging benign multilateral arrangements for adjudicating decision making by the engaged international community, given the unresolved juridical status of the region;

- maximising the benefits for Australia of international cooperation and collaboration, given such multilateral arrangements; and

- securing whatever economic advantage is consistent with the foregoing, probably largely based on the resources present in the area.

In general terms, these interests are well served by the present ATS. It was, after all, crafted to address the concerns of States, Australia included, so this is no very great surprise.

These are ordinarily the sorts of interests one hears argued in relation to Australia's territorial sovereignty position. On the face of it, however, they would seem to be the sorts of interests that Australia would naturally have merely by virtue of its relative proximity to Antarctica, and the real-world linkages between the two continents. They are not obviously directly coupled to Australia's sovereignty assertions.

So, what interests might arise particularly from being a *claimant*? Most obviously, securing some advantage from that claimant status, through either:

- actual control or access advantages (and the corollary – *denial* or diminution of those advantages to others, including the United Nations[5]), or

- instrumental advantage through the structural concessions to claimants embedded in the ATS or any other Antarctic regulatory structure.

Realistically, it is difficult to imagine that Australia will gain the conventional prerogatives of territorial sovereignty in any likely Antarctic future. But this need not mean there are no relative advantages over non-claimant States. These relative advantages may be bolstered by other Australian advantages (proximity, oceanic continuity between the two continents, economic capability, and participation in the de-facto condominium governing Antarctica). Further, such advantages need not be required to exist in perpetuity; if they merely offered benefits during the building of a post-claimant or post-ATS Antarctic dispensation, they may be valuable indeed. In our judgement, when one gets below the formalism of the legal basis to claim, Australia's continuing attachment to its territorial claim is very largely based on this instrumental calculus. Few officials, and, to the extent they give it any thought, politicians, realistically entertain the idea that the AAT will ever be shown on maps in green and gold. But there may be other perceived benefits from a formal assertion of

---

5   The Treaty is in Australia's interests, according to Patterson (2007: 71) in part because it helps "keep the UN sidelined".

territorial sovereignty, such as national prestige, status or even "nation building" (Bergin and Haward 2007: 17) – a sort of Antarctic "Manifest Destiny" argument, perhaps. We do not underestimate the populist potential of such stances in the Australian domestic context. But, what one loses in this stance may be the opportunity to argue idealist positions, and if one supposes this is naïve in Antarctica, one presumably sees no prospects for such positions anywhere.

To speak of Australian Antarctic interests is of course to beg the question whether there is now a consistent set of shared interests or values for this area – any more than for anywhere else. Is it likely that, to take just a few actors of the Australian polity, the Australian Conservation Foundation, the Australian Mining Industry Council, Austral Fishing and the government of the day, have similar Antarctic interests? Some perhaps, but probably we increasingly face the situation where divergent and not easily reconcilable valuations are the norm. We do not have the space here to pursue how Australia might deal with this, but it does seem likely that we shall need rather more developed and sophisticated mechanisms for debate and adjudication than has hitherto been the case for Antarctic policy issues.

As we noted above, a simple perusal of the AIIA series on *Australia in World Affairs* reveals the lumpiness of attention to Antarctica as a political/policy issue over the past half century. Looking at a higher resolution over the 22 years since the publication of *Australia's Antarctic Policy Options* (Harris 1984a) we see what this meant in terms of actual Australian activities in both the Antarctic and the key international forums.

Until the late 1980s, Australia had an Antarctic engagement which was politically unclear and financially under-resourced. The earlier focus on marine living resources, and adoption of the Convention on the Conservation of Antarctic Marine Living Resources (CCAMLR), notwithstanding the fact that Australia played a significant role and hosted the resulting Secretariat, did not appear to bring significantly greater clarity to Australia's broader political engagement with Antarctica. Then, during the negotiation of the Convention on the Regulation of Antarctic Mineral Resource Activities (CRAMRA), it developed a strongly articulated political goal (of rejecting CRAMRA and putting in its place something that prohibited mineral resource activities and securing greater environmental protection). In support of that political goal, Australia strengthened its station infrastructure and repositioned its science program to emphasise non-mineral resource research and the protection of the Antarctic environment. Through the period of the adoption of the Protocol on Environmental Protection to the Antarctic Treaty (Madrid Protocol) and its immediate bedding in, a very clear Australian priority to environmental protection was evident. From the later 1990s on, the national position became less clear. Whilst still an active ATS player, with a strong across-the-board science program, and at the progressive end of the spectrum on environmental management, new commercial interests (primarily fishing) became evident. In the past five years there have been perceptions that as a result of its approach to a variety of issues including illegal, unreported and unregulated (IUU) fishing, whaling and the extended continental shelf, Australia has become the most assertive claimant (Hemmings 2006b). The issue now is not lack of clarity about national interest, but attitudes to that national interest.

Domestically, there appears to have been a contraction in the number of agencies of state actively concerned with Antarctica over the past decade. Aside from a largely *pro forma* leadership role at Antarctic Treaty Consultative Meetings (ATCMs) (it doesn't even have this role at CCAMLR, where the Australian Antarctic Division (AAD) leads), the Department of Foreign Affairs and Trade is invisible apart from the occasional "big-ticket" issue such as the submission to the Commission on the Limits of the Continental Shelf. This seems to be largely a product of the massive reduction in staffing within the Department, which has left Antarctica as a part-time responsibility for officials really focused elsewhere. It is also in part a product of the unusual situation of AAD, administratively within the Department of the Environment and Water Resources. Already novel as an Antarctic science and logistics agency in having a mandated policy role, AAD has in recent years been the agency on which the Australian government has loaded prime responsibility for any and all international agreements having an Antarctic or Southern Ocean element. So, aside from the raft of ATS instruments that fall to it, it is heavily engaged in the International Whaling Commission (IWC) and Agreement on the Conservation of Albatrosses and Petrels (ACAP) issues. Whilst the Attorney-General's Department is periodically involved in Australian ATCM delegations, and the Australian Customs Service, Australian Fisheries Management Authority, Department of Agriculture, Fisheries and Forestry engage with CCAMLR, they do so in very narrow areas (primarily it seems in relation to IUU activity in the Heard Island and McDonald Islands EEZ) and often only at lower grade officials level. For all intents and purposes, AAD is the Australian government when it comes to Antarctic affairs. This is perhaps a mixed blessing. Notwithstanding the superb science role it performs, and an operational capacity and competence that other and larger Antarctic States eye enviously, it is both overstretched and (frankly) a bit out of its league when it comes to international diplomacy. This is hardly surprising. In our judgement, whilst it is probably unreasonable to expect Australia to maintain the sort of all-of-government commitment and participation of Ambassadorial-level officials in the development and international articulation of Australian Antarctic policy that was evident during its successful challenging of the minerals regime in the late 1980s and early 1990s, the game has to be lifted somewhat from its present situation. A further challenge is provided by the increasing number of fora in which Antarctic affairs are now discussed.

One option open to Australia that is better used by a number of other Antarctic States is to take advantage of the expertise that resides outside agencies of government. Australia, like some other States, has allowed representation on its delegations from environmental and industry advocacy groups, but it has no developed tradition of itself actively seeking external advice, let alone recruiting external experts for its delegations. We risk retorts of being self-serving, but it seems to us a fairly remarkable state of affairs that, with the obvious exception of this volume's AAD authors, none of the other Australian participants in the Looking South project have ever been approached formally for advice on any aspect of Australian Antarctic engagement in the international arena. This is a picture quite different from that found with a number of other Antarctic Treaty Consultative Parties, for example from non-claimants such as Italy, Germany and the Netherlands (whose legal representation has drawn heavily on expertise at the universities of Sienna, Heidelberg and Utrecht respectively) or claimants such as Chile or New Zealand (who have drawn on university scientists for environmental expertise). Australia's Antarctic representation is not merely drawn from a tiny fraction of the government's own agencies, it is drawn only from that small pool.

The International Polar Year now upon us will surely increase the profile of Antarctica, domestically and internationally. We hope that this enables our scientists to not only throw greater light on the challenges of our time – most obviously the critical issue of climate change – but to show both the political leadership and the wider public whom they serve why Antarctic science is important. Alongside this, we also hope that the legal and social sciences communities (the humanities) find both reason and the institutional space to examine Antarctica too. The present situation of the 10 per cent of the planet that is Antarctica is such that the full range of academic and wider intellectual resources needs to attend to it.

References

(AAD) Australian Antarctic Division, 1995, *Heard Island Wilderness Reserve Management Plan*, Department of Environment and Heritage.

AAD, 2000, *Looking South: The Australian Antarctic Program into the 21st Century*, Department of Environment and Heritage.

AAD, 2003, *Australia's Antarctic Science Program, Science Strategy 2004/05-2008/09*, <http://www.aad.gov.au/default.asp?casid=13950> (26 March 2007).

AAD, 2004a, *Australia's Antarctic Tourism Policy*, <www.aad.gov.au/default.asp?casid=20909> (12 January 2007).

AAD, 2004b, *Protecting Antarctica from Tourist Invasion*, <http://www.aad.gov.au/default.asp?casid=13979> (12 March 2007).

AAD, 2004c, *Unusual Animal Mortality Response Plan 04/05 Season*.

AAD, 2005a, *Antarctic Air Link Project Open for Business*, <http://www.aad.gov.au/default.asp?casid=19989> (12 March 2007).

AAD, 2005b, *Illegal Fishing in the Southern Ocean: The Problem, Practices and Perpetrators*, <http://www.aad.gov.au/default.asp?casid=11981> (24 January 2007).

AAD, 2005c, *Heard Island and McDonald Islands Marine Reserve Management Plan*, <http://www.heardisland.aq/protection/management_plan/index.html> (28 February 2007).

AAD, 2006, *Antarctic Non-Government Operations – Australian Antarctic Tour Operators*, <http://www.aad.gov.au/default.asp?casid=1985> (12 March 2007).

AAD, 2007a, Australian Antarctic Science Program, <http://www.aad.gov.au/default.asp?casid=13949> (15 March 2007).

AAD, 2007b, Australian Centre for Applied Marine Mammal Science, <http://www.aad.gov.au/default.asp?casid=23095> (15 March 2007).

(ABC) Australian Broadcasting Corporation, 2007a, *Japanese Pact Won't Cause Arms Race: PM* (14.03.07) <http://www.abc.net.au/news/newsitems/200703/s1871019.htm> (14 March 2007).

ABC, 2007b, *Foreign Correspondent*, ABC Television, 17 March.

(ACAP) Agreement on the Conservation of Albatrosses and Petrels, 2004, *Report of the First Session of the Meeting of the Parties*, Hobart, Australia, 10-12 November.

ACAP, 2006, *Report of the Second Session of the Meeting of the Parties*, Christchurch, New Zealand, 13-17 November.

(ACE CRC) Antarctic Climate and Ecosystems Cooperative Research Centre, 2007, Homepage, <http://www.acecrc.org.au> (26 March 2007).

(AFMA) Australian Fisheries Management Authority, 2001, *Sub-Antarctic Fisheries Bycatch Action Plan 2001, Background Paper*, Commonwealth of Australia.

AFMA, 2007, Figure <http://www.afma.gov.au/fisheries/fisheriesv3.gif> (19 January 2007).

(AIIA) Australian Institute of International Affairs, 2006, *Australia in World Affairs 1950-2000*, CD-ROM.

(ASAC) Antarctic Science Advisory Committee, 1986, *Australia's National Interests in Antarctica and International Considerations Affecting Australia's Antarctic Policy: Implications for Australia's Antarctic Scientific Research Program*, Department of Foreign Affairs, Occasional Paper 4.

ASAC, 1997, *Australia's Antarctic Program Beyond 2000*, <http://www.aad. gov.au/science/foresight/index.html/> (13 February 2007).

(ASOC) Antarctic and Southern Ocean Coalition, 2001a, *Antarctic Tourism*, Information Paper 40, ATCM XXIV, St Petersburg.

ASOC, 2001b, *ASOC Report on the XXIV Antarctic Treaty Consultative Meeting*.

ASOC, 2004a, *Report of the Antarctic and Southern Ocean Coalition*, Information Paper 66, ATCM XXVII, Cape Town.

ASOC, 2004b, *The Case for Concern about Antarctic Tourism*, ATME Paper 20 Rev 1, Antarctic Treaty Meeting of Experts on Tourism and Non-governmental Activities in Antarctica, Tromso-Trondheim.

ASOC, 2004c, *Tourism accreditation and inspection under the Antarctic Treaty*, Information Paper 108, ATCM XXVII, Cape Town.

ASOC, 2005a, *Some legal issues posed by Antarctic tourism*, Information Paper 71, ATCM XXVIII, Stockholm.

ASOC, 2005b, *Antarctic Marine Ecosystem Research in the CCAMLR Area*, SC-CAMLR-XXIV/BG/20.

ASOC, 2006a, Strategic Issues Posed by Tourism in the Antarctic Treaty Area, Information Paper 120, XXIX ATCM, Edinburgh.

ASOC, 2006b, *Managing Antarctic Tourism: A critical review of site-specific guidelines*, Information Paper 65, XXIX ATCM, Edinburgh.

ASOC, 2006c, *CCAMLR XXV: Meeting Report*, <http://www.asoc.org/pdfs/ ASOC%20Report%20CCAMLR%20XXV-2006.pdf> (24 March 2007).

(ATCM) Antarctic Treaty Consultative Meeting XIII, 1985, *Final Report of the Thirteenth Antarctic Treaty Consultative Meeting*, Belgium.

ATCM XXIII, 1999, *Final Report of the Twenty-Third Antarctic Treaty Consultative Meeting*, Lima.

ATCM XXVI, 2003, Decision 5 – Meeting of Experts on Tourism and Non-governmental Activities, *Final Report of the Twenty-Sixth Antarctic Treaty Consultative Meeting*, Madrid.

ATCM XXVII, 2004, *Final Report of the Twenty-Seventh Antarctic Treaty Consultative Meeting*, Cape Town.

ATCM XXVIII, 2005a, *Final Report of the Twenty-Eighth Consultative Meeting*, Stockholm.

ATCM XXVIII, 2005b, Resolution 5 (2005) Resolution on Site Guidelines for Visitors, *Final Report of the XXVIII ATCM – Part II: Measures, Decisions and Resolutions adopted at the XXVIII ATCM*, Stockholm.

ATCM XXIX, 2006, *Final Report of the Twenty-Ninth Antarctic Treaty Consultative Meeting*, Edinburgh.

(ATME) Antarctic Treaty Meeting of Experts, 2004, *Chairman's Report from Antarctic Treaty Meeting of Experts on Tourism and Non-governmental Activities in Antarctica*, Tromso-Trondheim.

(CCAMLR) Commission for the Conservation of Antarctic Marine Living Resources, 1984, *Report of the Third Meeting of the Commission*.

CCAMLR, 1989a, *Report of the Eighth Meeting of the Commission*: Annex G, paragraphs 133-140.

CCAMLR, 1989b, *Report of the Eighth Meeting of the Commission.*

CCAMLR, 1990a, *Report of the Ninth Meeting of the Scientific Committee.*

CCAMLR, 1990b, *Report of the Ninth Meeting of the Commission.*

CCAMLR, 1991, *Report of the Tenth Meeting of the Commission.*

CCAMLR, 1994, *Report of the Thirteenth Meeting of the Commission.*

CCAMLR, 2001, *Report of the Twentieth Meeting of the Commission.*

CCAMLR, 2002, *Report of the Twenty-first Meeting of the Commission.*

CCAMLR, 2003, *Report of the Twenty-second Meeting of the Commission.*

CCAMLR, 2004a, *CCAMLR's work on the elimination of seabird mortality associated with fishing,* CCAMLR Secretariat, <htpp://www.ccamlr.org/pu/e/sc/imaf/ie-intro.htm> (16 February 2007).

CCAMLR, 2004b, *Report of the Twenty-third Meeting of the Scientific Committee.*

CCAMLR, 2005, *Report of the Twenty-fourth Meeting of the Scientific Committee.*

CCAMLR, 2006, *Report of the Twenty-fifth Meeting of the Commission.*

CCAMLR, 2006/07, *Schedule of Conservation Measures in Force 2006/07,* CCAMLR Secretariat, <http://www.ccamlr.org/pu/E/e_pubs/cm/06-07/toc.htm> (11 April 2007).

CCAMLR, 2007, *Map,* <http://www.ccamlr.org/pu/E/conv/map.htm> (14 January 2007).

(CCSBT) Commission for the Conservation of Southern Bluefin Tuna, 2001, *Report of the Fourth Meeting of the Ecologically Related Species Working Group,* <http://www.ccsbt.org> (13 April 2007).

(CLCS) Commission on the Limits of the Continental Shelf, 2005, *Statement by the Chairman of the Commission on the Limits of the Continental Shelf on the progress of work of the Commission* (3 May).

(CMS) Convention on the Conservation of Migratory Species of Wild Animals, 1997, *Proceedings of the Fifth Meeting of the Conference of the Parties.*

CMS, 1999a, *Proceedings of the Sixth Meeting of the Conference of the Parties.*

CMS, 1999b, Final Statement of the First Meeting of the Valdivia Group's Ad hoc Working Group on Albatross, *Proceedings of the Sixth Meeting of the Conference of the Parties.*

CMS, 2007, *CMS Secretariat,* <http://www.cms.int> (10 February 2007).

(COMNAP) Council of Managers of National Antarctic Programs, 2003, *Worst Case and Less than Worst Case Environmental Scenarios,* Working Paper 9, ATCM XXVI, Madrid.

COMNAP, 2004, *Working Paper on the Applicability to the Antarctic of the IMO "Guidelines for Ships Operating in Arctic Ice-Covered Waters,"* Working Paper 9, ATCM XXVII, Cape Town.

COMNAP, 2006, *The Use of Ballast Water in Antarctica,* Information Paper 83, ATCM XXIX, Edinburgh.

(COMNAP and IAATO) Council of Managers of National Antarctic Programs and the International Association of Antarctica Tour Operators, 2005, Information Paper on the Use of Ballast Water in Antarctica, Information Paper 121, ATCM XXVIII, Stockholm.

(DEH) Department of Environment and Heritage, 2004, *Department of Environment and Heritage Annual Report 2003-04,* <http://www.deh.gov.au/about/annual-report/03-04/> (28 June 2005).

DEH, 2005, *Corporate Plan 2005-08,* Canberra.

(FAO) Food and Agriculture Organization of the United Nations, 1999, *International Plan of Action for Reducing Incidental Catch of Seabirds in Longline Fisheries. International Plan of Action for the Conservation and Management of*

Sharks. International Plan of Action for the Management of Fishing Capacity, FAO, Rome.

FAO, 2007, *International Plan of Action for Reducing Incidental Catch of Seabirds in Longline Fisheries*, <http://www.fao.org/fi/website/FIRetrieveAction. do?dom=org&xml=ipoa_seabirds.xml&xp_nav=2> (11 April 2007).

(HSI) Humane Society International, 2004, *Humane Society International goes to Federal Court over Japanese Whaling* (19 October), <www.hsi.org.au/> (9 January 2007).

(IAATO) International Association of Antarctica Tour Operators, 2004a, *Overview Summarizing the Terms of Reference*, ATME Paper 12, Antarctic Treaty Meeting of Experts on Tourism and Non-governmental Activities in Antarctica, Tromso-Trondheim.

IAATO, 2004b, *Report of the International Association of Antarctica Tour Operators 2003-2004 under Article III(2) of the Antarctic Treaty*, Information Paper 68, ATCM XXVII, Cape Town.

IAATO, 2004c, *IAATO's Formalization of an Accreditation Scheme and Internal Audit Process and the Association's Views on an ATCM Accreditation Scheme*, Information Paper 69, ATCM XXVII, Cape Town.

IAATO, 2005a, *Newsletter* (April).

IAATO, 2005b, *An Update on IAATO's Accreditation and Audit Scheme*, Information Paper 96, ATCM XXVIII, Stockholm.

IAATO, 2005c, *Update on Boot and Clothing Decontamination Guidelines and the Introduction and Detection of Diseases in Antarctic Wildlife: IAATO's Perspective*, Information Paper 97, ATCM XXVIII, Stockholm.

IAATO, 2006a, *IAATO Overview of Antarctic Tourism: 2005-2006 Antarctic Season*, Information Paper 86, ATCM XXIX, Edinburgh.

IAATO, 2006b, *Report of the International Association of Antarctica Tour Operators 2005-2006*, Information Paper 90, ATCM XXIX, Edinburgh.

IAATO, 2006c, *Tourism Statistics, 2005-2006 Tourists by Nationality (All) – Rev 1*, <http://www.iaato.org/tourism_stats.html> (13 March 2007).

IAATO, 2006d, *Land-Based Tourism and the Development of Land-Based Tourism Infrastructure in Antarctica: an IAATO Perspective*, Information Paper 85, ATCM XXIX, Edinburgh.

IAATO, 2006e, *An Update on the Antarctic Audit and Accreditation Scheme*, Information Paper 95, ATCM XXIX, Edinburgh.

IAATO, 2007, *Tourism Statistics*, <http://www.iaato.org> (31 January 2007).

(ICSU) International Council for Science, 2005, *About ICSU*, <http://www.icsu. org/5_abouticsu/INTRO.html> (28 June 2005).

(IPCC) Intergovernmental Panel on Climate Change, Working Group 1, 2007, *Climate Change 2007: The Physical Science Basis Summary for Policymakers*, <http://www.ipcc.ch> (27 March 2007).

(IPY) International Polar Year, 2004, *A Framework for the International Polar Year 2007-2008*, <http://216.70.123.96/images/uploads/framework.pdf> (10 January 2007).

(IUCN) World Conservation Union, 2007, *Red List of Threatened Species*, <http:// www.iucnredlist.org/> (6 February 2007).

(IWC) International Whaling Commission Bycatch Sub-Committee, 2004, *Report of the IWC Sub-Committee on Estimation of Bycatch and Other Human-Induced Mortality*, <http://www.iwcoffice.org/_documents/sci_com/ SCRepFiles 2004/56annexj.pdf> (6 February 2007).

(IWC) International Whaling Commission, 2001, Resolution 1, *Transparency Within the International Whaling Commission*, <http://www.iwcoffice.org/meetings/resolutions/> (13 February 2007).

IWC, 2006a, Submission by Japan, IWC/58/12, *Normalizing the International Whaling Commission*, <http://www.iwcoffice.org/meetings/resolutions/> (9 February 2007).

IWC, 2006b, Resolution 1, *St Kitts and Nevis Declaration*, <http://www.iwcoffice.org/meetings/resolutions/> (5 February 2007).

IWC, 2006c, *Report of the Scientific Committee*, IWC/58/Rep 1.

IWC, 2006d, *Report of the Conservation Committee*, IWC/58/Rep 7.

(IWC Chairman) International Whaling Commission Chairman, 2005, Chair's Report, 57th Annual IWC Meeting, at 3; draft resolution Doc. IWC/57/30 (2005).

(NOAA) National Oceanic and Atmospheric Administration, 2004, *Large Whale Ship Strike Database*, <http://www.nmfs.noaa.gov/pr/overview/publicat.html> (13 February 2007).

(NOO) National Oceans Office, 2002, *Resources: Macquarie Island's Picture*, Assessment Report, National Oceans Office.

(PWS) Parks and Wildlife Service, 1999, *Guidelines for Tourist Operations at Macquarie Island Nature Reserve 1999/2000*.

PWS, 2004, *Guidelines for Tourist Operations and Visits to Macquarie Island Nature Reserve World Heritage Area 2004–2005*.

PWS, 2006, *Macquarie Island Nature Reserve and World Heritage Area Management Plan*.

(SCAR) Scientific Committee on Antarctic Research, *Homepage*, <http://www.scar.org> (15 March 2007).

(SEAFO) South East Atlantic Fisheries Organisation Commission, 2007, *Conservation Measure 05/06 on Reducing Incidental By-catch of Seabirds in the SEAFO Convention Area*, <http://www.seafo.org/welcome.htm> (11 April 2007).

(UN FAO) United Nations Food and Agriculture Organization, 2001, *International Plan of Action to Prevent, Deter and Eliminate Illegal, Unreported and Unregulated Fishing* (IPoA-IUU), <http://www.fao.org/Legal/index_en.htm> (16 December 2006).

UN FAO, 2007, *Communications*, <http://www.fao.org/fi/website/FIRetrieveAction.do?dom=topic&fid=1478> (12 March 2007).

(UN) United Nations, 2004, *Report of the Secretary General: Sustainable Fisheries, including through the 1995 Agreement for the Implementation of the Provisions of the United Nations Convention on the Law of the Sea of 10 December 1982 relating to the Conservation and Management of Straddling Fish Stocks and Highly Migratory Fish Stocks, and related instruments*, UN publications: A/59/298.

(UNFCCC) United Nations Framework Convention on Climate Change, 2007, *Kyoto Protocol*, <http://unfccc.int/kyoto_protocol/items/2830.php> (3 March 2007).

(WCPFC) Western and Central Pacific Fisheries Commission, 2006, *Conservation and Management Measure to Mitigate the Impact of Fishing for Highly Migratory Fish Stocks on Seabirds*, <http://www.wcpfc.int/> (2 April 2007).

(WDCS) Whale and Dolphin Conservation Society, 2005, *A Review of the Impact of Noise on Cetaceans*, <http://www.wdcs.org.au/info_details.php?select=1076160600> (2 February 2007).

Agnew, D, 2000, The Illegal and Unregulated Fishery for Toothfish in the Southern Ocean and the CCAMLR Catch Documentation Scheme, *Marine Policy,* 24: 361-374.

Ainley, D, Ballard G, Ackley S, Blight L, Eastman J, Emslie S, Lescroel A, Olmastroni S, Townsend S, Tynan C, Wilson P and Woehler E, Paradigm Lost, or is Top-down Forcing No Longer Significant in the Antarctic Marine Ecosystem? *Antarctic Science,* [in press 2007].

Allison, G, 1992, Public and Private Management: Are They Fundamentally Alike in All Unimportant Respects, reprinted in *Public Administration: Concepts and Cases,* Stillman Jr, R, 5th edn, Houghton Mifflin: 292-298.

Animal Welfare Institute, 2006, Letter to WT Hogarth, Director, National Marine Fisheries Service, dated 27 December.

Antarctic Tasmania, 2006, *Tasmania: Your Gateway to Antarctica,* Department of Economic Development, Hobart.

Antarctic Treaty Secretariat, 2006, *Final Report of the Twenty-ninth Antarctic Treaty Consultative Meeting: Edinburgh, United Kingdom, 12–23 June 2006,* Secretariat of the Antarctic Treaty, Buenos Aires.

Atkinson, A, Siegel V, Pakhomov E and Rothery P, 2004, Long-term Decline in Krill Stock and Increase in Salps Within the Southern Ocean, *Nature,* 432: 100-3.

Auburn, FM, 1982, *Antarctic Law and Politics,* Croom-Helm.

Australia, 1998, *Australia's Oceans Policy: Caring, Understanding, Using Wisely,* Commonwealth of Australia.

Australia, 2004a, *An Analysis of Potential Threats and Opportunities Offered by Antarctic Tourism,* ATME Paper # 17 at Attachment A, Antarctic Treaty Meeting of Experts on Tourism and Non-governmental Activities in Antarctica, Tromso-Trondheim.

Australia, 2004b, *Accreditation of Non-Government Operations,* ATME Paper #15, Antarctic Treaty Meeting of Experts on Tourism and Non-governmental Activities in Antarctica, Tromso-Trondheim.

Australia, 2004c, *Accreditation Scheme for Antarctic Tour Operators,* Working Paper 38, ATCM XXVII, Cape Town.

Australia, 2005a, *Protection of Antarctica's Intrinsic Values: Policy on Non-Government Activities,* Working Paper 38, ATCM XXVIII, Stockholm.

Australia, 2005b, *Measures to Address the Unintentional Introduction and Spread of Non-Native Biota and Disease to the Antarctic Treaty Area,* Working Paper 28, ATCM XXVIII, Stockholm.

Australian Attorney-General, 2005, Outline of Submissions of the Attorney-General of the Commonwealth as *Amicus Curiae,* at 2, <http://www.hsi.org.au/> (24 June 2005).

Australian Government, 1998, *Our Antarctic Future: Australia's Antarctic Program Beyond 2000: The Howard Government Response,* Australian Government Publishing Service.

Australian Law Reform Commission, 2006, Report: *Same Crime, Same Time – Sentencing of Federal Offenders,* Australian Government.

Baird, Ruth, 2004, Can Australia assert an Extended Continental Shelf off the Australian Antarctic Territory Consistent with the Law of the Sea and Within the Constraints of the Antarctic Treaty? *Maritime Studies,* 138: 1-19.

Baird, Rachel, 2004, Testing the Waters: Fine Tuning the Provisions of the Fisheries Management Act 1991 (Cth) Applicable to Foreign Fishing Boats, *University of Western Australia Law Review,* 32: 63.

Baker, GB, Double, M, Gales, R, Tuck, G, Abbott, C, Ryan, P, Petersen, S, Robertson, C, Baird, S-J and Alderman, R, A Global Assessment of the Impact of Fisheries-Related Mortality on Shy and White-Caped Albatrosses: Conservation Implications, *Biological Conservation,* [in press 2007].

Baker, GB, Gales, R, Hamilton, S and Wilkinson, V, 2002, Albatrosses and Petrels in Australia: A Review of Their Conservation and Management, *Emu,* 102: 71-97.

Bakhtiari, AS, 2006, Crude Ideas, *Australian Antarctic Magazine,* Spring: 10.

Barsh R, 2001, Food Security, Food Hegemony, and Charismatic Animals, in *Toward a Sustainable Whaling Regime,* (ed) Friedheim, R, CCI Press.

Bastmeijer, K, 2003, Tourism in Antarctica: Increasing Diversity and the Legal Criteria for Authorisation, *New Zealand Journal of Environmental Law,* 7: 85.

Bastmeijer, K, 2004, Regulating Antarctic Tourism and the Precautionary Principle, *American Journal of International Law,* 98: 763-81.

Bello, W, 2002, *Deglobalization: Ideas for a New World Economy,* Zed Books.

Benderm, P and Lugten, G, 2007, Taxing Illegal Fishing (A Proposal for Using Taxation Law to Reduce Profiteering from IUU Fishing Offences), *International Journal of Marine and Coastal Law,* 22:1.

Bergin, A, 1991, The Politics of Antarctic Minerals: The Greening of White Australia, *Australian Journal of Political Science,* 26: 216-39.

Bergin, A and Haward, M, 2007, Frozen Assets: Securing Australia's Antarctic Future, *Strategic Insights 34,* Australian Strategic Policy Institute.

Best, P, Peddemors, V, Cockcroft, V and Rice, N, 2005, Mortalities of Right Whales and Related Anthropogenic Factors in South African Waters 1963 – 1998, *Journal of Cetacean Research and Management,* Special Issue 2: 171-6.

BirdLife International, 2004, *Tracking Ocean Wanderers: The Global Distribution of Albatrosses and Petrels.* Results from the Global Procellariiform Tracking Workshop, 1-5 September 2003, Gordon's Bay, South Africa, BirdLife International.

Birnie, P, 1985, *International Regulation of Whaling: From Conservation of Whaling to Conservation of Whales and Regulation of Whale-watching* (Vols 1 and 2), Oceana Publications.

Birnie, P and Boyle, A, 1992, *International Law and the Environment,* Clarendon Press.

Birnie, P and Boyle, A, 2002, *International Law and the Environment,* 2nd edn, Oxford University Press.

Blay, S and Bubna-Litic, K, 2006, The Interplay of International Law and Domestic Law: The Case of Australia's Efforts to Protect Whales, *Environmental and Planning Law Journal,* 23: 465-89.

Bonner, W, 1985, Birds and Mammals – Antarctic Seals, in *Key Environments: Antarctica,* (eds) Bonner, W and Walton, D, Pergamon: 202-22.

Boyle, AE, 1991, Saving the World? Implementation and Enforcement of International Environmental Law Through International Institutions, *Journal of Environmental Law,* 3: 229-46.

Branch, T and Butterworth, D, 2001, Southern Hemisphere Minke Whales: Standardised Abundance Estimates From the 1978/79 to 1997/98 IDCR-SOWER Surveys, *Journal of Cetacean Research and Management,* 3: 143-74.

Brook, J, 1984, Australia's Policy Towards Antarctica, in *Australia's Antarctic Policy Options,* (ed) Harris, S, Centre for Resource and Environmental Studies, Australian National University: 255-64.

Brownlie, I, 1990, *Principles of Public International Law*, 4th edn, Clarendon Press.

Brownlie, I, 2003, *Principles of Public International Law*, 6th edn, Oxford University Press.

Burns, WCG, 2003, Climate Change and the International Whaling Commission in the 21st Century, in *The Future of Cetaceans in a Changing World*, (eds) Burns, WCG and Gillespie, A, Transnational.

Busbee, D, Tizard I, Ferrick D and Ott-Reeves E, 1999, Environmental Pollutants and Marine Mammal Health: the Potential Impact of Hydrocarbons and Halogenated Hydrocarbons on Immune System Dysfunction, *Journal of Cetacean Research and Management*, Special Issue 1: 223-48.

Bush, W, (compiler) 1982, *Antarctica and International Law: A Collection of Interstate and National Documents*, Oceana.

Bush, W, 2000, Means and Methods of Implementation of Antarctic Environmental Regimes and National Environmental Instruments: An Exercise in Comparison in *Implementing the Environmental Protection Regime for the Antarctic*, (ed) Vidas, D, Kluwer Academic Publishers, 21-43.

Bush, W, 2001, The Next 40 Years: The Challenge of Economic Globalisation and 21st Century Security Threats, in *The Antarctic: Past, Present and Future*, (eds) Jabour-Green, J and Haward, M, Cooperative Research Centre for the Antarctic and Southern Ocean, Research Report 28: 126-46.

Calvert, A, 2000, *Secretary's Speech: Australian Foreign Policy and the Trans-Tasman Relationship*, <http://www.dfat.gov.au/media/speeches/department/001122trans_tasman.html> (26 March 2007).

Cameron, I, 1974, *Antarctica: The Last Continent*, Cassell.

Campbell, Senator the Hon I, 2005a, *Whaling – Back to the Bad Old Days, Warns Campbell*, Media Release (1 April), <http://www.deh.gov.au/minister/env/2005/mr01apr205.html> (1 February 2007).

Campbell, Senator the Hon I, 2005b, *Whale protection: Australia leads the way*, Media Release (20 May), <www.deh.gov.au/minister/env/2005/mr20may2005.html> (23 May 2005).

Campbell, Senator the Hon I, 2005c, Minister for the Environment and Heritage, Interview with Fran Bailey on Radio National Breakfast program, (21 June), <http://www.deh.gov.au/minister/env/2005/tr21jun05.html> (30 March 2007).

Cessford, G and Dingwall, P, 1994, Tourism on New Zealand's Sub-Antarctic Islands, *Annals of Tourism Research*, 21: 318-32.

Chapman, R, 1990, Public Policy, Federalism, Intergovernmental Relations: The Federal Factor, *Publius*, 20: 69-84.

Chaturvedi, S, 1990, *Dawning of Antarctica: A Geopolitical Analysis*, Segment Books.

Chester, J, 1986, *Going to Extremes: Project Blizzard and Australia's Antarctic Heritage*, Doubleday.

Chia, E, 2000, *Middle Powers in the Modern State System: A Case Study of Australia's Role as a Regional Actor*, Unpublished PhD Thesis, Institute of Antarctic and Southern Ocean Studies, University of Tasmania.

Christianson, G, 1999, *Greenhouse: The 200-Year Story of Global Warming*, Constable.

Clifton, R, 2004, Planning for Contingencies, *Australian Antarctic Magazine*, 7: 4-5.

Coghlan, A, 2002, Extreme Mercury Levels Revealed in Whalemeat, *New Scientist*, 6 June.

Commonwealth of Australia, 1953, *Gazette* No 56, 11 September 1953.

Commonwealth of Australia, 1994, *Gazette* No S 290, 29 July 1994.

Commonwealth of Australia, 2004, *Continental Shelf Submission of Australia: Executive Summary*, <http://www.un.org/Depts/los/clcs_new/submissions_files/submission_aus.htm> (12 January 2007).

Cooper, J and Riviera, K, 2004, *FAO IPOA-Seabirds: Progress to Date and a Comparative Analysis of Existing Plans*, Presentation at the Third International Albatross and Petrel Conference, IAPC, Montevideo, Uruguay, 23-27 August.

Cooper, J, Baker, B, Double, M, Gales, R, Papworth, W, Tasker, M and Waugh, S, 2006, Agreement on the Conservation of Albatrosses and Petrels: Rationale, History, Progress and the Way Forward, *Marine Ornithology*, 34:1-5.

Copson, G and Whinam, J, 2001, Review of Ecological Restoration Programme on Sub-Antarctic Macquarie Island: Pest Management Progress and Future Directions, *Ecological Restoration and Management*, 2: 129-38.

Couratier, J, 1983, The Regime For the Conservation of Antarctica's Living Resources, in *Antarctic Resources Policy*, (ed) Vicuña, F, University of Cambridge.

Crawford, J and Rothwell, DR, 1992, Legal Issues Confronting Australia's Antarctica, *Australian Year Book of International Law*, 13: 53-88.

Crosbie, K, 2005, Towards Site Guidelines: A Preliminary Analysis of Antarctic Peninsula Site Landing Data, 1999/00 – 2003/04, Information Paper 81, Antarctic Treaty Consultative Meeting XXVIII.

Croxall, J and Nicol, S, 2004, Management of Southern Ocean fisheries: global forces and future sustainability, *Antarctic Science*, 16: 569-84.

Dastidar, P and Persson, O, 2005, Mapping the Global structure of Antarctic research *vi-a vis* Antarctic Treaty System, *Current Science*, 89: 1552-4.

Davis, C, Li, Y, McConnell, J, Frey, M and Hanna, E, 2005, Snowfall-driven Growth in East Antarctic Ice Sheet Mitigates Recent Sea-level Rise, *Science*, 308: 1898-1901.

Davis, J, 2000, Monitoring Control Surveillance and Vessel Monitoring System Requirements to Combat IUU Fishing, Published by Australian Fisheries Management Authority (AFMA) as IUU/2000/14, <http://www.fao.org/DOCREP/005/Y3274E/y3274e)g.htm> (10 February 2007).

Dodds, K, 1997, *Geopolitics in Antarctica: Views from the Southern Oceanic Rim*, Wiley.

Dodds, K, 2002, *Pink Ice: Britain and the South Atlantic Empire*, Tauris.

Doern, G and Phidd, R, 1983, *Canadian Public Policy: Ideas, Structure, Process*, Methuen.

Downer, A, Ruddock, P and MacFarlane, I, 2004, Joint Media Release – *Australia Lodges Continental Shelf Submission*, 16 November, <http://www.foreign minister.gov.au/releases/2004/joint_continental_shelf_submission_16110 4.html> (12 January 2007).

Doyle, T, 1985, Antarctica and the Science of Exploitation, *Habitat*, 13: 12-14.

Doyle, T and Kellow, A, 1995, *Environmental Politics and Policy Making in Australia*, Macmillan.

Embassy of Australia, 2003, Note 44/2003, 5 February, to the State Department of the United States.

Environment Australia, 1997, *A Universal Metaphor: Australia's Opposition to Commercial Whaling,* Report of the National Task Force on Whaling, Commonwealth of Australia.

Environment Australia, 2001, *Macquarie Island Marine Park Management Plan.*

Environment Australia, 2002, *Assessment of the Heard Island and McDonald Islands Fishery.*

Etheridge, D, Steele, L, Langenfelds, R, Francey, R, Barnola, J-M, and Morgan, V, 1996, Natural and Anthropogenic Changes in Atmospheric CO2 over the Last 1000 Years from Air in Antarctic Ice and Firn, *Journal of Geophysics Research,* 101: 4115-28.

Evans, G and Grant, B, 1991, *Australia's Foreign Relations: In the World of the 1990s,* Melbourne University Press: 321-33.

Fallon, L and Kriwoken, LK, 2004, International Influence of an Australian Non-government Organisation in the Protection of Patagonian Toothfish, *Ocean Development and International Law,* 35: 221-66.

Farman, J, Gardiner, B and Shanklin, J, 1985, Large Losses of Total Ozone in Antarctica Reveal Seasonal ClOx/NOx Interaction, *Nature,* 315: 207-10.

Fisheries Agency of Japan, 2007, Conference for the Normalization of the International Whaling Commission, document dated 27 January, available online (Japanese language version only) at <http://www.jfa.maff.go.jp/release/index.html> (2 February 2007).

Fothergill, A, 1994, *Life in the Freezer – A Natural History of the Antarctic,* BBC Books.

France, 2005, Permanent Mission of France to the United Nations, *Note No 05.29130* (28 March 2005) <www.un.org/Depts/los/clcs_new/submissions_files/aus04/clcs_03_2004_los_fra_en.pdf> (4 January 2007).

Frenot, Y, Chown, S, Whinam, J, Selkirk, P, Convey, P, Skotnicki, M and Bergstrom, D, 2005, Biological Invasions in the Antarctic: Extent, Impacts and Implications, *Biological Reviews,* 80: 45-72.

Frith, D, 2007, Business Embraces Change, *The Weekend Australian,* 24-25 March: 12.

Frost, S, 1978, *Report on the Inquiry into Whales and Whaling,* Commonwealth of Australia.

Germany, 2005, Permanent Mission of Germany to the United Nations, *Note No 88/2005* (5 April 2005) <www.un.org/Depts/los/clcs_new/submissions_files/aus04/clcs_03_2004_los_deu.pdf> (4 January 2007).

Gill, A, Kriwoken, LK, Dodson, S and Fallon, L, 2003, The Challenges of Integrating Tourism into Canadian and Australian Coastal Zone Management, *Dalhousie Law Journal,* 26: 85-147.

Government of Japan, 2005, Note to the UN Commission on the Limits of the Continental Shelf: CLCS.03.2004.LOS/JPN, dated 4 February, <http://www.un.org/Depts/los/clcs_new/submissions_files/submission_aus.htm> (6 February 2007).

Grewe, WG, 2000, *The Epochs of International Law,* Walter de Gruyter.

Greig, D, 1984, Australian Sovereignty in Antarctica: Comments, in *Australia's Antarctic Policy Options,* (ed) Harris, S, Centre for Resource and Environmental Studies, Australian National University: 66-81.

Griggs, L and Lugten, G, 2007, Veil Over the Nets: Unraveling Corporate Liability for IUU Fishing Offences, *Marine Policy,* 31: 159.

Haas, P, 1989, Do Regimes Matter? Epistemic Communities and Mediterranean Pollution Control, *International Organization,* 43: 377.

Hall, HR, 2002, Casey and the Negotiation of the Antarctic Treaty, in *The Antarctic: Past, Present and Future*, (eds) Jabour-Green, J and Haward, M, Proceedings of a conference celebrating the 40th anniversary of the entry into force of the Antarctic Treaty on 23 June 1961, Cooperative Research Centre for the Antarctic and Southern Ocean, Research Report 28: 27-33.

Hanessian Jnr, H, 1965, National Interests in Antarctica, in *Antarctica*, (ed.) Hatherton, T, Methuen.

Harris, S, (ed), 1984a, *Australia's Antarctic Policy Options*, Centre for Resource and Environmental Studies, Australian National University.

Harris, S, 1984b, A Review of Australia's Antarctic Policy Options, in *Australia's Antarctic Policy Options*, (ed) Harris, S, Centre for Resource and Environmental Studies, Australian National University: 1-28.

Harry, R, 1981, The Antarctic Regime and the Law of the Sea Convention: An Australian View, *Virginia Journal of International Law*, 21: 727-46.

Haward, M, 2005, Australian Antarctic Science, paper presented to Australia's Antarctic Agenda workshop, 7 July 2005, ACE CRC.

Haward, M, 2006, Consensus in Antarctica: A Fragile Image?" *Island*, 105: 19-22.

Haward, M, Antarctica, in *The Oxford Companion to Australian Politics*, (ed) Galligan, B, Oxford [in press].

Haward, M, Rothwell D, Jabour J, Hall R, Kellow A, Kriwoken L, Lugten, G and Hemmings A, 2006, Australia's Antarctic Agenda, *Australian Journal of International Affairs*, 60: 439-56.

Hemmings, AD, 2004, Managing the Southern Ocean – The 2003 Meeting of the Commission for the Conservation of Antarctic Marine Living Resources, *New Zealand Yearbook of International Law*, 1: 199-205.

Hemmings, AD, 2005, A Question of Politics: Bioprospecting and the Antarctic Treaty System, in *Antarctic Bioprospecting*, (eds) Hemmings, AD and Rogan-Finnemore, M, 2005a, Gateway Antarctica Special Publication Series 0501: 98-129.

Hemmings, AD, 2006b, Problems Posed by Attempts to Apply Claimant Domestic Legislation Beyond its Own Nationals in Antarctica, *Whales, Antarctica, Diplomacy and the Law: Humane Society International v Kyodo (or Australia v Japan)*, Centre for International and Public Law and Australian Centre for Environmental Law, Australian National University, Canberra, 4 September.

Hemmings, AD, 2006a, Regime Overlap in the Southern Ocean: The Case of Southern Bluefin Tuna and CCSBT in the CCAMLR Area, *New Zealand Yearbook of International Law*, 3: 207-17.

Hemmings, AD, 2006c, Antarctica's tourism peril, *Adelaide Advertiser – Review*, 21 October: W3.

Hemmings, AD and Rogan-Finnemore, M (eds), 2005a, *Antarctic Bioprospecting*, Gateway Antarctica Special Publication Series 501.

Hemmings, AD and Rogan-Finnemore, M, 2005b, The Issues Posed by Bioprospecting in Antarctica, in *Antarctic Bioprospecting*, (eds) Hemmings, AD and Rogan-Finnemore, M, 2005a, Gateway Antarctica Special Publication Series 501: 234-44.

Hemmings, AD and Rogan-Finnemore, M, in press, Access, Obligations and Benefits: Regulating Bioprospecting in the Antarctic, in *Biodiversity, Law and Livelihoods: Bridging the North-South Divide*, IUCN Academy of Environmental Law Research Studies Series, Cambridge University Press.

Henry, D, 2007, Households Must Act Now to Become Energy Efficient, *The Weekend Australian*, 24-25 March: 4.

Herber, B, 2007, *Protecting the Antarctic Commons: Problems of Economic Efficiency*, Udall Center Fellows Monographs, Udall Center for Studies in Public Policy, The University of Arizona.

Herr, R and Hall, R, 1989, Science as Currency and the Currency of Science, in *Antarctica: Policies and Policy Development*, (ed) Handmer, J, Centre for Resource and Environmental Studies, Australian National University: 13-24.

High Seas Task Force, 2006, Report: *Closing the Net: Stopping Illegal Fishing on the High Seas*, Governments of Australia, Canada, Chile, Namibia, New Zealand, and the United Kingdom, WWF, IUCN and the Earth Institute at Columbia University.

Holmes, N, Giese, M and Achurch, H, 2003, *The effects of small boats and pedestrians on the numbers, distribution and behaviour of Giant petrels at Sandy Bay, Macquarie Island during tourism visits, 2003*. Report to the Tasmanian Parks and Wildlife Service and the Macquarie Island Research Activities Group.

Holmes, N, Giese, M and Kriwoken, LK, 2005, Testing the Minimum Approach Distance Guidelines for Incubating Royal Penguins *Eudyptes schlegeli*, *Biological Conservation*, 126: 339-50.

Homeshaw, J, 1995, Policy Community, Policy Networks and Science Policy in Australia, *Australian Journal of Public Administration*, 54: 520-32.

House of Representatives, 1989, Standing Committee on Environment, *Tourism in Antarctica*, Report of the House of Representatives Standing Committee on Environment, Recreation and the Arts, Australian Government Publishing Service.

House of Representatives, 1992, Standing Committee on Legal and Constitutional Affairs, Australian Law in Antarctica: *The Report of the Second Phase of an Inquiry into the Legal Regimes of Australia's External Territories and the Jervis Bay Territory*, Australian Government Printing Service.

Jabour, J, 2006, High Latitude Diplomacy: Australia's Antarctic Extended Continental Shelf, *Marine Policy*, 30: 197-98.

Jabour-Green, J and Nicol, D, 2003, Bioprospecting in Areas Outside National Jurisdiction: Antarctica and the Southern Ocean, *Melbourne Journal of International Law*, 4: 76-111.

Jackson, A, 2006, Looking to Australia's Antarctic Future, *Australian Antarctic Magazine*, Spring: 34.

Jackson, A, Senior Policy Adviser, AAD, Personal Communication, 30 March 2007.

Johnson, M, 2002, *Regulating Ship-Based Antarctic Protected Area Tourism Within the AAT*, Unpublished Honours Dissertation, Faculty of Law, The University of Sydney, Sydney.

Jones, A, Chown, S, Ryan, P, Gremmen, N and Gaston, K, 2003, A Review of Conservation Threats on Gough Island: A Case Study for Terrestrial Conservation in the Southern Oceans, *Biological Conservation*, 113: 75-87.

Jones, B, 1984, *Bulletin*, January 24: 39.

Joyner, C, 1992, *Antarctica and the Law of the Sea*, Martinus Nijhoff.

Joyner, C, 2000, The Role of Non-Binding Norms in the International Legal System, in *Commitment and Compliance*, (ed) Shelton, D, Oxford University Press.

Kaye, S, 2001, The Outer Continental Shelf in the Antarctic, in *The Law of the Sea and Polar Maritime Delimitation and Jurisdiction*, Oude Elferink, A and Rothwell, DR (eds), Martinus Nijhoff Publishers: 125-37.

Kaye, S and Rothwell, DR, 1995, Australia's Antarctic Maritime Claims and Boundaries, *Ocean Development and International Law*, 26: 195-226.

Kaye, S and Rothwell, DR, 2002, Southern Ocean Boundaries and Maritime Claims: Another Antarctic Challenge for the Law of the Sea? *Ocean Development and International Law*, 33: 359-89.

Kaye, S, Rothwell, DR and Dando, S, 1999, The Laws of the Australian Antarctic Territory, *Antarctic and Southern Ocean Law and Policy Occasional Papers* 8, University of Tasmania Law Press.

Keage, P, 1981, *Conservation of Heard Island and the McDonald Islands*, Environmental Studies Occasional Paper 13, Centre for Environmental Studies, University of Tasmania.

Keating, M, 1996, Defining the Policy Advising Function, in *Evaluating Policy Advice: Learning From Commonwealth Experience*, (eds) Uhr, J and Mackay, K, Federalism Research Centre, Australian National University.

Kimpton, P, 2004, Current Legal Developments – Australia, *International Journal of Marine and Coastal Law*, 19: 537-44.

Kolbert, E, 2006, The Darkening Sea: What Carbon Emissions Are Doing To The Ocean, Annals of Science, *The New Yorker*, 20 November: 66-75.

Kriwoken, LK and Williamson, J, 1993, Hobart, Tasmania: Antarctic and Southern Ocean Connections, *Polar Record*, 29: 93-102.

Kriwoken, LK, and Rootes, D, 2000, Tourism on Ice: Environmental Impact Assessment and Antarctic Tourism, *Impact Assessment and Project Appraisal*, 18: 138-50.

Kriwoken, LK, Ellis, C and Holmes, N, 2006, Macquarie Island, Australia, in *Extreme Tourism: Lessons from the World's Cold Water Islands*, (ed) Baldacchino, G, Elsevier: 193-203.

Kriwoken, LK, Hay, P, and Keage, P, 1989, Environmental Policy Implementation: The Case of Sea Dumping off Sub-Antarctic Heard Island, Australia, *Maritime Studies*, 48: 11-21.

Kuhnel, I and Coates, I, 2000, El Niño-Southern Oscillation: Related Probabilities of Fatalities From Natural Perils in Australia, *Natural Hazards*, 22: 117-38.

Law, P, 1962, *Australia and the Antarctic*, John Murtagh Macrossan Memorial Lecture.

Letts, D, 2000, The Use of Force in Patrolling Australia's Fishing Zones, *Marine Policy*, 24: 149-57.

Lewis, P, Hewitt, C, Riddle, M and McMinn, A, 2003, Marine Introductions in the Southern Ocean: An Unrecognised Hazard to Biodiversity, *Marine Pollution Bulletin*, 46: 213-23.

Lowy Institute, 2007, Homepage, <http://www.lowyinstitute.org> (2 April 2007).

Lugten, G, 1999, Report: A Review of Measures Taken by Regional Marine Fishery Bodies To Address Contemporary Fishery Issues, UNFAO.

Lyster, S, 1985, *International Wildlife Law*, Grotius Publications.

Marsden, S, 2005, *Strategic Environmental Assessment and Protected Areas Management in the Sub-Antarctic: Are Some Areas Better Than Others?* Paper presented to the International Association for Impact Assessment Conference, International Experience and Perspectives on SEA, Prague, September.

Mason, P and Legg, S, 2000, The Growth of Tourism in Antarctica, *Geography*, 85: 358-62.

Mawson, D, 1911, *Australasian Association for the Advancement of Science Report*, 13: 398-400.

McDorman, T, 2002, The Role of the Commission on the Limits of the Continental Shelf: A Technical Body in a Political World, *International Journal of Marine and Coastal Law*, 17: 301-24.

Metcalfe, L, 1994, International Policy Coordination and Public Management Reform, *International Review of Administrative Sciences*, 60: 271-90.

Meyer, L, Constable, A and Williams, R, 2000, *Conservation of Marine Habitats in the Region of Heard Island and McDonald Islands*, Paper presented to HIMI Marine Habitats Review, Australian Antarctic Division, Kingston, Tasmania.

Molenaar, E, 2001, Southern Ocean Fisheries and the CCAMLR Regime, in *The Law of the Sea and Polar Maritime Delimitation and Jurisdiction*, (eds) Oude Elferink, A and Rothwell, DR, Martinus Nijhoff: 293-315.

Molenaar, E, 2003, Marine Mammals: The Role of Ethics and Ecosystem Considerations, *Journal of International Wildlife Law & Policy*, 6: 31-51.

Molenaar, E, 2004, Multilateral Hot Pursuit and Illegal Fishing in the Southern Ocean: The Pursuits of the *Viarsa 1* and the *South Tomi* in 2004, *The International Journal of Marine and Coastal Law*, 19: 19-42.

Molenaar, E, 2005, Sea-Borne Tourism in Antarctica: Avenues for Further Intergovernmental Regulation, *The International Journal of Marine and Coastal Law*, 20: 1-49.

Morishita, J, 2006, Multiple Analysis of the Whaling Issue: Understanding the Dispute by a Matrix, *Marine Policy*, 30: 802-08.

Mortimer, G, 2004, Antarctic Tourism – Past, Present and Future, 3rd Annual Phillip Law Lecture, Antarctic Midwinter Festival, Hobart.

Mosley, G, 1984, The Natural Option: The Case for an Antarctic World Park, in *Australia's Antarctic Policy Options*, (ed) Harris, S, Centre for Resource and Environmental Studies, Australian National University: 307-27.

Murray, C and Jabour, J, 2004, Independent Expeditions and Antarctic Tourism Policy, *Polar Record*, 40: 309-17.

Nadelman, E, 1990, Global Prohibition Regimes: The Evolution of Norms in International Society, *International Organisation*, 44: 482.

Namias, J, 1978, Multiple Causes of the North American Abnormal Winter, *Monthly Weather Review*, 106: 279-95.

Naveen, R, 2003, *Compendium of Antarctic Peninsula Visitor Sites*, 2nd edn, Oceanites.

Naveen, R, Forrest, S, Dagit, R, Blight, L, Trivelpiece, W and Trivelpiece, S, 2001, Zodiac Landings by Tourist Ships in the Antarctic Peninsula Region, 1989-99, *Polar Record*, 37: 121.

New Zealand, 2004a, *An Analysis of the Existing Legal Framework for the Management of Tourism and Non-Governmental Activities in Antarctica: Issues, Some Proposals and Comments*, ATME Paper 7, Antarctic Treaty Meeting of Experts on Tourism and Non-governmental Activities in Antarctica, Tromso-Trondheim.

New Zealand, 2004b, *Practical Experience of an Observer Scheme for Antarctic and Sub-Antarctic Tourism*, ATME Paper 10, Antarctic Treaty Meeting of

Experts on Tourism and Non-governmental Activities in Antarctica, Tromso-Trondheim.

New Zealand, 2004c, *Tourism and Non-Governmental Activities in Antarctica: Monitoring Compliance and Environmental Impact*, Information Paper 23, ATCM XXVII, Cape Town.

New Zealand, 2005, Land-based Tourism in Antarctica, Working Paper 12, ATCM XXVIII, Stockholm.

New Zealand and Australia, 2006, *Regulation of Land-Based Infrastructure to Support Tourism in Antarctica*, Working Paper 15 rev. 1, ATCM XXIX, Edinburgh.

Ocean Conserve, 2004, *Japanese Charged with Whaling Inside Sanctuary* (19 October 2004) <http://www.oceanconserve.info/articles/reader.asp?linkid=35793> (23 June 2005).

Opeskin, B and Rothwell, DR, 1991, Australia's Territorial Sea: International and Federal Implications of its Extension to 12 Miles, *Ocean Development and International Law*, 22: 395-431.

Oude Elferink, A, 2002, The Continental Shelf of Antarctica: Implications of the Requirement to Make a Submission to the CLCS under Article 76 of the LOS Convention, *International Journal of Marine and Coastal Law*, 17: 485-520.

Parker, D, 2007, Farmers Need Facts to Play Their Part and Insurers Study Danger Signs, *The Weekend Australian*, 24-25 March: 3.

Parsons, W, 1995, *Public Policy: An Introduction to the Theory and Practice of Policy Analysis*, Edward Elgar.

Patterson, B, 2007, Slicing the Ice, *The Diplomat*, 6: 68-71.

Pauly, D, Christensen, V, Froese, R and Palomares, M, 2000, Fishing Down Aquatic Food Webs, *American Scientist*, 88: 46-51.

Peters, B, 1996, *The Policy Capacity of Governments*, Research Paper No 18, Canadian Centre for Management Development.

Peters, B, 1998, Managing Horizontal Government: The Politics of Coordination, *Public Administration*, 76: 295-311.

Plass, G, 1956, The Carbon Dioxide Theory of Climatic Change, *Tellus*, 8: 140-154.

Powell, S, 2006, *Antarctic Tourism: The call of the ice growing in popularity*, Conference Program, 2nd National Wildlife Tourism Conference: 155-63.

Press, T, 2001, Antarctica and the Future, in *The Antarctic: Past Present and Future*, (eds) Jabour-Green, J and Haward, M, Proceedings of a conference celebrating the 40th anniversary of the entry into force of the Antarctic Treaty on 23 June 1961, Cooperative Research Centre for the Antarctic and Southern Ocean, Research Report 28: 153-66.

Pross, A, 1992, *Group Politics and Public Policy*, 2nd edn, Oxford University Press.

Putnam, R, 1988, Diplomacy and Domestic Politics: The Logic of Two level Games, *International Organization*, 42: 427-60.

Revelle, R and Suess, H, 1957, Carbon Dioxide Exchange between the Atmosphere and Ocean and the Question of an Increase of Atmospheric CO2 during the Past Decades, *Tellus*, 9: 18-27.

Richardson, J and Jordan, A, 1979, *Governing Under Pressure: The Policy Process in a Post-Parliamentary Democracy*, Martin Robertson.

Richardson, M, 2000, Regulating Tourism in the Antarctic: Issues of Environment and Jurisdiction, in *Implementing the Environmental Protection Regime for the Antarctic*, (ed) Vidas, D, Kluwer Academic Publishers, 71-90.

Riddle, M, 2006, A New Science Programme, *Australian Antarctic Magazine*, Spring: 28.

Robertson, G, 1998, The Culture and Practice of Longline Tuna Fishing: Implications for Seabird By-catch Mitigation, *Bird Conservation International*, 8: 211-21.

Robertson, G, 2001, Can Albatrosses and Longline Fisheries Co-exist? *Australian Antarctic Magazine*, 1, Autumn.

Robertson, G, 2005, Seabird Safe Longline Fishing at Heard Island, *Australian Antarctic Magazine*, 8: 18-19.

Rothwell, DR and Davis, R, 1997, *Antarctic Environmental Protection: A Collection of Australian and International Instruments*, The Federation Press.

Ross, G, Weaver, K and Greig, J (eds), 1996, *The Status of Australia's Seabirds: Proceedings of the National Seabird Workshop, Canberra, 1–2 November, 1993*, Biodiversity Group, Environment Australia.

Rothwell, DR, 1996, *The Polar Regions and the Development of International Law*, Cambridge University Press.

Rothwell, DR, 2000, Polar Environmental Protection and International Law: The 1991 Antarctic Protocol, *European Journal of International Law*, 11: 591-92.

Rothwell, DR, 2001, Antarctic Baselines: Flexing the Law for Ice-Covered Baselines, in *The Law of the Sea and Polar Maritime Delimitation and Jurisdiction*, (eds) Oude Elferink, A and Rothwell, DR, Martinus Nijhoff Publishers: 49-68.

Rowe, R, 2002, Antarctic Treaty: Past and Present, in *The Antarctic: Past Present and Future*, (eds) Jabour-Green, J and Haward, M, Proceedings of a conference celebrating the 40th anniversary of the entry into force of the Antarctic Treaty on 23 June 1961, Cooperative Research Centre for the Antarctic and Southern Ocean, Research Report 28: 7-17.

Russia, 2001, *Russian Studies of the Antarctic 2000 Under the Subprogram 'Study and Research of the Antarctic'*, Working Paper 27, ATCM XXIV, St Petersburg.

Ruttimann, J, 2006, Sick Seas, *Nature*, 442: 978-80.

Sandford, R, 2006, Australia's Future in Antarctica and the Southern Ocean, submission to Australian Antarctic Division, Antarctic Futures Project, 8 August 2006.

Sanson, L, 1994, An Ecotourism Case Study in Sub-Antarctic Islands, *Annals of Tourism Research*, 21: 318-31.

Saul, J, 2005, *The Collapse of Globalism and the Reinvention of the World*, Viking.

Schaffer, B, 1977, On the Politics of Policy, *Australian Journal of Politics and History*, 23: 146-55.

Scott, J, 2000, *Marine Conservation at Macquarie Island: A Marine Conservation Strategy and an Account of the Marine Environment*, Parks and Wildlife Service, Ocean Rescue 2000.

Scott, SV, 1997, Universalism and Title to Territory in Antarctica, *Nordic Journal of International Law*, 66: 33-53.

Scott, SV, 1999, Japan's Renunciation of Territorial Rights in Antarctica and Australian Diplomacy, *Polar Record*, 35: 99.

Scott, SV, 2001, How Cautious is Precautious? Antarctic Tourism and the Precautionary Principle, *International and Comparative Law Quarterly*, 4: 963.

Scovazzi, T, 2000, Towards Guidelines for Antarctic Shipping: A Basis for Co-operation Between the Antarctic Treaty Consultative Parties and the IMO, in

Implementing the Environmental Protection Regime for the Antarctic, (ed) Vidas, D, Kluwer Academic: 243-59.

Siegenthaler, U, Stocker, T, Monnin, E, Lüthi, D, Schwander, J, Stauffer, B, Raynaud, D, Barnola, J-M, Fischer, H, Masson-Delmotte, V and Jouzel, J, 2005, Stable Carbon Cycle–Climate Relationship During the Late Pleistocene, *Science*, 310: 1313.

Simeon, R, 1976, Studying Public Policy, *Canadian Journal of Political Science*, 9: 548-80.

Small, C, 2005, *Regional Fisheries Management Organisations: Their Duties and Performance in Reducing Bycatch of Albatrosses and Other Species*, BirdLife International.

Steger, M, 2003, *Globalization: A Very Short Introduction*, Oxford University Press.

Steger, M, 2005a, Ideologies of Globalization, *Journal of Political Ideologies*, 10: 11-30.

Steger, M, 2005b, *Globalism: Market Ideology Meets Terrorism*, 2nd edn, Rowman and Littlefield.

Stephens, T, 2004, Enforcing Australian Fisheries Laws: Testing the Limits of Hot Pursuit in Domestic and International Law, *Public Law Review*, 15: 12-16.

Stiglitz, J, 2006, *Making Globalization Work*, Allen Lane.

Stoddart, M, 2001, The Science Program – The Present, in *The Antarctic: Past Present and Future*, (eds) Jabour-Green, J and Haward, M, Proceedings of a conference celebrating the 40th anniversary of the entry into force of the Antarctic Treaty on 23 June 1961, Cooperative Research Centre for the Antarctic and Southern Ocean, Research Report 28: 61-70.

Stoddart, M, 2007, Antarctica – In From the Cold, *Year Book Australia 2007*: 25-32.

Stonehouse, B, 2000, *The Last Continent: Discovering Antarctica*, Shuttlewood Collinson.

Tepper, R and Haward, M, 2005, The Development of Malaysia's Position on Antarctica: 1982-2004, *Polar Record*, 41: 113-24.

The Royal Society, 2005, Ocean Acidification Due to Increasing Atmospheric Carbon Dioxide, Policy document 12/05, <http://www.royalsoc.ac.uk> (22 April 06).

Tønnessen, J and Johnsen, A, 1982, *The History of Modern Whaling*, Hurst.

Towns, D and Broome, K, 2003, From Small Maria to Massive Campbell: Forty Years of Rat Eradications from New Zealand Islands, *New Zealand Journal of Zoology*, 30: 377-98.

Traavik, K, 2004, Opening remarks by Deputy Minister Kim Traavik Ministry of Foreign Affairs of Norway, *Annex 5: Chairman's Report from Antarctic Treaty Meeting of Experts on Tourism and Non-governmental Activities in Antarctica*, Tromso-Trondheim.

Tracey, P, 2001, *Managing Antarctic Tourism*, Unpublished PhD Thesis, Institute of Antarctic and Southern Ocean Studies, University of Tasmania, Hobart.

Triggs, G, 1984, Australian Sovereignty in Antarctica: Traditional Principles of Territorial Acquisition Versus a "Common Heritage", in *Australia's Antarctic Policy Options*, (ed) Harris, S, Centre for Resource and Environmental Studies, Australian National University: 55-60.

Triggs, G, 1986, *International Law and Australian Sovereignty in Antarctica*, Legal Books.

Triggs, G, 2005, Australian Broadcasting Corporation, Four Corners Inter-view, 18.07.05, <http://www.abc.net.au/4corners/content/2005/s1414042.htm> (23 February 2007).

Truss, W, 2006, Australia-Japan FTA Negotiation a Valuable Opportunity, Senator the Hon Warren Truss, Minister for Trade, Media release 13 December, <http://www.trademinister.gov.au/releases/2006/wtt028_06.html> (13 February 2007).

Turnbull, M, 2007, Australian Government Condemns Sea Shepherd Actions, Senator the Hon. Malcolm Turnbull, Minister for the Environment and Water Resources, Media release 12 February, <http://www.environment.gov.au/minister/env/2007/index.html> (13 February 2007).

United Kingdom Sentencing Advisory Panel, 2000, Report: *Environmental Offences: The Panel's Advice to the Court of Appeal*, <http://www.sentencing-advisory-panel.gov.uk> (16 March 2007).

United Kingdom, 2004, *Tourism and Self- Regulation: A Commentary on IAATO*, ATME Paper 4, Antarctic Treaty Meeting of Experts on Tourism and Non-governmental Activities in Antarctica, Tromso-Trondheim.

United Kingdom, 2005, *Report of the Intersessional Contact Group on Accreditation Scheme for Antarctic Tour Operators*, Working Paper 18, ATCM XXVIII, Stockholm.

United Kingdom, Argentina, Australia, Norway and the United States, 2006, *Policy Issues Arising From On-Site Review of Guidelines for Visitor Sites in the Antarctic Peninsula*, Working Paper 2, ATCM XXIX, Edinburgh.

Velicogna, I and Wahr, J, 2006, Measurements of Time-variable Gravity Snow Mass Loss in Antarctica, *Scienceexpress*, 2 March.

Vicuña, F, 2000, Port State Jurisdiction in Antarctica: A New Approach to Inspection, Control and Enforcement, in *Implementing the Environmental Protection Regime for the Antarctic*, (ed) Vidas, D, Kluwer Academic: 45-69.

Vidas, D, 2000, Entry Into Force of the Environmental Protocol and Imple-mentation Issues: An Overview, in *Implementing the Environmental Protection Regime for the Antarctic*, (ed) Vidas, D, Kluwer Academic: 1-17.

Vincent, R, 2005, *Atlas Cove, Heard Island Cultural Heritage Management Plan*, Australian Antarctic Division.

Wace, N, 1983, Resources, Research, Sovereignty and Logistics in Antarctica, *Maritime Studies*, 9, January/February.

Watkins, D and Jaensch, R, 2003, *A Strategic Assessment of Nationally Important Wetlands Managed by the Commonwealth in Relation to the Listing of Wetlands of International Importance*, Environment Australia.

Watts, A, 1992, *International Law and the Antarctic Treaty System*, Grotius.

Wearing, S and Neil, J, 1999, *Ecotourism: Impacts, Potentials and Possibilities*, Butterworth-Heinemann.

Western Australia, 2002, Water and Rivers Commission, Office of Water Regu-lation, and Water Corporation, *Climate Change*, Information Sheet, July.

Whinam, J, Chilcott, N and Bergstrom, D, 2005, Sub-Antarctic Hitchhikers: Expeditioners as Vectors for the Introduction of Alien Organisms, *Biolo-gical Conservation*, 121: 207-19.

Wilder, M, 1995, The Settlement of Disputes under the Protocol on Environ-mental Protection to the Antarctic Treaty, *Polar Record*, 31: 399.

Williams, D, 2005, Australian Antarctic Division Report: *Antarctic Marine Living Resources Program – A History of the Patagonian Toothfish Fishery*, <http:// www.aad.gov.au/default.asp?casid+2112> (3 December 2006).

Woolcott, R, 2003, *The Hot Seat: Reflections on Diplomacy from Stalin's Death to the Bali Bombings*, Harper Collins.

Young, O, 1989, *International Cooperation: Building Regimes for Natural Resources and the Environment*, Cornell University Press.

Young, O, 1994, *International Governance: Protecting the Environment in a Stateless Society*, Cornell University Press.

Zwally, H, Giovinetto, M, Li, J, Cornejo, H, Beckley, M, Brenner, A, Saba, J and Yi, D, 2005, Mass changes of the Greenland and Antarctic Ice Sheets and Contributions to Sea-level Rise: 1992-2002, *Journal of Glaciology*, 51: 509-27.

Index

Climate Law in Australia

Professor Tim Bonyhady and Dr Peter Christoff (eds)

Just as climate change is a dominant issue in Australian politics, so climate law has become one of the most significant areas of Australian law.

Climate Law in Australia brings together a combination of leading academics in environmental law and policy and senior environmental law practitioners who have been at the forefront of climate law in Australia.

The book examines the current state of the law and considers its future directions within an international dimension but with a focus on Australia at the national, state and local levels. It contains many important contributions including:

Tim Bonyhady on *The New Australian Climate Law*

Peter Christoff & Robyn Eckersley on *Kyoto and the Asia Pacific Partnership*

Andrew McIntosh on *The Greenhouse Trigger*

Allison Warburton on *Geosequestration Law*

Martin Wilder & Monique Miller on *Carbon Trading Markets & the Law*

Peter Christoff on *Carbon Emissions Trading*

Rob Fowler on *Emissions Reduction Targets Legislation*

Ron Levy on *Nuclear Law Making;* and

Jan McDonald on *Managing the Legal Risks.*

Climate Law in Australia combines scholarly research with clear prose accessible for both legal and general readers. It is essential reading for anyone with an interest in the futures of coal, emissions trading, renewable energy and nuclear power.

2008 • ISBN 978 1 86287 673 6 • paperback • 288 pages • $59.95

Fisheries Management in Australia
Daryl McPhee

This book offers a comprehensive analysis of fisheries management in Australia, an industry which has undergone such significant change that Australia is now recognised as a world leader.

Dr Daryl McPhee has been at the centre of this transformation, a leading scholar who has hands-on experience in several States. His book provides practical insight into the cross disciplinary tools of fisheries management and moves the focus away from the outdated notion of "managing fish" to the reality of managing human behaviour. It does so without losing track of the fundamental need to consider the ecosystem and its components.

The book covers a diverse range of contemporary topics including:

- sharing fisheries resources between commercial and recreational fishers,
- marine park planning,
- current regulatory and policy environments,
- consultative and participatory frameworks,
- by-catch mitigation and fisheries habitat management, and
- key challenges for fisheries management – including population growth, reducing costs of commercial production; environmental concerns and the maintenance of the structure and function of ecosystems.

Fisheries resources are economically and socially important for many Australians. This book is a must for tertiary students studying fisheries, fisheries management professionals, the fishing industry and anyone else with an interest in how our valuable but finite fisheries resources are managed.

2008 • ISBN 978 1 86287 684 2 • paperback • c.224 pages • $64.95

Environment and Sustainability Policy
Creation, Implementation, Evaluation
Stephen Dovers

Dovers argues that better public policy is the key to creating a more sustainable environment and shows what this might involve. This is an intensely practical book, intellectually original and rigorous, and written in a concise and accessible style.

> *... a seminal contribution to the literature on learning for sustainability, a truly comprehensive analysis of the issues and policy implications. ... Dovers' insights on participation, integration and institutional change in particular will be welcomed by educators and policy professionals, students, change managers and administrators at the cutting edge of sustainability.*
>
> Adjunct Professor Paul J Perkins

> *Dovers masterfully explains why researchers, land managers, and environmental professionals are all deeply enmeshed in government policy making and how all these different players can work more effectively together to achieve environmental sustainability. This book is essential reading for anyone involved in Natural Resource Management.*
>
> Professor David Bowman

> *Clear and accessible in style, tone, organisation and presentation, it will be a useful resource for all those associated with sustainability and policy.*
>
> Rural Society

> *... an important book [which] should be mandatory reading for every minister responsible for an environment or natural resource portfolio, every government policy officer responsible for environmental issues, and every environmental management student.*
>
> Hearsay

> *This is a very valuable book ... Dover uses refreshingly transparent language, and he makes no prior assumption about familiarity with the public policy or ecological literature. ... almost every point Dovers made prompted reflection ... it is one of the most engaging books I have read for some time.*
>
> Reviews in Australian Studies

2005 • ISBN 1 86287 540 5 • paperback • 208 pages • $49.95

For further details, visit our website at *www.federationpress.com.au*

Environmental Impact Assessment in Australia 4th edn
Ian Thomas & Mandy Elliott

Ian Thomas is joined by Mandy Elliott in this new edition of what *Rural Society* has described as "one of Australia's key texts in the field of environmental impact assessment".

From reviews of earlier editions

The book is comprehensive in scope and the author has drawn on a very wide range of sources. ... The book is successful in providing a comprehensive, readable and non-technical overview of EIA. ... it would be a very useful text for those needing a non-technical introduction to EIA and an overview of EIA procedures in the various Australian jurisdictions. This could include undergraduate and postgraduate students in scientific and non-scientific disciplines, as well as EIA practitioners and others with an interest in EIA. I commend the book to this audience and to readers of this journal.

Australian Journal of Environmental Management

This is an excellent handbook on the theory and practice of Environmental Impact Assessment in Australia. The coverage of the topic is broad and comprehensive.

Eingana

[the book] contains much of interest for legal practitioners involved in environmental and planning law.

NSW Bar News

Ian Thomas' respected book provides a thorough analysis of the operation of the environmental impact assessment system in Australia. Solidly grounded in theory, it discusses fundamental questions such as What is EIA? What is its role? How does it relate to other assessment procedures?

Building Construction Materials & Equipment

Thomas' book is a comprehensive analysis of the theory and practical application of Australia's impact-assessment regime covering its origins, current operations and future directions. ... The book is well researched and a wonderful reference source.

Proctor

2005 • ISBN 978 1 86287 538 8 • paperback • 286 pages • $49.95

For further details, visit our website at *www.federationpress.com.au*

Safety, Security, Health and Environment Law in Australia

Michael Tooma
Partner, Deacons and Adjunct Lecturer, School of Safety Science,
University of NSW

This new book by one of Australia's leading experts on occupational health and safety takes a groundbreaking integrated approach to the law and practice of safety, security and environment management. This approach recognises the common grounding in risk management that underlies the methodology of practice in Safety, Security, Health and Environment areas and the similarity in legislative treatment by all jurisdictions.

The contents include:

- Occupational safety law – comprehensive and national in approach
- Occupational security law – discusses the emerging discipline of security law, including major hazard facilities and security plans, ports, airports and security requirements, emergency preparedness
- Security and anti-terrorism laws as they apply to business
- Occupational health law – includes material on asbestos law, synthetic fibres, nanoparticles, noise management, stress, depression and mental health
- Environmental and sustainability law – takes account of environmental law affecting the workplace, nationally, including pollution law and environmental sustainability
- Safety, Security, Health and Environment Risk Management, Management systems and Performance measurement.

Each chapter contains extensive references to relevant legislation, with case summaries extracted to illustrate principles along with discussion of relevant literature and expert commentary.

Publishing 2008 – see our website for further details

Law & Liberty in the War on Terror

Andrew Lynch, Edwina MacDonald and George Williams (eds)

Defending the community from the threat of terrorism has involved changes to our laws which impact upon the liberties that define our society. Is this impact too great? Is the cure worse than the disease?

Law & Liberty in the War on Terror debates the challenge of ensuring national security in the modern era. It brings together diverse views from leading Australian and domestic commentators drawn from politics, government, the academy and media.

Contributors address questions such as the difficulty of defining 'terrorism'; the extent to which the criminal justice system can accommodate terrorism offences; the acceptability of torture as an interrogative method; the role of the judiciary in times of emergency; how Australia's laws compare with those of the United Kingdom and New Zealand; and how our communities and politics are affected by responses to terrorism.

Law & Liberty in the War on Terror is written so as to be accessible to a general informed audience and is an indispensable book for all Australians who want to know more about our anti-terrorism laws and their wider significance for our society.

The book is an excellent resource for law and politics students.

2008 • ISBN 978 186287 674 3 • paperback • 240 pages • $49.95

For further details, visit our website at *www.federationpress.com.au*